Standard C
A Reference

Prentice Hall Series on Programming Tools and Methodologies

P.J. Plauger — *Series Advisor*

Lipkin — *String Processing and Text Manipulation In C Selected Data Structures and Techniques*

Plauger — *Standard C: A Reference*

The Standard C Library

Programming on Purpose I: Essays on Programming Design

Programming on Purpose II: Essays on Software People

Programming on Purpose III: Essays on Software Technology

The Standard C++ Library

Jongerius — *Writing Bug-Free C Code for Windows*

Standard C
A Reference

P.J. Plauger
Jim Brodie

Prentice Hall PTR
Upper Saddle River, New Jersey 07458

Plauger, P. J.,
Standard C / P.J. Plauger, Jim Brodie.
p. cm. --
Includes index.
ISBN 0-13-436411-2
1. C (Computer program language I. Brodie, Jim.
II Title.
QA76.73.C15P56 1995 95-15055
005.13'3--dc20 CIP

Editorial/production supervision: **Ann Sullivan**
Cover manager: **Jerry Votta**
Manufacturing manager: **Alexis R. Heydt**
Acquisitions editor: **Paul Becker**
Editorial assistant: **Maureen Diana**

Published by Prentice Hall PTR
Prentice-Hall, Inc.
A Simon and Schuster Company
Upper Saddle River, NJ 07458

The publisher offers discounts on this book when ordered in bulk quantities.
For more information, contact:

Corporate Sales Department
Prentice Hall PTR
One Lake Street
Upper Saddle River, NJ 07458

Phone: 800-382-3419
Fax: 201-236-7141
email: corpsales@prenhall.com

Printed in the United States of America

10 9 8 7 6 5 4 3 2 1

ISBN: 0-13-436411-2

Prentice-Hall International (UK) Limited, *London*
Prentice-Hall of Australia Pty. Limited, *Sydney*
Prentice-Hall Canada Inc., *Toronto*
Prentice-Hall Hispanoamericana, S.A., *Mexico*
Prentice-Hall of India Private Limited, *New Delhi*
Prentice-Hall of Japan, Inc., *Tokyo*
Simon & Schuster Asia Pte. Ltd., *Singapore*
Editora Prentice-Hall do Brasil, Ltda., *Rio de Janeiro*

for Tana and Sarah

TRADEMARKS

TYPOGRAPHY

This book was typeset in Palatino, Avant Garde bold, and Courier bold by the authors using a Gateway2000 Nomad 425DXL computer running Ventura Publisher 4.1.1 under Microsoft Windows 3.1.

Contents

Preface

This book describes the C programming language as completely, precisely, and succinctly as possible. The focus is on what is true of C across all implementations that conform to the international C Standard. (See **ISO90** in ***Appendix C: References***). It includes the extensive support for manipulating large character sets added with Amendment 1 to that standard. (See **ISO94**.) And it incorporates refinements and clarifications developed in response to formal Defect Reports against the international C Standard. Put briefly, this book is as comprehensive as the C Standard, but considerably more readable.

We named the initial version of this book *Standard C* as an act of faith. (See **P&B89**.) At that time, no standard for the C programming language had been formally adopted. ANSI, the American National Standards Institute, was close to accepting the work of Committee X3J11. We crossed our fingers and went to press with what we thought would be an accurate description of ANSI C. We guessed right.

ISO, the International Standards Organization, was a bit farther from consensus. Their Committee SC22/WG14 was still addressing issues that might lead to a new dialect of C. Our hope and expectation was that they would eventually adopt a standard identical to ANSI C. That, too, has proved to be the case.

Standard C is a sensible term for this common language with worldwide acceptance. It is also easier to pronounce, and write, than ANSI/ISO C. Some programmers, mostly American, still refer parochially to ANSI C. Others make a point of referring only to ISO C. But the term Standard C has become widely accepted, and used, in all circles.

This book takes on a larger, more open format than even its immediate predecessor, which expanded on the original. (See **P&B92**.) A complete description of a programming language, however succinct, involves considerable detail. And the addition of Amendment 1 added still more detail. Those of us with aging eyes welcome the relief that the new format brings, particularly in a book we refer to almost daily.

Our basic approach is to describe Standard C as a monolithic language, outside of any historical context. We make one important concession, however. The additions mandated by Amendment 1 are all marked as such. We believe the material is too new to many programmers for us to pretend that it has always been there.

We confess to having corrected a number of technical errors over the years. For all our careful reading, we let an embarrassing number creep in. To put the best spin on things, we note that the material has been continually refined over years of usage in the field. We think it's pretty accurate now.

Where possible, however, we have left well enough alone. *Standard C* is now widely used as an approachable version of the C Standard. Whatever we did right at the outset we want to keep on doing.

Acknowledgments

Paul Becker, our Publisher at Prentice Hall, saw merit in issuing an updated version of our sturdy little reference to Standard C. We appreciate the opportunity to make the description more complete and more widely available.

We gratefully acknowledge the assistance of Randy Hudson, Rex Jaeschke, Tom Plum, and David Prosser in reviewing the first edition of this book. We thank Jack Litewka for his patience and meticulous editing of that edition. We also note the untiring efforts of all the members of X3J11, over many years, in producing such an effective standard for the C programming language.

Geoffrey Plauger helped refine the layout and typographic design of this book. And our wives, Tana Plauger and Sarah Brodie, provided support in ways too numerous to count. We thank them.

P.J. Plauger
Concord, Massachusetts

Jim Brodie
Motorola
Phoenix, Arizona

Chapter 0: Introduction

This book provides all the information you need to read and write programs in the Standard C programming language. It describes all aspects of Standard C that are the same on all implementations that conform to the standard for C. Whenever your goal is to produce code that is as portable as possible, this book tells you what you can count on. And by omission, it lets you know what you *cannot* count on — nothing in this book is peculiar to any nonstandard dialect of C.

This is not a tutorial on Standard C, nor is it a lesson on how to write computer programs. It does not describe how to use any particular implementation of Standard C. Consult the documentation that comes with the particular translator (compiler or interpreter) that you are using for specific instructions on translating and executing programs.

STANDARD C

The Standard C programming language described in this book corresponds to the American National Standards Institute (ANSI) standard for the C language — ANSI X3.159-1989. An identical standard was approved by the International Organization for Standardization (ISO) — ISO/IEC 9899:1990. This common standard was developed through the joint efforts of the ANSI-authorized C Programming Language Committee X3J11 and the ISO authorized Committee JTC1 SC22 WG14.

Standard C is designed to "codify existing practice." Most of the C code written before the advent of Standard C is still acceptable to one or more Standard C translators. Nevertheless, Standard C is a new language:

- It adds features, such as function prototypes, to correct some known deficiencies in the C language.
- It resolves conflicting practices, such as ones found among the differing rules for redeclaring objects.
- It clarifies ambiguities, such as whether the objects manipulated by library functions are permitted to overlap.

This book presents Standard C as a distinct language, not as a historical outgrowth of any particular earlier dialect of C. If you are new to C or are familiar with just a specific dialect, you have a new language to learn.

AMENDMENTS

Amendment 1 The C Standard has more recently been amended and clarified. Amendment 1 (approved in 1994) adds extensive support for manipulating *wide characters,* which represent large character sets, and some additional support for writing source code in national variants of the ISO 646 character set. Most of these new features are additions to the library, and most library additions are defined or declared in three new headers — `<iso646.h>`, `<wchar.h>`, and `<wctype.h>`. Many Standard C translators have yet to add these new features, so this book labels such additions as **Amendment 1**. For maximum near-term portability, you may wish to avoid them.

Technical Corrigendum 1 (also approved in 1994) supplies a number of clarifications and corrections to the C Standard. These are in response to ANSI Requests for Interpretation or ISO Defect Reports received and processed by X3J11 and WG14 since the C Standard was first issued. None are intended to alter the original definition of Standard C, merely to make its definition more unambiguous and precise. This book reflects the effect of Technical Corrigendum 1, but does not identify any specific changes.

BRIEF OVERVIEW

This book is organized into two parts and three appendixes. **PART I** describes the Standard C language proper. **PART II** describes the Standard C library. **PART I** includes seven chapters:

Chapter 1: Characters — You can use many *character* sets, both for writing C source files and when executing programs. This chapter describes the constraints on character sets and the various ways you can specify characters within Standard C.

Chapter 2: Preprocessing — C is translated (at least logically) in two stages. *Preprocessing* first rewrites the C source text. More conventional language translation then parses and translates the resulting *translation unit.* This chapter describes the steps of preprocessing and the preprocessing facilities you can use.

Chapter 3: Syntax — Detailed *syntax* rules exist for each of the Standard C program constructs you create, directly or as a result of preprocessing. This chapter summarizes the syntax of each construct. (Later chapters in Part I cover the underlying meaning, or *semantics,* for each construct in more detail.)

Chapter 4: Types — The *types* you specify capture many of the important properties of the objects you manipulate in a Standard C program. This chapter describes the various types, the values they specify, and how the program represents them.

Chapter 5: Declarations — You express all parts of a Standard C program, its executable code and the objects to be manipulated, as a series of *declarations.* This chapter describes how to name these parts and how to specify their types and their contents.

Chapter 6: Functions — The *functions* are the parts of a Standard C program that contain executable code. This chapter describes how to declare functions, specify their contents by writing statements, and call them from other functions.

Chapter 7: Expressions — You express computations by writing *expressions.* The translator itself evaluates some expressions to determine properties of the program. The program executes code to evaluate other expressions. This chapter explains the common rules for writing all expressions, determining their types, and computing their values.

PART II of this book includes 19 chapters:

Chapter 8: Library — Standard C provides an extensive *library* of functions that perform many useful services. This chapter describes how to use the library in general. The chapters that follow describe in detail each of the 18 standard headers that define or declare library entities.

Chapter 9: **`<assert.h>`** — The macro **`assert`** helps you document and debug functions that you write.

Chapter 10: **`<ctype.h>`** — You can classify characters in many useful ways with these functions.

Chapter 11: **`<errno.h>`** — The macro **`errno`** records several kinds of errors that can occur when the library executes.

Chapter 12: **`<float.h>`** — This header summarizes important properties of the floating-point types.

Amendment 1

Chapter 13: **`<iso646.h>`** — A number of macros help you write more readable programs when the source character set has alternate graphics for certain punctuation characters.

Chapter 14: **`<limits.h>`** — This header summarizes important properties of the integer types.

Chapter 15: **`<locale.h>`** — You can adapt to the conventions of various cultures by changing and inspecting *locales.*

Chapter 16: **`<math.h>`** — This header declares the common math functions for arguments of type *double.*

Chapter 17: **`<setjmp.h>`** — You can perform a non-local *goto* by calling the functions **`setjmp`** and **`longjmp`**.

Chapter 18: **`<signal.h>`** — You can specify how to handle a variety of extraordinary events called *signals* while the program executes.

Chapter 19: **`<stdarg.h>`** — This header defines the macros you need to access a varying number of arguments in a function call.

Chapter 20: **`<stddef.h>`** — This header defines several widely used types and macros.

Chapter 21: **`<stdio.h>`** — The library includes a rich assortment of functions that perform input and output.

Chapter 22: **`<stdlib.h>`** — This header declares a variety of functions.

Chapter 23: **`<string.h>`** — The library includes an assortment of functions that manipulate character arrays of different sizes.

Chapter 24: **`<time.h>`** — You can represent times in several formats and convert among them.

Amendment 1 *Chapter 25:* **<wchar.h>** — Wide-character analogs exist for many of the functions declared in **<stdio.h>** that read and write single-byte characters, for the functions declared in **<stdlib.h>** that convert (single-byte) strings to numeric representations, and for the functions declared in **<string.h>** that manipulate (single-byte) strings.

Amendment 1 *Chapter 26:* **<wctype.h>** — Wide-character analogs exist for the functions declared in **<ctype.h>** that classify and map character codes.

The **Appendixes** section contains three appendixes:

Appendix A: Portability — One of the great strengths of the Standard C language is that it helps you write programs that are powerful, efficient, and portable. You can move a portable program with little extra investment of effort to a computer that differs from the one on which you originally developed the program. This appendix describes aspects to be aware of when writing a portable program. It outlines the large subset of Standard C that is also valid C++ code. And it lists the minimum requirements imposed on all Standard C implementations.

Appendix B: Names — Standard C predefines many *names,* most of which name functions in the library. You must avoid duplicating these names when you create your own names. This appendix provides a list of all predefined names.

Appendix C: References — This appendix lists all books and other publications referred to in the text.

RAILROAD-TRACK DIAGRAMS

Syntax rules appear in the form of *railroad-track diagrams.* The diagrams summarize all valid ways that you can form explicit computer text for a given form. Not all forms that you can generate from a railroad-track diagram are necessarily valid. Often semantic restrictions also apply. These are described in separate tables or in running text.

A railroad-track diagram contains boxes that indicate the components you use to create a form. Arrows connect the boxes to indicate the ways that you can combine the components. You can create different text for a form by taking different paths between the boxes. The name of the form appears next to the arrow leading out to the right from the diagram.

Figure 0.1 shows the syntax rule for writing a ***name*** in Standard C.

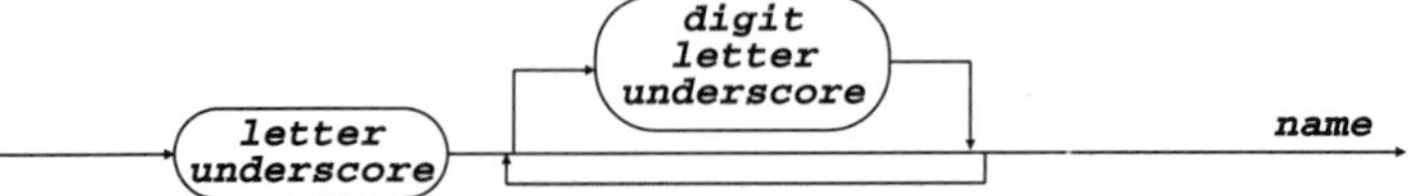

Figure 0.1: *Syntax of* ***name.***

You generate a valid ***name*** by following the arrows. You begin with the arrow leading in from the left and continue until you follow the arrow leading out to the right. In a complex diagram, an arrow followed by an ellipsis (**...**) connects to the arrow preceded by an ellipsis immediately below.

Each time you come to a box, you must add the text in the box to the item being created. If the box contains a form, you must add text that matches the form. If the box contains more than one entry, you must add one of the choices. If you come to an intersection with two arrows leading away from it, you can follow either arrow. You cannot follow an arrow in the direction opposite to the way it points.

The railroad-track diagram in Figure 0.1 tells you:

- Every name in Standard C begins with either an uppercase or lowercase ***letter*** (such as **A** or **x**) or an ***underscore*** (_).
- A name need not contain more than one character.
- The initial character might be followed by a ***digit*** (such as **3**), a ***letter***, or an ***underscore***.
- The initial character might be followed by an indefinite number of these characters.

A name can therefore be any of the following:

```
A                    A3                _x
timer                box_2             z173ab
an_extremely_long_name_that_also_contains_1_digit
```

The syntax rule does *not* tell you about the following semantic limitations:

- Some implementations can limit the length of the name. (The limit cannot be less than 509 characters.)
- An implementation might use only the first 31 characters when comparing names.
- An implementation might use only the first 6 characters and ignore the difference in case between **a** and **A** when comparing names with external linkage from separate translation units.
- Names beginning with an ***underscore*** are generally reserved for use by an implementation.

Some diagrams require boxes that permit anything *except* one or a few items. In these cases, **bold text** describes the matching rule. For example, **not *NL*** matches any character except a newline character.

NOTATION

A type face that differs from the running text has a special meaning:

- *definition* — a term that has a special definition in Standard C.
- **computer text** — any item that can appear explicitly in a text file, such as C source text, input to a program, or output from a program.
- ***form*** — a name that stands for one or more explicit computer text patterns. For example:

    digit **0 1 2 3 4 5 6 7 8 9**

`digit` is a form that you can replace with any of the explicit characters **`0`**, **`1`**, **`2`**, and so on.

- **comments** — remarks that are not an actual part of the computer text being presented.
- **SECTION HEAD** in ***Chapter x: Title*** — a reference to another section of this book.

PART I

The Standard C Language

Chapter 1: Characters

Characters play a central role in Standard C. You represent a C program as one or more *source files*. A source file is a *text file* consisting of characters that you can read when you display the file on a terminal screen or produce hard copy with a printer. You often manipulate text when a C program executes. The program might produce a text file that people can read, or it might read a text file entered by someone typing at a keyboard or modified using a text editor. This chapter describes the characters that you use to write C source files and that you manipulate when executing C programs.

CHARACTER SETS

When you write a program, you express C source files as lines of text containing characters from the *source character set*. When a program executes in the *target environment*, it uses characters from the *target character set*. These character sets are related, but need not have the same encoding or all the same members.

Every character set contains a distinct code value for each character in the *basic C character set*. A character set can also contain additional characters with other code values. For example:

- The *character constant* **'x'** becomes the value of the code for the character corresponding to **x** in the target character set.
- The *string literal* **"xyz"** becomes a sequence of character constants stored in successive bytes of memory, followed by a byte containing the value zero:

```
{'x', 'y', 'z', 0}
```

A string literal is one way to specify a *null-terminated string*.

Table 1.1: *Visible graphic characters in the basic C character set.*

Form	Members
letter	A B C D E F G H I J K L M N O P Q R S T U V W X Y Z a b c d e f g h i j k l m n o p q r s t u v w x y z
digit	0 1 2 3 4 5 6 7 8 9
underscore	_
punctuation	! " # % & ' ( ) * + , - . / : ; < = > ? [\ ] ^ {	} ~

Table 1.1 shows the visible graphic characters in the basic C character set. Table 1.2 shows the remaining characters in this set. The code value zero is reserved for the *null character* which is always in the target character set. Code values for the basic C character set are positive when stored in an object of type *char*. Code values for the digits are contiguous, with increasing value. For example, **'0' + 5** equals **'5'**. Code values for any two letters are *not* necessarily contiguous.

Table 1.2: *Additional characters in the basic C character set.*

Character	Meaning
space	leave blank *space*
BEL	signal an alert (*bell*)
BS	go back one position (*backspace*)
FF	go to top of page (*form feed*)
NL	go to start of next line (*newline*)
CR	go to start of this line (*carriage return*)
HT	go to next *horizontal tab* stop
VT	go to next *vertical tab* stop

Character Sets and Locales

An implementation can support multiple *locales*, each with a different character set. A locale summarizes conventions peculiar to a given culture, such as how to format dates or how to sort names. To change locales and, therefore, target character sets while the program is running, use the function **setlocale** (declared in **<locale.h>**). The translator encodes character constants and string literals for the **"C"** locale, which is the locale in effect at program startup.

ESCAPE SEQUENCES

Within character constants and string literals, you can write a variety of *escape sequences*. Each escape sequence determines the code value for a single character. You use escape sequences:

- to represent character codes you cannot otherwise write (such as **\n**)
- that can be difficult to read properly (such as **\t**)
- that might change value in different target character sets (such as **\a**)
- that must not change in value among different target environments (such as **\0**)

An escape sequence takes the form shown in Figure 1.1.

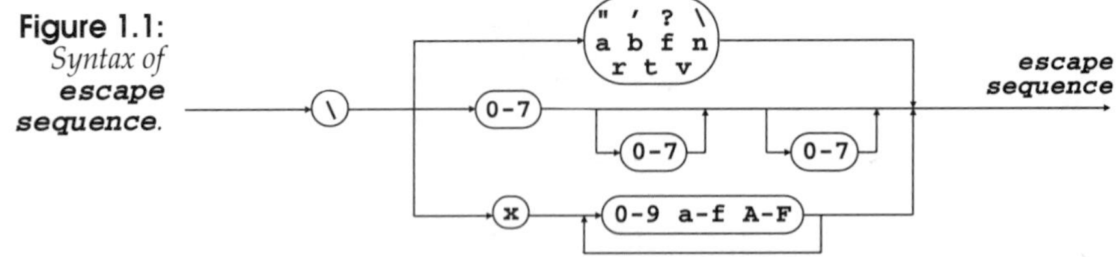

Figure 1.1: *Syntax of* ***escape sequence****.*

Some escape sequences are *mnemonic,* to help you remember the characters they represent. Table 1.3 shows all the characters and their mnemonic escape sequences.

Table 1.3: *Character escape sequences.*

Character	Escape Sequence	Character	Escape Sequence
`"`	`\"`	*FF*	`\f`
`'`	`\'`	*NL*	`\n`
`?`	`\?`	*CR*	`\r`
`\`	`\\`	*HT*	`\t`
BEL	`\a`	*VT*	`\v`
BS	`\b`		

Numeric Escape Sequence

You can also write *numeric escape sequences* using either octal or hexadecimal digits. An *octal escape sequence* takes one of the forms:

`\d` or `\dd` or `\ddd`

The escape sequence yields a code value that is the numeric value of the 1-, 2-, or 3-digit octal number following the backslash (`\`). Each *d* can be any digit in the range `0-7`. A *hexadecimal escape sequence* takes one of the forms:

`\xh` or `\xhh` or `...`

The escape sequence yields a code value that is the numeric value of the arbitrary-length hexadecimal number following the backslash (`\`). Each *h* can be any decimal digit `0-9`, or any of the letters `a-f` or `A-F`. The letters represent the digit values 10–15, where either `a` or `A` has the value 10.

A numeric escape sequence terminates with the first character that does not fit the digit pattern. Here are some examples:

- You can write the null character as `'\0'`.
- You can write a newline character (*NL*) within a string literal by writing:

  `"hi\n"` which becomes the array `{'h', 'i', '\n', 0}`
- You can write a string literal that begins with a specific numeric value:

  `"\3abc"` which becomes the array `{3, 'a', 'b', 'c', 0}`
- You can write a string literal that contains the hexadecimal escape sequence `\xF` followed by the digit `3` by writing two string literals:

  `"\xF" "3"` which becomes the array `{0xF, '3', 0}`

TRIGRAPHS

A *trigraph* is a sequence of three characters that begins with two question marks (`??`). You use trigraphs to write C source files with a character set that does not contain convenient graphic representations for some punctuation characters. (The resultant C source file is not necessarily more readable, but it is unambiguous.) Table 1.4 shows all defined trigraphs. These are the only trigraphs. The translator does not alter any other sequence that begins with two question marks.

Table 1.4: *Trigraph sequences.*

Character	Trigraph
[	??(
\	??/
]	??)
^	??'
{	??<
|	??!
}	??>
~	??-
#	??=

For example, the expression statements:

```
printf("Case ??=3 is done??/n");
printf("You said what????/n");
```

are equivalent to:

```
printf("Case #3 is done\n");
printf("You said what??\n");
```

The translator replaces each trigraph with its equivalent single character representation in an early phase of translation. (See **PHASES OF TRANSLATION** in ***Chapter 2: Preprocessing***.) You can always treat a trigraph as a single source character.

MULTIBYTE CHARACTERS

A source character set or target character set can also contain *multibyte characters* (sequences of one or more bytes). Each sequence represents a single character in the *extended character set*. You use multibyte characters to represent large sets of characters, such as Kanji. A multibyte character can be a one-byte sequence that is a character from the basic C character set, an additional one-byte sequence that is implementation-defined, or an additional sequence of two or more bytes that is implementation-defined. (See **WRITING PORTABLE PROGRAMS** in ***Appendix A: Portability*** for a description of implementation-defined behavior.)

Multibyte characters can have a *state-dependent encoding*. How you interpret a byte in such an encoding depends on a state determined by bytes earlier in the sequence of characters. In the *initial shift state*, any byte whose value matches one of the characters in the basic C character set represents that character. A subsequent code can determine an *alternate shift state*, after which all byte sequences can have a different interpretation. A byte containing the value zero always represents the null character. It cannot occur as any of the bytes of another multibyte character.

You can write multibyte characters in C source text as part of a comment, a character constant, a string literal, or a filename in an *include* directive. How such characters print is implementation defined. Each sequence of multibyte characters that you write must begin and end in the initial shift state.

The program can also include multibyte characters in null-terminated character strings used by several library functions, including the format strings for **printf** and **scanf**. Each such character string must begin and end in the initial shift state.

Each character in the extended character set also has an integer representation, called a *wide-character encoding*. Each extended character has a unique wide-character value. The value 0 always corresponds to the null wide character. The type definition **wchar_t**, defined in **<stddef.h>**, specifies the integer type that represents wide characters.

Amendment 1 You write a wide character constant as **L'mbc'**, where **mbc** represents a single multibyte character. You write a wide character string literal as **L"mbs"**, where **mbs** represents a sequence of zero or more multibyte characters. The library functions **mblen**, **mbstowcs**, **mbtowc**, **wcstombs**, and **wctomb** (declared in **<stdlib.h>**) — as well as **btowc**, **mbrlen**, **mbrtowc**, **mbsrtowcs**, **wcrtomb**, **wcsrtombs**, and **wctob** (declared in **<wchar.h>**, with Amendment 1) — help you convert between the multibyte and wide-character representations of extended characters.

The macro **MB_LEN_MAX** (defined in **<limits.h>**) specifies the length of the longest possible multibyte sequence required to represent a single character defined by the implementation across supported locales. And the macro **MB_CUR_MAX** (defined in **<stdlib.h>**) specifies the length of the longest possible multibyte sequence required to represent a single character defined for the *current locale*.

For example, the string literal **"hello"** becomes an array of six *char*:

```
{'h', 'e', 'l', 'l', 'o', 0}
```

while the wide-character string literal **L"hello"** becomes an array of six integers of type **wchar_t**:

```
{L'h', L'e', L'l', L'l', L'o', 0}
```

Chapter 2: Preprocessing

The translator processes each source file in a series of phases. *Preprocessing* constitutes the earliest phases, which produce a *translation unit.* Preprocessing treats a source file as a sequence of text lines. You can specify *directives* and *macros* that insert, delete, and alter source text. This chapter describes the operations that you can perform during preprocessing. It shows how the translator parses the program as white space and preprocessing tokens, carries out the directives that you specify, and expands the macros that you write in the source files.

PHASES OF TRANSLATION

Preprocessing translates each source file in a series of distinct phases. The translator performs the following steps, in order:

1. Terminates each line with a newline character (*NL*), regardless of the external representation of a text line.
2. Converts trigraphs to their single-character equivalents.
3. Concatenates each line ending in a backslash (`\`) with the line following.
4. Replaces each comment (beginning with `/*` that is not inside a character constant, a string literal, or a standard header name and ending with a `*/`) with a ***space*** character.
5. Parses each resulting *logical line* as preprocessing tokens and white space.
6. Recognizes and carries out directives (that are not skipped) and expands macros in all non-directive lines (that are not skipped).
7. Replaces escape sequences within character constants and string literals with their single character equivalents.
8. Concatenates adjacent string literals to form single string literals.
9. Converts the remaining preprocessing tokens to C tokens and discards any white space to form the translation unit.

The remainder of the translator then parses the translation unit as one or more *declarations* and translates each declaration. You combine (or *link*) one or more separately processed translation units, along with the Standard C library, to form the program.

A translation unit can contain entire include files, which can contain entire if-groups (see **CONDITIONAL DIRECTIVES** later in this chapter), which can contain entire directives and macro invocations, which can contain entire comments, character constants, string literals, and other preprocessing tokens.

You cannot write a comment inside a string literal, as in:

```
"hello /* ignored */"    comment is NOT ignored
```

You cannot write a macro to begin comments, as in:

```
#define BEGIN_NOTE /*    still inside comment
```

You cannot include a source file that contains an *if* directive without a balancing *endif* directive within the same file. Nor can you include a source file that contains only part of a macro invocation.

You write a directive on one logical line. (Use line concatenation, described above, to represent a long directive on multiple source lines.) Every directive begins with a number character (**#**). You can write any number of ***space*** and ***HT*** characters (or comments) before and after the **#**. You cannot write ***FF*** or ***VT*** characters to separate tokens on a directive line. Every line that begins with a **#** must match one of the forms described in this chapter.

WHITE SPACE

Preprocessing parses each input line as *preprocessing tokens* and *white space.* You use white space for one or more purposes.

- to separate two tokens that the translator might otherwise parse as a single token, as in:

```
case 3:
```

- to separate the macro name and a macro definition that begins with a left parenthesis, to signal that there are no macro parameters, as in:

```
#define neg_pi     (-3.1415926535)
```

- to separate two tokens of a macro argument that you are using to create a string literal, to create a ***space*** in the string literal, as in:

```
#define str(x)      #x
str(hello there)   which becomes "hello there"
```

- to improve readability

White space takes one of three distinct forms:

- *vertical white space* (the characters ***FF*** and ***VT***), which you can use within any non-directive line, as shown in Figure 2.1

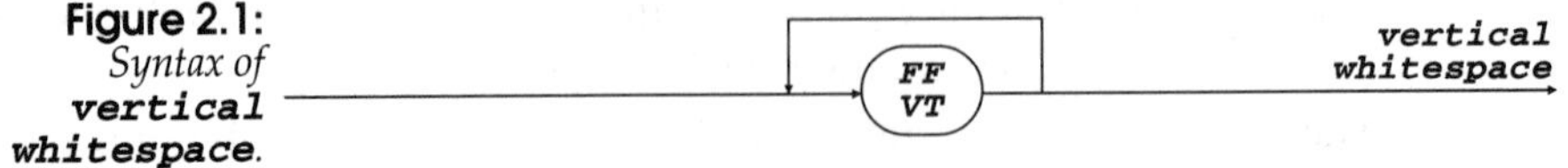

Figure 2.1: *Syntax of* ***vertical whitespace.***

- *horizontal white space* (comments and the characters ***space*** and ***HT***), which you can use in any line, as shown in Figure 2.2

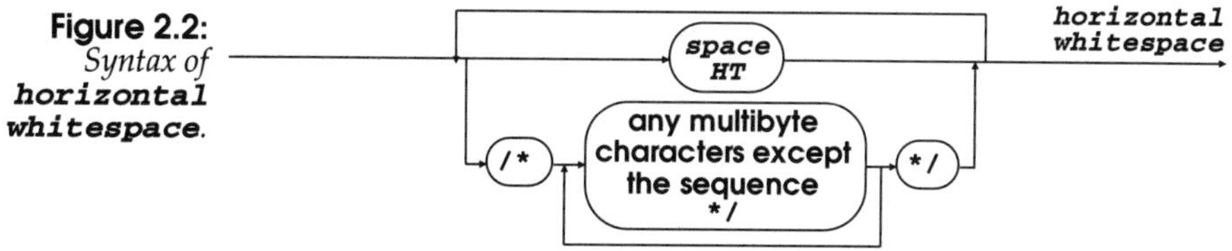

Figure 2.2: *Syntax of* **horizontal whitespace**.

- *end of line* (the character **NL**), which you use to terminate directives or to separate tokens on non-directive lines, as shown in Figure 2.3

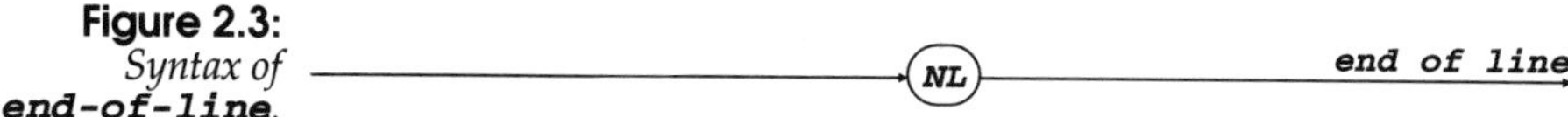

Figure 2.3: *Syntax of* **end-of-line**.

For a directive, you can write horizontal white space wherever an arrow appears in its railroad-track diagram.

PREPROCESSING TOKENS

A preprocessing token is the longest sequence of characters that matches one of the following patterns.

A *name* is a sequence of letters, underscores, and digits that begins with a letter or underscore, as shown in Figure 2.4. Distinct names must differ within the first 31 characters.

Figure 2.4: *Syntax of* **name**.

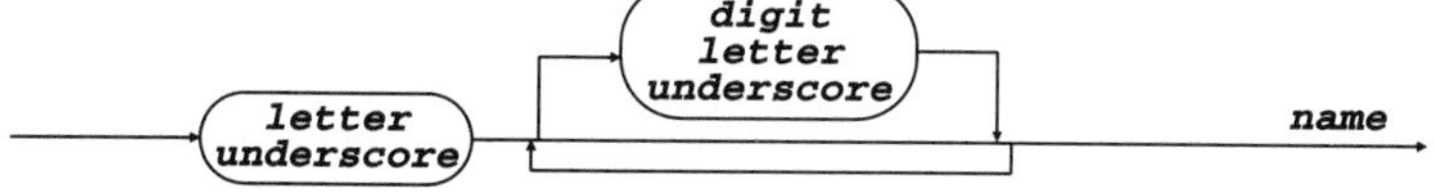

Some valid names, all of which are distinct, are:

```
abc        Version13    old_sum
ABC        _Abc         X1_Y2_Z3
```

A *preprocessing number* subsumes all integer and floating-point constants (see **C TOKENS** in ***Chapter 3: Syntax***) plus a number of other forms, as shown in Figure 2.5.

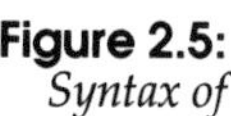

Figure 2.5: *Syntax of* **number**.

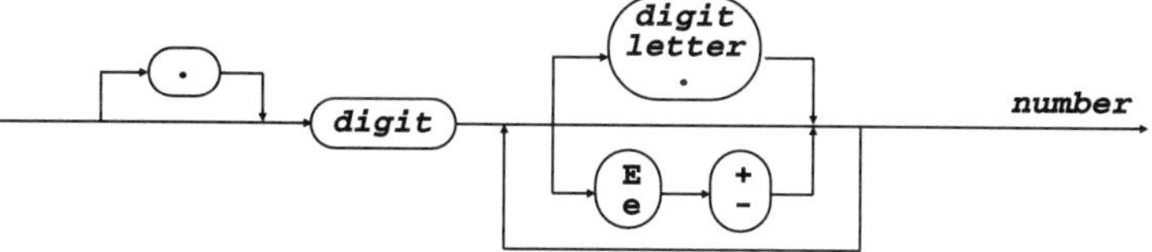

Some valid preprocessing numbers are:

```
0          .123          3E
123        123E0F        3e+xy
123LU      0.123E-005    2for1
```

The third column shows several of the additional forms.

You use the additional forms:

- to build string literals from macro arguments during macro expansion
- to build other tokens by concatenating tokens during macro expansion
- as part of text that you skip with conditional directives

Some valid preprocessing numbers are:

```
314        3.14      .314E+1
0xa5       .14E+     1z2z
```

A *character constant* consists of one or more multibyte characters enclosed in single quotes, as shown in Figure 2.6. (See **ESCAPE SEQUENCES** in ***Chapter 1: Characters.***)

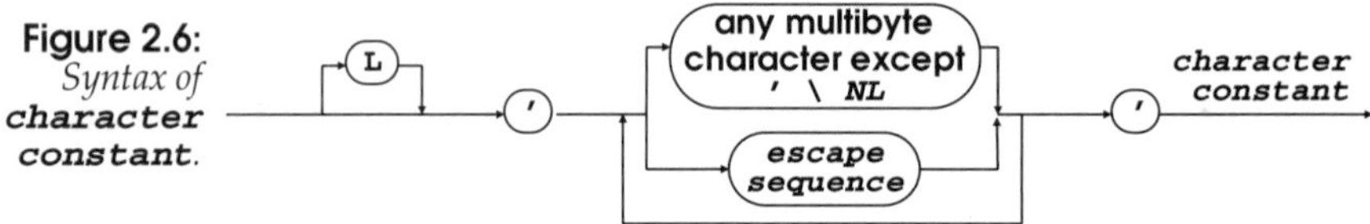

Figure 2.6: *Syntax of* **`character constant`**.

To make a wide character constant, precede the character constant with an **`L`**. Some valid character constants are:

```
'a'        '\n'      L'x'
'abc'      '\0'      L'□'
```

A *string literal* consists of zero or more multibyte characters enclosed in double quotes, as shown in Figure 2.7. To make a wide character string literal, precede the string literal with an **`L`**.

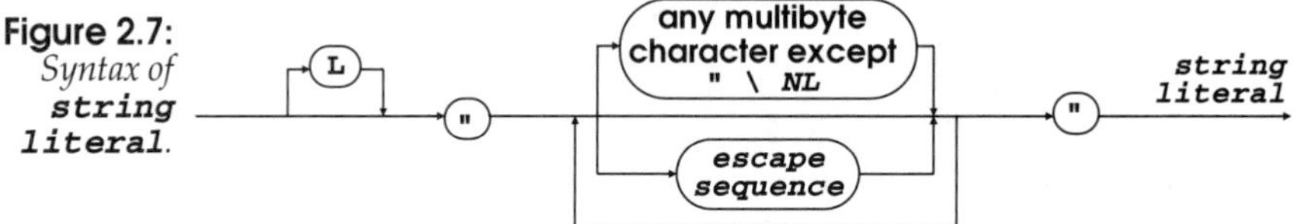

Figure 2.7: *Syntax of* **`string literal`**.

Some valid string literals are:

```
""        "Good Night!\n"       L"Kon ban wa"
"abc"     "\5hello\0Hello"      L"exit is □"
```

Amendment 1 Table 2.1 lists all valid *operator* or *punctuator* tokens. Tokens in the rightmost column are added by Amendment 1.

Table 2.1: *List of valid* **`operator`** *or* **`punctuator`** *tokens.*

<table>
<tr><td>...</td><td>&&</td><td>-=</td><td>>=</td><td>~</td><td>+</td><td>;</td><td>]</td><td><:</td></tr>
<tr><td><<=</td><td>&=</td><td>-></td><td>>></td><td>%</td><td>,</td><td><</td><td>^</td><td>:></td></tr>
<tr><td>>>=</td><td>*=</td><td>/=</td><td>^=</td><td>&</td><td>-</td><td>=</td><td>{</td><td><%</td></tr>
<tr><td>!=</td><td>++</td><td><<</td><td>|=</td><td>(</td><td>.</td><td>></td><td>|</td><td>%></td></tr>
<tr><td>%=</td><td>+=</td><td><=</td><td>||</td><td>)</td><td>/</td><td>?</td><td>}</td><td>%:</td></tr>
<tr><td>##</td><td>--</td><td>==</td><td>!</td><td>*</td><td>:</td><td>[</td><td>#</td><td>%:%:</td></tr>
</table>

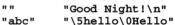

Any character standing alone *other* than one from the basic C character set forms a preprocessing token by itself. For example, some other characters often found in character sets are **`@`** and **`$`**.

You use other characters for one of two purposes:

- to build string literals, when you create string literals from macro arguments during macro expansion
- as part of text that you skip with conditional directives

Thus, almost any form that you write will be recognized as a valid preprocessing token. Do not, however, write an unbalanced single or double quote alone on a source line and outside other enclosing quotes, as in:

```
#define str(x) #x
char *name1 = str(O'Brien);        INVALID
char *name2 = "O'Brien";           valid
```

INCLUDE DIRECTIVES

You include the contents of a standard header or another source file in a translation unit by writing an *include* directive, as shown in Figure 2.8. The contents of the specified standard header or source file replace the *include* directive.

Figure 2.8: *Syntax of* include *directive.*

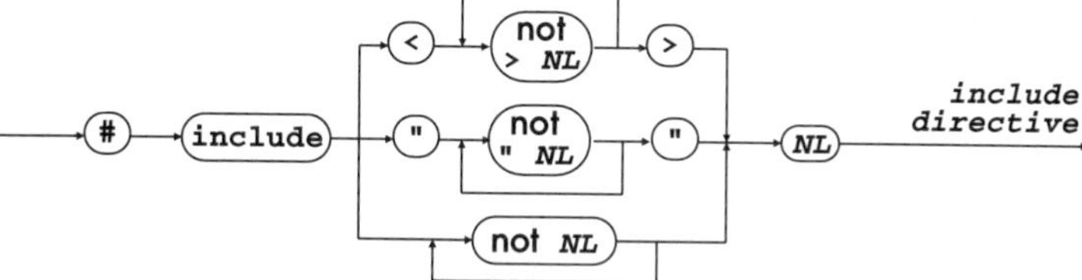

Following the directive name **include**, write one of the following:

- a standard header name between angle brackets
- a filename between double quotes
- any other form that expands to one of the two previous forms after macro replacement

Some examples are:

```
#include <stdio.h>        declare I/O functions
#include "mydecs.h"       and custom ones
#include MACHDEFS         MACHDEFS defined earlier
```

A standard header name:

- cannot contain a right angle bracket (`>`)
- should not contain the sequence that begins a comment (`/*`)

A filename:

- cannot contain a double quote (`"`)
- should not contain the sequence that begins a comment (`/*`)

For maximum portability, filenames should consist of from one to six lowercase letters, followed by a dot (`.`), followed by a lowercase letter. Some portable filenames are:

```
"salary.c"        "defs.h"      "test.x"
```

DEFINE DIRECTIVES

You define a macro by writing a *define* directive, as shown in Figure 2.9. Following the directive name **define**, you write one of two forms:

- A name *not* immediately followed by a left parenthesis, followed by any sequence of preprocessing tokens — to define a macro without parameters.
- A name immediately followed by a left parenthesis with *no* intervening white space, followed by zero or more distinct *parameter names* separated by commas, followed by a right parenthesis, followed by any sequence of preprocessing tokens — to define a macro with as many parameters as names that you write inside the parentheses.

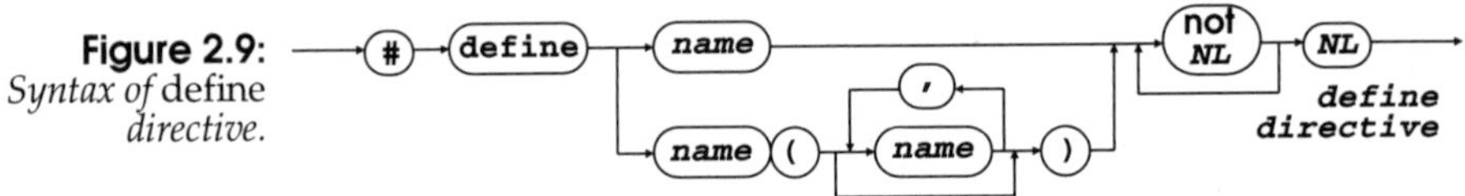

Figure 2.9: *Syntax of* define *directive.*

Three examples are:

```
#define  MIN_OFFSET     (-17)           no parameters
#define  quit()     exit(0)             zero parameters
#define add(x, y) ((x) + (y))           two parameters
```

Write a *define* directive that defines a name currently defined as a macro *only* if you write it with the identical sequence of preprocessing tokens as before. Where white space is present in one definition, white space must be present in the other. (The white space need not be identical.)

To remove a macro definition, write an *undef* directive, as shown in Figure 2.10. You might want to remove a macro definition so that you can define it differently with a *define* directive or to unmask any other meaning given to the name. (See **LIBRARY ORGANIZATION** in ***Chapter 8: Library***.)

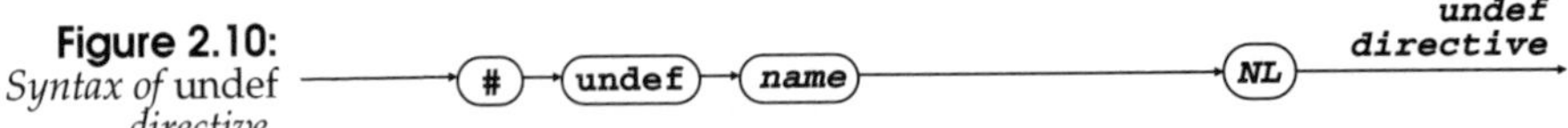

Figure 2.10: *Syntax of* undef *directive.*

The name whose definition you want to remove follows the directive name **undef**. If the name is not currently defined as a macro, the *undef* directive has no effect.

Expanding Macros

Preprocessing *expands* macros in all non-directive lines and in parts of some directives that are not skipped as part of an if-group. In those places where macros are expanded, you *invoke* a macro by writing one of the two forms: the name of a macro without parameters; or the name of a macro with parameters, followed by a left parenthesis, followed by zero or more *macro arguments* separated by commas, followed by a right parenthesis.

A macro argument consists of one or more preprocessing tokens. You must write parentheses only in balanced pairs within a macro argument. You must write commas only within these pairs of parentheses. For example, using the macros defined in the previous example, you can write:

```
if (MIN_OFFSET < x)        invokes MIN_OFFSET
    x = add(x, 3);          invokes add
```

Following the name of a macro with parameters, you *must* write one macro argument for each parameter and you *must* write at least one preprocessing token for each macro argument. Following the name of a macro with parameters, you *must not* write any directives within the invocation and you *must not* write the invocation across more than one file. Following the name of a macro with parameters, you *can* write arbitrary white space before the left parenthesis and you *can* write the invocation across multiple source lines.

The translator expands a macro invocation by replacing the preprocessing tokens that constitute the invocation with a sequence of zero or more preprocessing tokens. It determines the replacement sequence in a series of steps. This example illustrates most of the steps.

```
#define sh(x) printf("n" #x "=%d, or %d\n",n##x,alt[x])
#define sub_z 26
    sh(sub_z)                    macro invocation
```

The steps, in order, are:

1. The translator takes the replacement list from the sequence of any preprocessing tokens (and intervening white space) in the macro definition. It does not include leading and trailing white space as part of the list.

```
printf("n" #x "=%d, or %d\n",n##x,alt[x])
```

Amendment 1 2. A macro parameter name must follow each **#** token (or **%:** token, with Amendment 1) in the replacement list. The translator replaces the **#** token and parameter name with a string literal made from the corresponding (unexpanded) macro argument. How the translator creates the string literal is shown below.

```
printf("n" "sub_z" "=%d, or %d\n",n##x,alt[x])
```

Amendment 1 3. Preprocessing tokens must both precede and follow each **##** token (or **%:%:** token, with Amendment 1) in the replacement list. If either token is a macro parameter name, the translator replaces that name with the corresponding (unexpanded) macro argument. The translator then replaces the **##** token and its preceding and following tokens with a single preprocessing token that is the concatenation of the preceding and following tokens. The result must be a valid preprocessing token.

```
printf("n" "sub_z" "=%d, or %d\n",nsub_z,alt[x])
```

4. For any remaining macro parameter names in the replacement list, the translator expands the corresponding macro argument. The translator replaces the macro parameter name in the replacement list with the resulting sequence.

```
printf("n" "sub_z" "=%d, or %d\n",nsub_z,alt[26])
```

5. The translator remembers not to further expand the macro (**sh** in the example) while it rescans the replacement list to detect macro invocations in the original replacement list or that it may have constructed as a result of any of these replacements. The replacement list can provide the beginning of an invocation of a macro with parameters, with the remainder of the invocation consisting of preprocessing tokens following the invocation.

In the example shown, no further expansion occurs. After string literal concatenation, the resulting text is:

```
    printf("nsub_z=%d, or %d\n",nsub_z,alt[26])
```

You can take advantage of rescanning by writing macros such as:

```
#define add(x, y) ((x) + (y))
#define sub(x, y) ((x) - (y))
#define math(op, a, b) op(a, b)
    math(add, c+3, d) becomes ((c+3) + (d))
```

Creating String Literals

The translator creates a string literal from a macro argument by performing the following steps, in order:

1. The translator discards leading and trailing white space.
2. Each preprocessing token in the macro argument appears in the string literal exactly as you spelled it, except that the translator adds a `\` before each `\` and `"` within a character constant or string literal.
3. Any white space between preprocessing tokens in the macro argument appears in the string literal as a ***space*** character.

For example:

```
#define show(x)   printf(#x "= %d\n", x)
    show(a    +/* same as space */-1);
                   becomes
    printf("a + -1= %d\n", a + -1);
```

You can also create a wide-character string literal:

```
#define wcsl(x)    L ## #x
    wcsl(arigato)  becomes L"arigato"
```

CONDITIONAL DIRECTIVES

You can selectively skip groups of lines within source files by writing *conditional* directives. The conditional directives within a source file form zero or more *if-groups,* as shown in Figure 2.11. Within an if-group, you write conditional directives to bracket one or more groups of lines, or *line-groups,* as shown in Figure 2.12. The translator retains no more than one line-group within an if-group. It skips all other line-groups. An if-group has the following general form:

- It begins with an *if, ifdef,* or *ifndef* directive, followed by the first line-group that you want to selectively skip.

- Zero or more *elif* directives follow this first line-group, each followed by a line-group that you want to selectively skip.
- An optional *else* directive follows all line-groups controlled by *elif* directives, followed by the last line-group you want to selectively skip.
- An if-group ends with an *endif* directive.

Figure 2.11: *Syntax of if-group.*

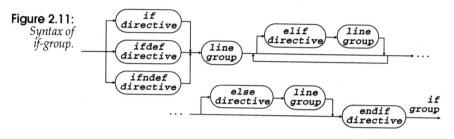

A *line-group* is zero or more occurrences of either an if-group or any line other than an *if, ifdef, ifndef, elif, else,* or *endif* directive. The translator retains no more than one alternative line-group:

- If the condition is true in the leading *if, ifdef,* or *ifndef* directive, the translator retains the first line-group and skips all others.
- Otherwise, if a condition is true in a subsequent *elif* directive, the translator retains its alternative line-group and skips all others.
- Otherwise, if an *else* directive is present, the translator retains its alternative line-group.
- Otherwise, the translator skips all line-groups within the if-group.

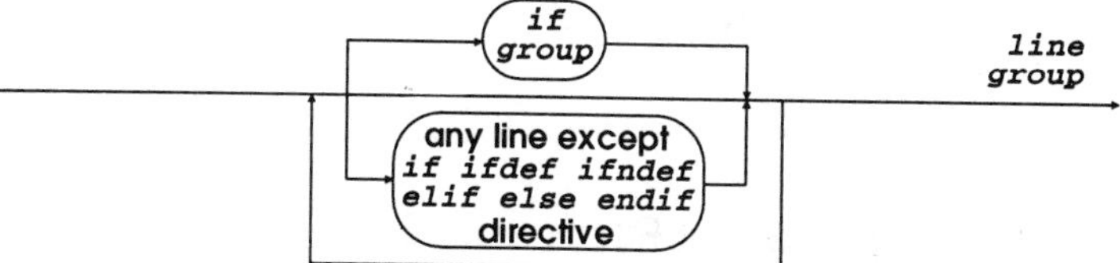

Figure 2.12: *Syntax of line-group.*

For example, to retain a line-group in a header file at most once, regardless of the number of times the header is included:

```
#ifndef _SEEN
#define _SEEN
/* body of header */
#endif
```

And to retain only one of three line-groups, depending on the value of the macro **MACHINE** defined earlier in the translation unit:

```
#if MACHINE == 68000
     int x;
#elif MACHINE == 8086
     long x;
#else     /* all others */
     #error UNKNOWN TARGET MACHINE
#endif
```

Conditional Expressions

For an *if* directive, write a *conditional expression* following the directive name **if**, as shown in Figure 2.13. If the expression you write has a nonzero value, then the translator retains as part of the translation unit the line-group immediately following the *if* directive. Otherwise, the translator skips this line-group.

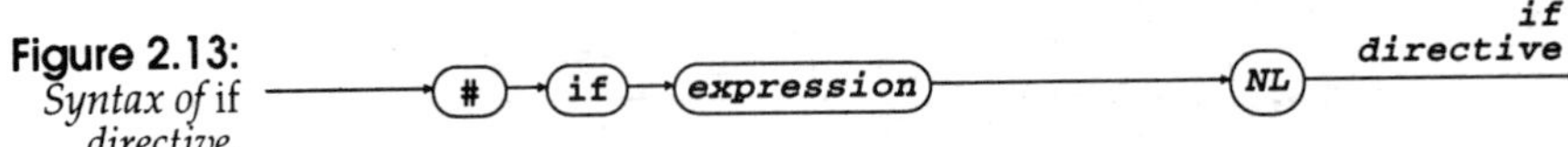

Figure 2.13: *Syntax of* if *directive.*

The translator evaluates the expression you write by performing the following steps. This example illustrates most of the steps, in order:

```
#define VERSION    2
#if defined x || y || VERSION < 3
```

1. The translator replaces each occurrence of the name **defined**, followed by another name or by another name enclosed in parentheses. The replacement is **1** if the second name is defined as a macro; otherwise, the replacement is **0**.

```
#if           0 || y || VERSION < 3
```

2. The translator expands macros in the expression.

```
#if           0 || y || 2 < 3
```

3. The translator replaces each remaining name with **0**.

```
#if           0 || 0 || 2 < 3
```

4. The translator converts preprocessing tokens to C tokens and then parses and evaluates the expression.

```
#if           1
```

Thus, the translator retains the line-group following the *if* directive.

Restrictions on Conditional Expressions

In the expression part of an *if* directive, you write only integer constant expressions (described under **CLASSES OF EXPRESSIONS** in ***Chapter 7: Expressions***), with the following additional considerations:

- You cannot write the *sizeof* or *type cast* operators. (The translator replaces all names before it recognizes keywords.)
- The translator may be able to represent a broader range of integers than the target environment.
- The translator represents type *int* the same as *long*, and *unsigned int* the same as *unsigned long*.
- The translator can translate character constants to a set of code values different from the set for the target environment.

To determine the properties of the target environment by writing *if* directives, test the values of the macros defined in **<limits.h>**.

Other Conditional Directives

The *ifdef* directive tests whether a macro name is defined, as shown in Figure 2.14. The directive:

```
#ifdef xyz
```

is equivalent to:

```
#if defined xyz
```

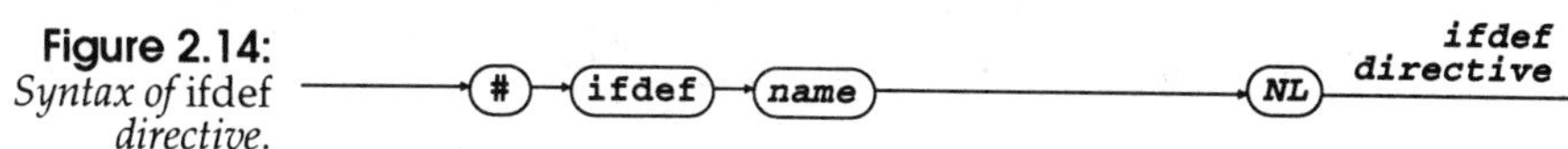

Figure 2.14: *Syntax of* ifdef *directive.*

The *ifndef* directive tests whether a macro name is *not* defined, as shown in Figure 2.15. The directive:

```
#ifndef xyz
```

is equivalent to:

```
#if !defined xyz
```

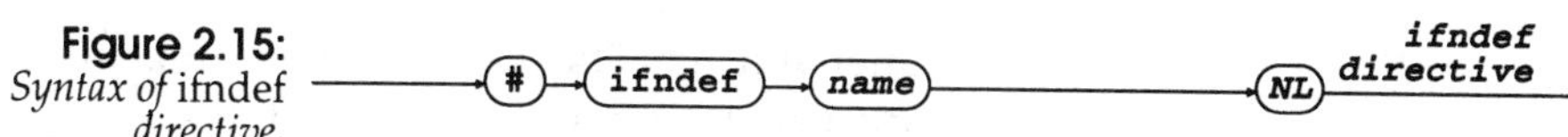

Figure 2.15: *Syntax of* ifndef *directive.*

You can provide an alternative line-group within an if-group by writing an *elif* directive, as shown in Figure 2.16. Following the directive name **elif**, you write an expression just as for an *if* directive. The translator retains the alternative line-group following the *elif* directive if the expression is true and if no earlier line-group has been retained in the same if-group.

Figure 2.16: *Syntax of* elif *directive.*

You can also provide a last alternative line-group by writing an *else* directive, as shown in Figure 2.17.

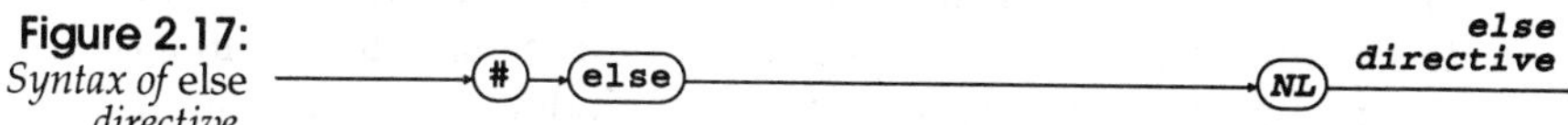

Figure 2.17: *Syntax of* else *directive.*

You terminate the last alternative line-group within an if-group by writing an *endif* directive, as shown in Figure 2.18.

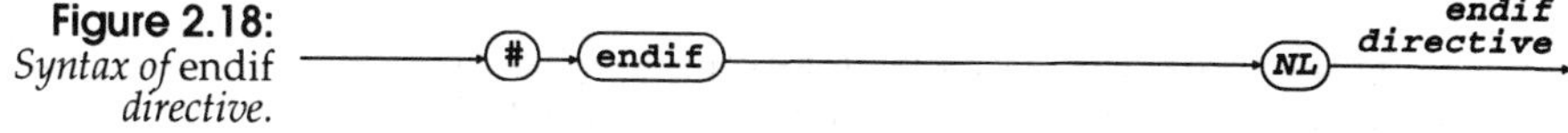

Figure 2.18: *Syntax of* endif *directive.*

OTHER DIRECTIVES

You alter the source line number and filename by writing a *line* directive, as shown in Figure 2.19. The translator uses the line number and filename to alter the values of the predefined macros **`__FILE__`** and **`__LINE__`**.

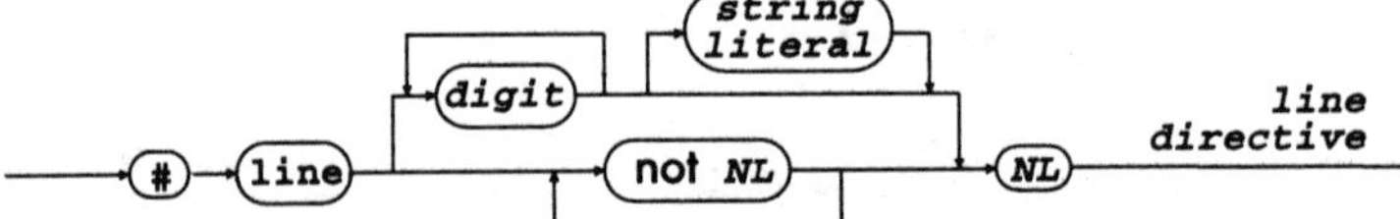

Figure 2.19: *Syntax of* line *directive.*

Following the directive name **`line`**, write one of the following:

- a decimal integer (giving the new line number of the line following)
- a decimal integer as before, followed by a string literal (giving the new line number and the new source filename)
- any other form that expands to one of the two previous forms after macro replacement

You generate an unconditional diagnostic message by writing an *error* directive, as shown in Figure 2.20. Following the directive name **`error`**, write any text that the translator can parse as preprocessing tokens. The translator writes a diagnostic message that includes this sequence of preprocessing tokens.

Figure 2.20: *Syntax of* error *directive.*

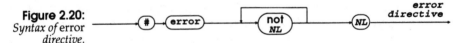

For example:

```
#if !defined VERSION
  #error You failed to specify a VERSION
#endif
```

You convey additional information to the translator by writing a *pragma* directive, as shown in Figure 2.21. Following the directive name **`pragma`**, write any text that the translator can parse as preprocessing tokens. Each translator interprets this sequence of preprocessing tokens in its own way and ignores those *pragma* directives that it does not understand.

Figure 2.21: *Syntax of* pragma

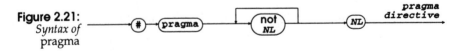

You introduce comments or additional white space into the program by writing the *null* directive, as shown in Figure 2.22.

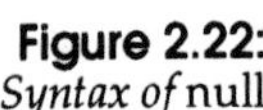

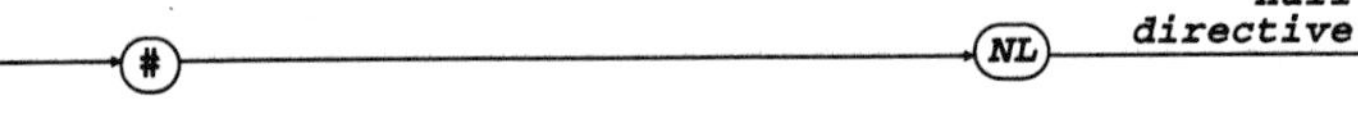

Figure 2.22: *Syntax of* null *directive.*

The *null* directive is the only directive that does not have a directive name following the **#** token. For example:

```
#
#    /* this section for testing only */ valid

#define comment     /* comment only */
#
#    comment                            INVALID
```

PREDEFINED MACROS

The translator predefines several macro names.

The macro **__DATE__** expands to a string literal that gives the date you invoked the translator. Its format is: **"Mmm dd yyyy"**. The month name **Mmm** is the same as for dates generated by the library function **asctime**, declared in **<time.h>**. The day part **dd** ranges from **" 1"** to **"31"** (a leading **0** becomes a ***space***).

The macro **__FILE__** expands to a string literal that gives the remembered filename of the current source file. You can alter the remembered filename by writing a *line* directive.

The macro **__LINE__** expands to a decimal integer constant that gives the remembered line number within the current source file. You can alter the remembered line number by writing a *line* directive.

The macro **__STDC__** expands to the decimal integer constant **1**. The translator should provide another value (or leave the macro undefined) when you invoke it for other than a Standard C environment. For example, you can write:

```
#if __STDC__ != 1
  #error NOT a Standard C environment
#endif
```

Amendment 1 The macro **__STDC_VERSION__** expands to the decimal integer constant **199409L**. The translator should provide another value (or leave the macro undefined) when you invoke it for other than a Standard C environment that incorporates Amendment 1.

The macro **__TIME__** expands to a string literal that gives the time you invoked the translator. Its format is **"hh:mm:ss"**, which is the same as for times generated by the library function **asctime**, declared in **<time.h>**.

You cannot write these macro names, or the name **defined**, in an *undef* directive. Nor can you redefine these names with a *define* directive.

Chapter 3: Syntax

The final stage of preprocessing is to convert all remaining preprocessing tokens in the translation unit to C tokens. The translator then parses these C tokens into one or more *declarations*. In particular:

- Declarations that define *objects* specify the storage for data that a program manipulates.
- Declarations that are *function definitions* specify the actions that a program performs.

You use *expressions* in declarations to specify values to the translator or to specify the computations that the program performs when it executes. This chapter shows the forms of all C tokens. It also summarizes the syntax of declarations, function definitions, and expressions. You use these syntactic forms, with preprocessing directives and macros, to write a C program.

C TOKENS

Each C token derives from a preprocessing token. Additional restrictions apply, however, so not all preprocessing tokens form valid C tokens. You must ensure that only valid C tokens remain in the translation unit after preprocessing.

Every preprocessing name forms a valid C token. Some of the names that you write are *keyword* C tokens (names that have special meaning to the translator). Table 3.1 lists all defined keywords.

Table 3.1: *List of keywords.*

`auto`	`double`	`int`	`struct`
`break`	`else`	`long`	`switch`
`case`	`enum`	`register`	`typedef`
`char`	`extern`	`return`	`union`
`const`	`float`	`short`	`unsigned`
`continue`	`for`	`signed`	`void`
`default`	`goto`	`sizeof`	`volatile`
`do`	`if`	`static`	`while`

A *name* C token is a preprocessing name that is not a keyword, as shown in Figure 3.1. You must ensure that distinct names with external linkage differ within the first 6 characters, even if the translator does not distinguish between lowercase and uppercase letters when comparing names. (See **WRITING PORTABLE PROGRAMS** in ***Appendix A: Portability***.)

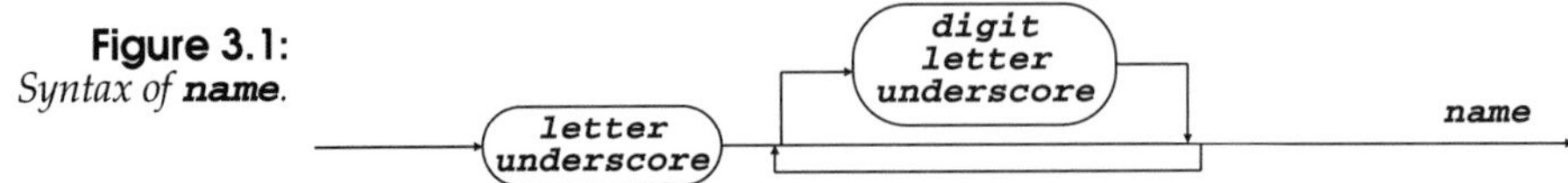

Figure 3.1: *Syntax of* **name**.

Integer and Floating-Point Constants

Every preprocessing number in the translation unit must be either an *integer constant* or a *floating-point constant* C token. An integer constant is a preprocessing number that represents a value of an integer type, as shown in Figure 3.2.

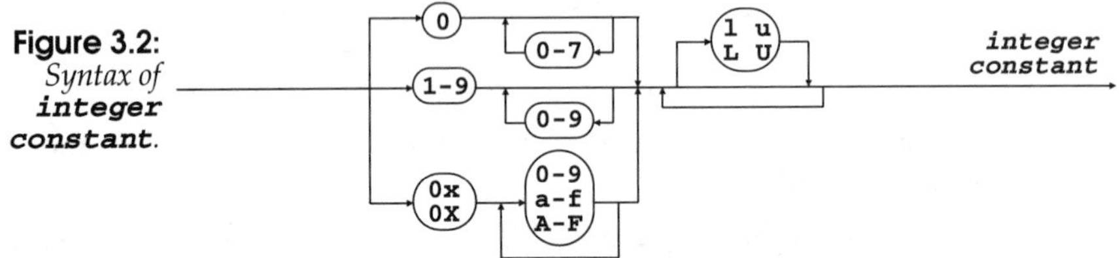

Figure 3.2: *Syntax of* **integer constant**.

An integer constant takes one of three forms:

- a leading `0x` or `0X` indicates a hexadecimal (base 16) integer
- a leading `0` indicates an octal (base 8) integer
- a leading nonzero digit indicates a decimal (base 10) integer

You write any combination of:

- at most one `l` or `L` suffix to indicate a *long* type
- at most one `u` or `U` suffix to indicate an *unsigned* type

(See **READING EXPRESSIONS** in ***Chapter 7: Expressions.***)

A floating-point constant is a preprocessing number that represents a number of a floating-point type, as shown in Figure 3.3.

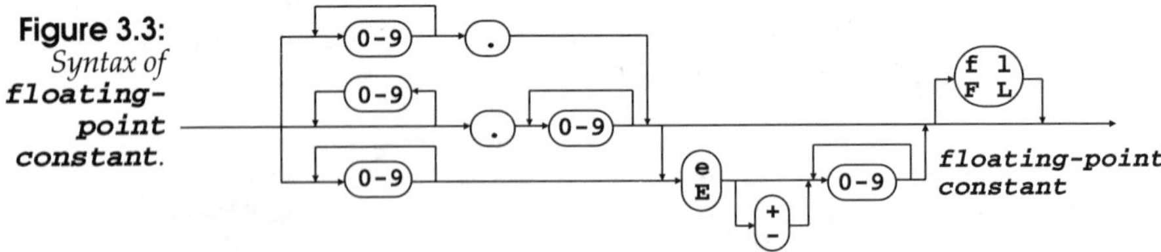

Figure 3.3: *Syntax of* **floating-point constant**.

You write:

- either a decimal point or an exponent or both to distinguish a floating-point constant from an integer constant
- at most one `f` or `F` suffix to indicate type *float*, or at most one `l` or `L` suffix to indicate type *long double*

(See **READING EXPRESSIONS** in ***Chapter 7: Expressions.***)

Character Constants and String Literals

A *character constant* C token has the same form as a preprocessing character constant, as shown in Figure 3.4.

Figure 3.4: *Syntax of* **`character constant`**.

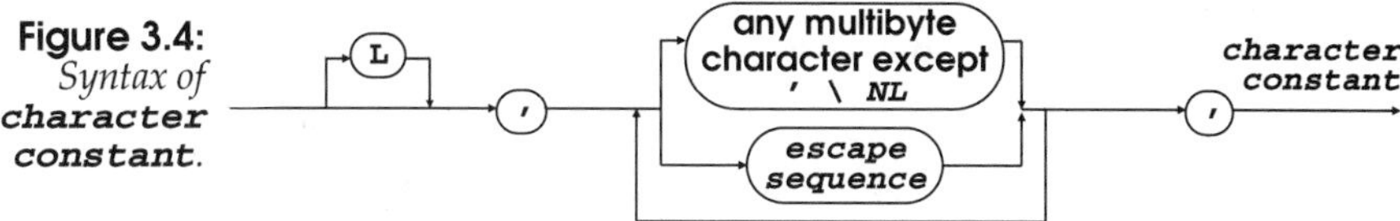

A *string literal* C token has the same form as a preprocessing string literal, as shown in Figure 3.5.

Figure 3.5: *Syntax of* **`string literal`**.

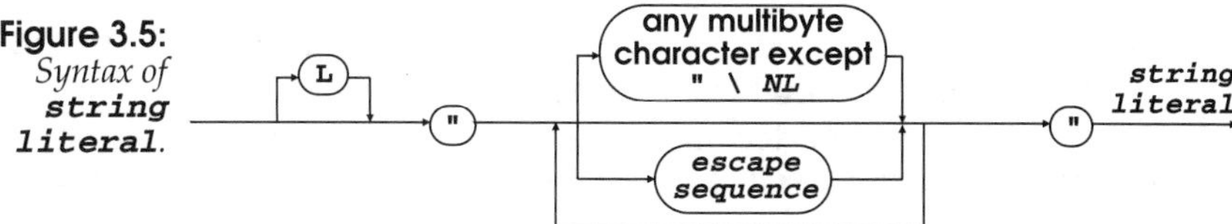

An escape sequence has the same form as within a preprocessing character constant or string literal, as shown in Figure 3.6.

Figure 3.6: *Syntax of* **`escape sequence`**.

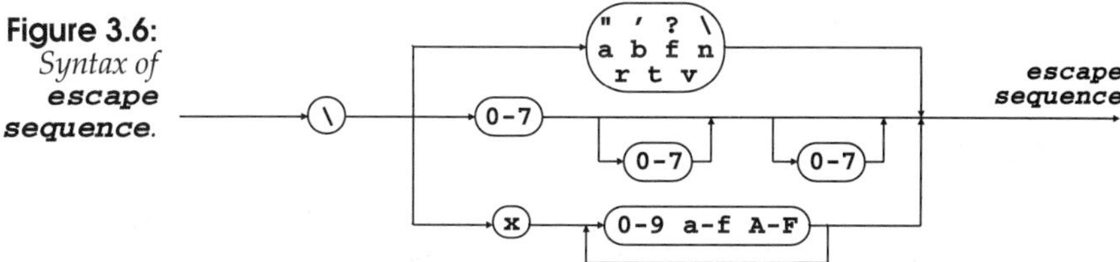

Amendment 1

An *operator* or *punctuator* C token has the same form as a preprocessing operator or punctuator, except that the tokens `#` and `##` (and `%:` and `%:%:`, with Amendment 1) have meaning only during preprocessing. Moreover, the remaining Amendment 1 additions map to other C tokens:

- `<:` becomes `[`
- `:>` becomes `]`
- `<%` becomes `{`
- `%>` becomes `}`

Table 3.2 shows all operators and punctuators.

Table 3.2: *List of* **`operator`** *and* **`punctuator`** *tokens.*

<table>
<tr><td>...</td><td>&&</td><td>-=</td><td>>=</td><td>~</td><td>+</td><td>;</td><td>]</td></tr>
<tr><td><<=</td><td>&=</td><td>-></td><td>>></td><td>%</td><td>,</td><td><</td><td>^</td></tr>
<tr><td>>>=</td><td>*=</td><td>/=</td><td>^=</td><td>&</td><td>-</td><td>=</td><td>{</td></tr>
<tr><td>!=</td><td>++</td><td><<</td><td>|=</td><td>(</td><td>.</td><td>></td><td>|</td></tr>
<tr><td>%=</td><td>+=</td><td><=</td><td>||</td><td>)</td><td>/</td><td>?</td><td>}</td></tr>
<tr><td></td><td>--</td><td>==</td><td>!</td><td>*</td><td>:</td><td>[</td><td></td></tr>
</table>

DECLARATION SYNTAX

The translator parses all C tokens that constitute a translation unit, as shown in Figure 3.7, as one or more *declarations,* some of which are *function definitions.* A declaration (other than a function definition) takes a variety of forms, as shown in Figure 3.8.

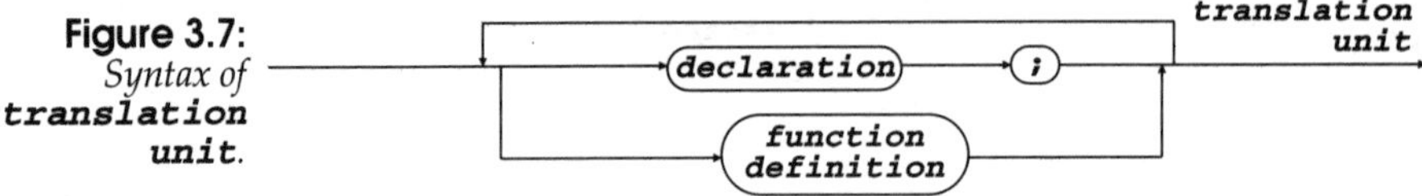

Figure 3.7: *Syntax of* **`translation unit`**.

Declarations can contain other declarations. You cannot write a function definition inside another declaration, however. (See **FUNCTION DEFINITION SYNTAX** later in this chapter.) There are many contexts for declarations. Some forms of declarations are permitted only in certain contexts. (See **DECLARATION CONTEXTS AND LEVELS** in ***Chapter 5: Declarations.***)

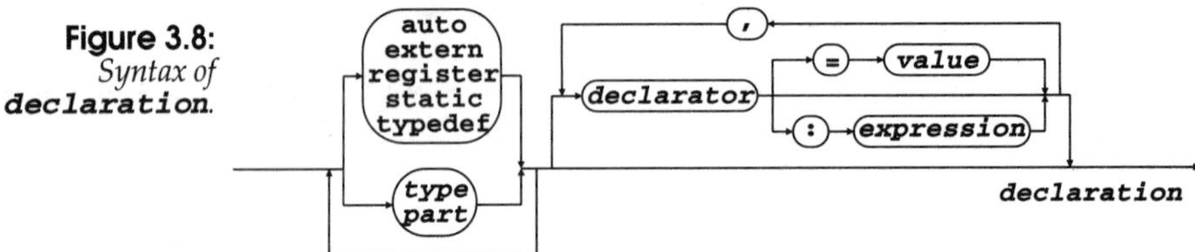

Figure 3.8: *Syntax of* **`declaration`**.

Storage Class and Type Parts

You begin a declaration with an optional storage class keyword, intermixed with zero or more *type parts,* as shown in Figure 3.9. The storage class keyword is from the set:

```
auto      extern      register    static      typedef
```

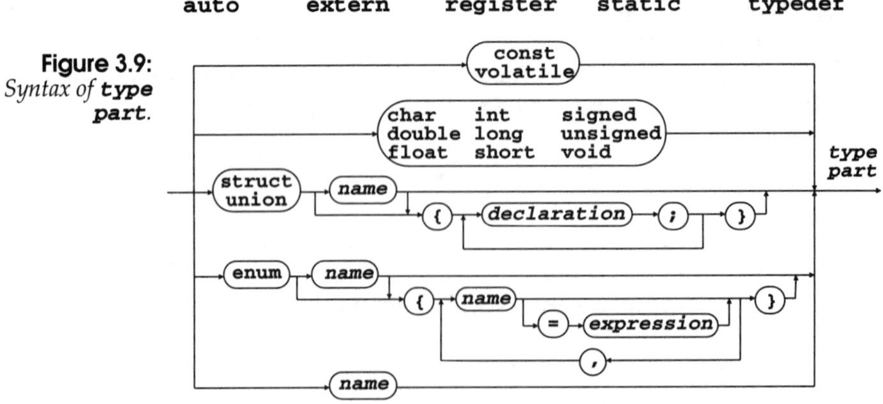

Figure 3.9: *Syntax of* **`type part`**.

You write a type part as any one of the following.

- a type qualifier keyword, from the set:

```
const          volatile
```

- a type specifier keyword, from the set:

`char`	**`double`**	**`float`**	**`int`**	**`long`**
`short`	**`signed`**	**`unsigned`**	**`void`**	

- a structure, union, or enumeration specification
- a type definition name

You can write only certain combinations of type parts. (See **ARITHMETIC TYPES** and **TYPE QUALIFIERS** in ***Chapter 4: Types.***)

Declarators

You can follow the storage class and type part of a declaration with a list of *declarators* separated by commas. Each declarator can specify a name for the entity that you are declaring as well as additional type information, as shown in Figure 3.10.

Figure 3.10: *Syntax of* ***`declarator`***.

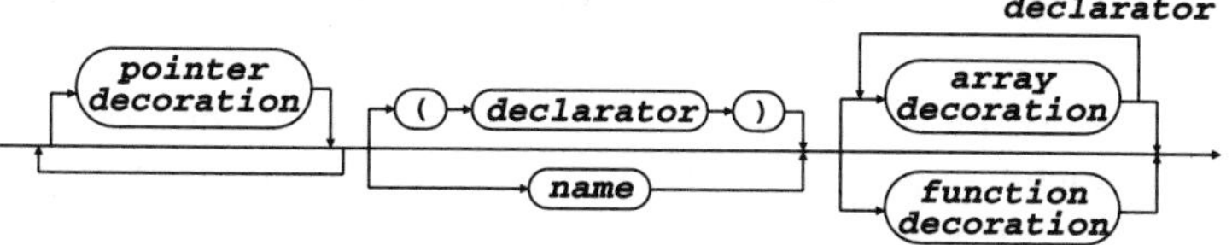

You write a declarator as, in order:

1. zero or more *pointer decorations*
2. an optional name or a declarator in parentheses
3. zero or more *array decorations* or at most one *function decoration*

A pointer decoration consists of an asterisk (`*`) followed by an optional list of type qualifier keywords, as shown in Figure 3.11.

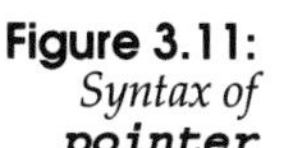

Figure 3.11: *Syntax of* ***`pointer`***

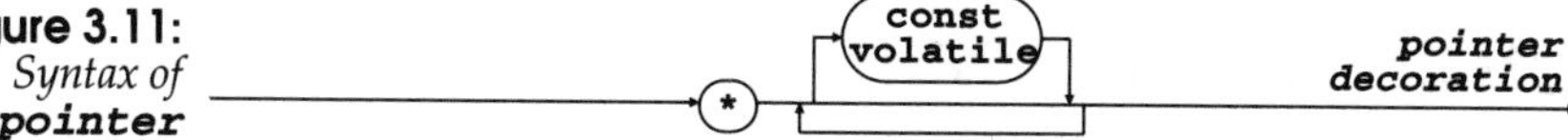

An array decoration consists of an optional expression enclosed in brackets (`[]`), as shown in Figure 3.12.

Figure 3.12: *Syntax of* ***`array decoration`***.

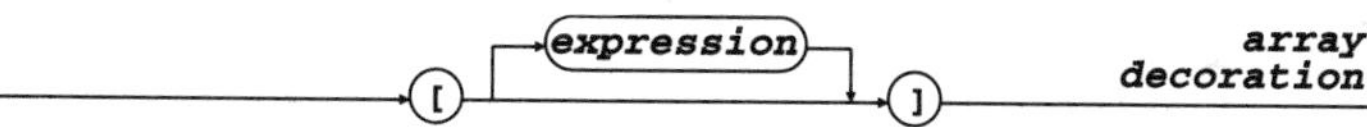

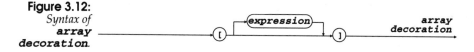

A function decoration is a sequence of one of the following:

- zero or more parameter names
- one or more parameter declarations

In either sequence, the parameters are separated by commas and enclosed in parentheses, as shown in Figure 3.13. Some of these forms are permitted in certain contexts and not in others. (See ***Chapter 6: Functions.***)

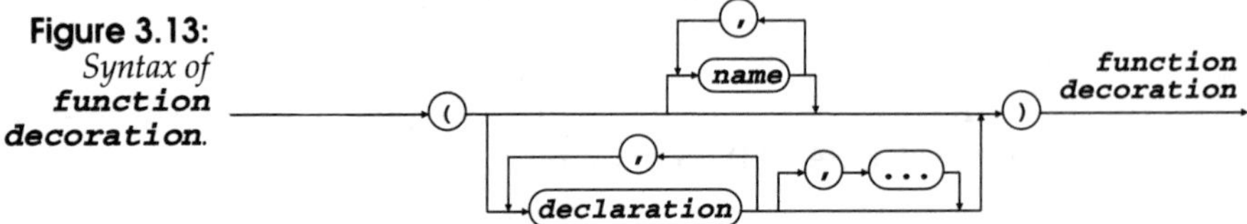

Figure 3.13: *Syntax of* **`function decoration`**.

Object Initializers and Bitfield Specifications

You can follow each declarator with one of the following:

- an optional object initializer, consisting of an equal sign (`=`) followed by a value
- an optional bitfield size, consisting of a colon (`:`) followed by an expression

You write an object initializer *value* as either an expression or a list of such values separated by commas and enclosed in braces `{}`, as shown in Figure 3.14.

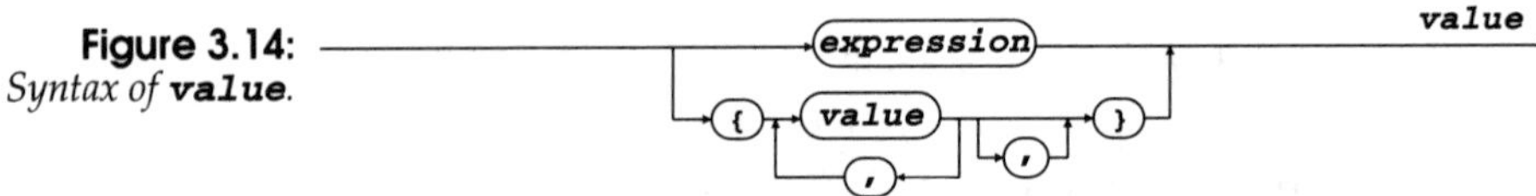

Figure 3.14: *Syntax of* **`value`**.

You can write a trailing comma after the last value in a comma separated list of object initializers. (See **OBJECT INITIALIZERS** in ***Chapter 5: Declarations.***)

FUNCTION DEFINITION SYNTAX

A function definition declares a function and specifies the actions it performs when it executes, as shown in Figure 3.15.

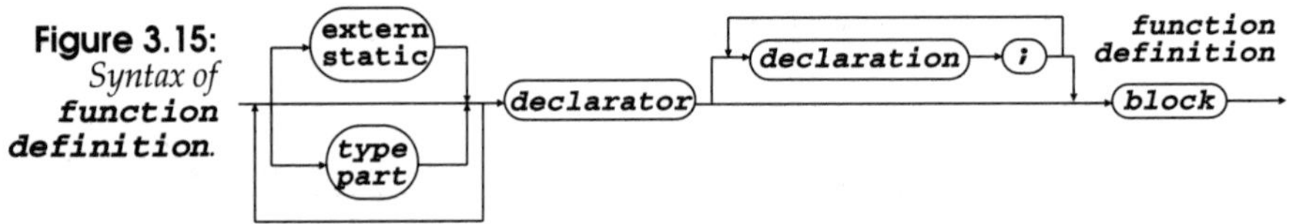

Figure 3.15: *Syntax of* **`function definition`**.

You write a function definition as, in order:

1. an optional set of storage class and type parts
2. a declarator
3. zero or more parameter declarations each terminated by a semicolon
4. a *block*

The declarator contains a function decoration that describes the parameters to the function. You can write parameter declarations before the block only if the function decoration contains a list of parameter names.

A block, shown in Figure 3.16, consists of braces surrounding, in order:

1. zero or more declarations each terminated by a semicolon
2. zero or more statements

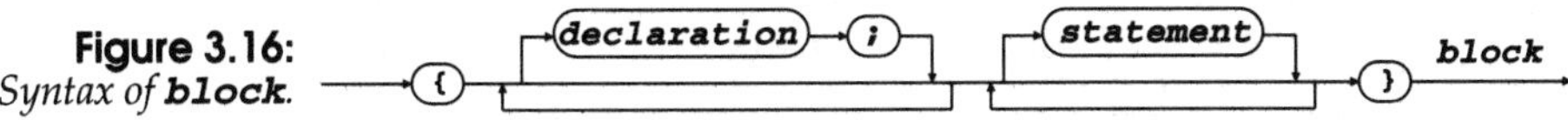

Figure 3.16: *Syntax of* **block**.

A block contains a sequence of *statements* that specifies the actions performed by the block when it executes, as shown in Figure 3.17.

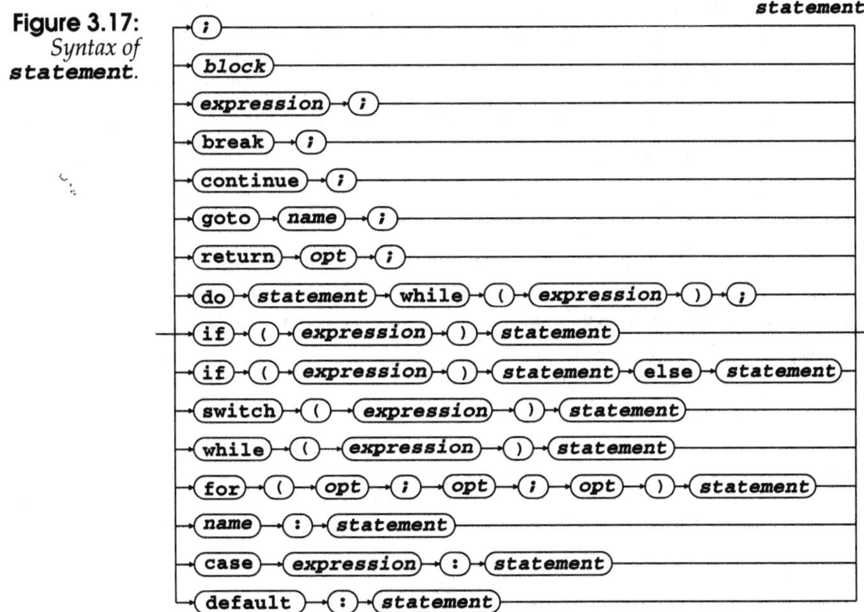

Figure 3.17: *Syntax of* **statement**.

opt represents an optional expression, as shown in Figure 3.18.

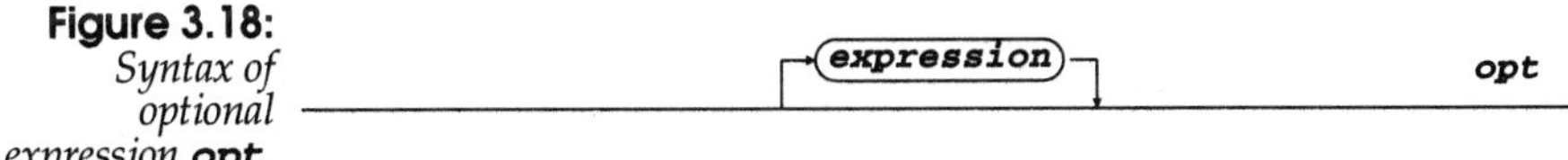

Figure 3.18: *Syntax of optional expression* **opt**.

Statements specify the flow of control through a function when it executes. A statement that contains expressions also computes values and alters the values stored in objects when the statement executes.

EXPRESSION SYNTAX

You use expressions to specify values to the translator or to specify the computations that a program performs when it executes.

- You write an expression as one or more *terms* separated by *infix* operators.
- Each term is preceded by zero or more *prefix* operators. Each term is followed by zero or more *postfix* operators, as shown in Figure 3.19.

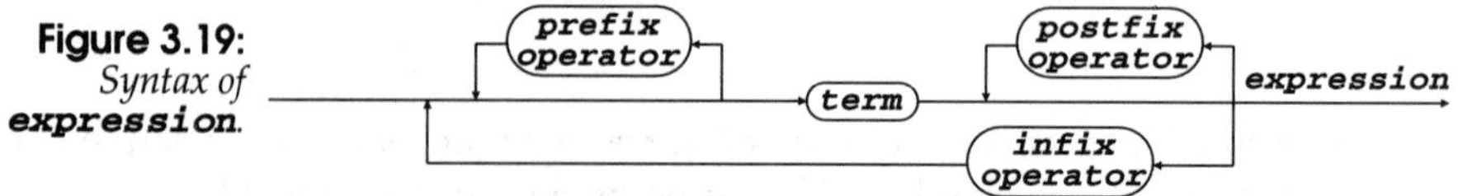

Figure 3.19: *Syntax of* **expression**.

(See **OPERATOR SUMMARY** in ***Chapter 7: Expressions*** for a description of how operators and terms form subexpressions.)

You write a term, as shown in Figure 3.20, as one of the following:

- a name that is declared as a function, object, or enumeration constant
- an integer constant
- a floating-point constant
- a character constant
- a string literal
- the *sizeof* operator followed by a declaration enclosed in parentheses
- an expression enclosed in parentheses

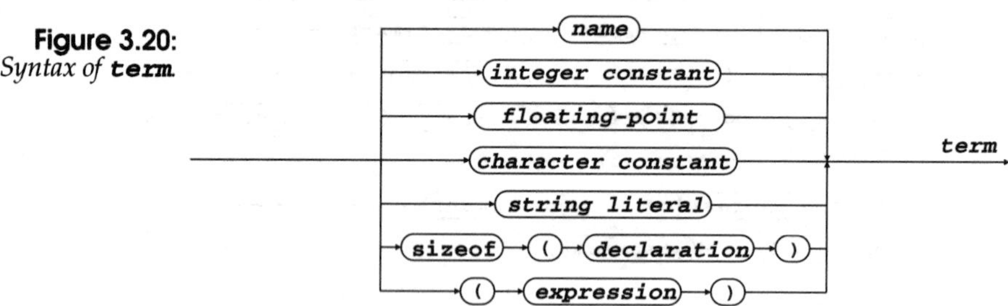

Figure 3.20: *Syntax of* **term**.

You write an infix operator, as shown in Figure 3.21, as one of the following:

- one of the infix operator tokens
- the conditional operator pair **? :** enclosing another expression

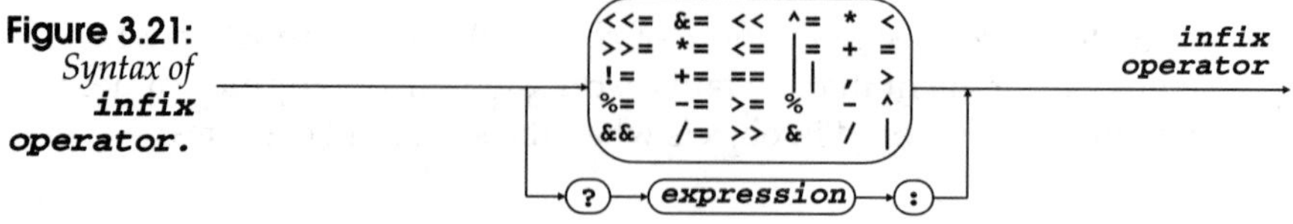

Figure 3.21: *Syntax of* **infix operator.**

You write a prefix operator, as shown in Figure 3.22, as one of the following:

- the keyword **`sizeof`**
- one of the prefix operator tokens
- a *type cast* (consisting of a declaration enclosed in parentheses)

Figure 3.22: *Syntax of* **`prefix operator`**.

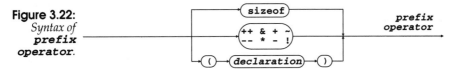

You can write only certain forms of declarations in a type cast. (See **DECLARATION CONTEXTS AND LEVELS** in ***Chapter 5: Declarations.***)

You write a postfix operator, as shown in Figure 3.23, as one of the following:

- the postfix operator token `++`
- the postfix operator token `--`
- an array subscript expression, enclosed in brackets `[]`
- a function call argument expression list, enclosed in parentheses `()`
- the member selection operator (a period), followed by the name of a structure or union member
- the member selection operator `->`, followed by the name of a structure or union member

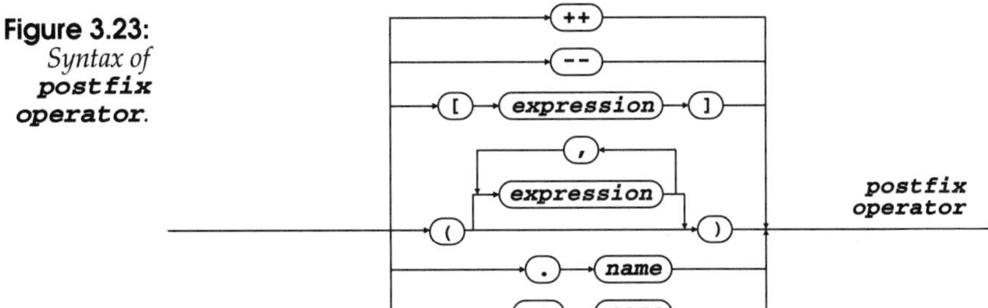

Figure 3.23: *Syntax of* **`postfix operator`**.

You can write only certain forms of expressions in some contexts. (See ***Chapter 7: Expressions.***)

Chapter 4: Types

Type is a fundamental concept in Standard C. When you declare a name, you give it a type. Each expression and subexpression that you write has a type. This chapter shows each type you can write and how to classify it as either a *function type,* an *object type,* or an *incomplete type.* You see how an implementation can represent *arithmetic types* and how to derive more complex *pointer types* as well as others that are not *scalar types.* You learn how to use *type qualifiers* to specify access limitations for objects. The chapter ends with rules for forming a *composite type* from two *compatible types.*

TYPE CLASSIFICATION

Types have a number of classifications, as summarized in Figure 4.1. The diagram shows you, for example, that the type *short* is an integer type, an arithmetic type, a scalar type, and an object type. Similarly, a *pointer to function* is a pointer type, a scalar type, and an object type.

Figure 4.1: *Type classification.*

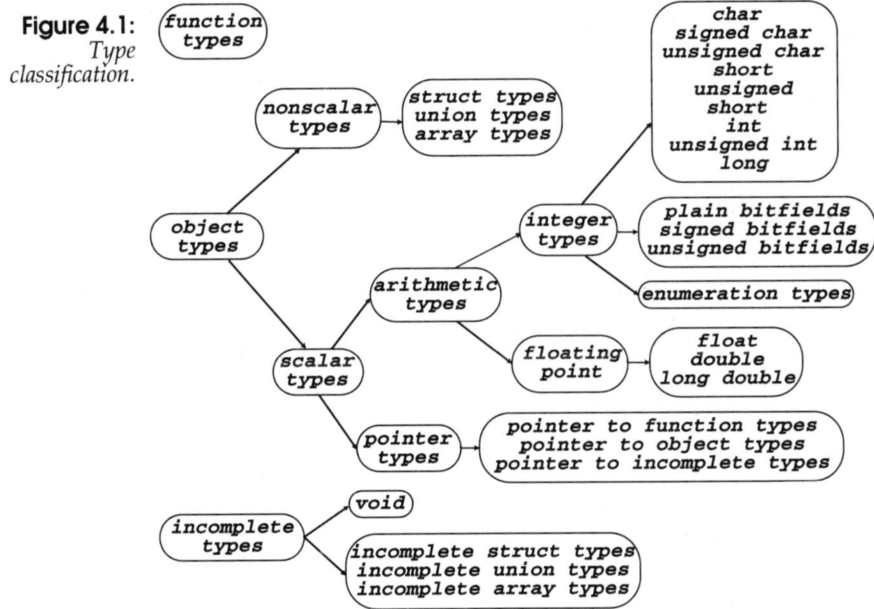

A type can be in any of three major classes. A function type determines what type of result a function returns, and possibly what argument types it accepts when you call it. An object type determines how an object is represented, what values it can express, and what operations you can perform on its values. An incomplete type determines whether you can complete the type and with what object types the type is compatible.

Object types have a number of subclassifications. This book uses these subclassifications to simplify a number of descriptions. For example, you can declare a member of a structure to have any object type, you can compare against zero any value that has scalar type, you can multiply any two values that have arithmetic types, and you can form the inclusive OR of any two values that have integer types.

ARITHMETIC TYPES

The arithmetic types describe objects that represent numeric values. You use *integer types* to represent whole numbers, including zero or negative values. The three subclassifications of integer types are:

- the predefined *basic integer types*
- the *bitfield types*
- the *enumeration types*

You use *floating-point types* to represent signed numbers that can have a fractional part. The range of values that you can represent with floating-point types is always much larger than those you can represent with integer types, but the precision of floating-point values is limited. The translator predefines three floating-point types:

- *float*
- *double*
- *long double*

Basic Integer Types

The translator predefines nine basic integer types. You can designate some of these types in more than one way. For a designation that has more than one type specifier, you can write the type specifiers in any order. For example, you can write the designation **unsigned short int** as:

```
unsigned short int    unsigned int short
short unsigned int    short int unsigned
int unsigned short    int short unsigned
```

Table 4.1 lists the properties of all basic integer types.

If you write no type specifiers in a declaration, the type you specify is *int*. For example, the following declarations both declare **x** to have type *int*.

```
extern int x;
extern x;
```

This book refers to each predefined type by its first designation listed in the table, but written in italics. For example, *unsigned short* refers to the type you designate as **`unsigned short`** or as **`unsigned short int`**.

Table 4.1: *Properties of basic integer types.*

Alternate Designations	Minimum Range	Restrictions on Representation
`char`	[0, 128)	same as either *signed char* or *unsigned char*
`signed char`	(–128, 128)	at least an 8-bit signed integer
`unsigned char`	[0, 256)	same size as *signed char;* no negative values

`short`
`signed short`
`short int`
`signed short int`
	$(-2^{15}, 2^{15})$	at least a 16-bit signed integer; at least as large as *char*

`unsigned short` `unsigned short int`	$[0, 2^{16})$	same size as *short;* no negative values

`int`
`signed`
`signed int`
none
	$(-2^{15}, 2^{15})$	at least a 16-bit signed integer; at least as large as *short*

`unsigned int` `unsigned`	$[0, 2^{16})$	same size as *int;* no negative values

`long`
`signed long`
`long int`
`signed long int`
	$(-2^{31}, 2^{31})$	at least a 32-bit signed integer; at least as large as *int*

`unsigned long` `unsigned long int`	$[0, 2^{32})$	same size as *long;* no negative values

In Table 4.1, and in the tables that follow in this chapter, each minimum range is written as one or more ranges of values. The leftmost value is the lowest value in the range, and the rightmost is the highest. A left or right bracket indicates that the endpoint is included in the range. A left or right parenthesis indicates that the endpoint is *not* included in the range. Thus, the notation [0, 256) describes a range that includes 0 through 255.

Table 4.2 lists the powers of 2 used in the other tables in this chapter. An implementation can represent a broader range of values than shown here, but not a narrower range.

Table 4.2: *Relevant powers of two.*

Power of 2	Decimal Value
2^{15}	32,768
2^{16}	65,536
2^{31}	2,147,483,648
2^{32}	4,294,967,296

Bitfields

A bitfield is an integer that occupies a specific number of contiguous bits within an object that has an integer type. You can declare bitfields based on any of three different sets of integer type designations to designate three different kinds of bitfields:

- *plain bitfields*
- *signed bitfields*
- *unsigned bitfields*

You declare bitfields only as members of a structure or a union. The expression you write after the colon specifies the size of the bitfield in bits. You cannot portably specify more bits than are used to represent type *int*.

How the translator packs successive bitfield declarations into integer type objects is implementation-defined. (See ***Chapter 5: Declarations*** for additional information on declaring bitfields.)

Table 4.3 lists the properties of various kinds of bitfields. For example, you can declare the flags register of some Intel 80X86 processors as:

```
struct flags {
     unsigned int
          cf:1, :1, pf:1, :1,
          af:1, :1, zf:1, sf:1,
          tf:1, if:1, df:1, of:1,
          iopl:2, nt:1, :1;
     };
```

assuming that the translator packs bitfields from least significant bit to most significant bit within a 16-bit object.

Table 4.3: *Properties of bitfield types.*

Alternate Designations	Minimum Range	Restrictions on Representation
`int` none	$[0, 2^{N-1})$	same as either *signed bitfields* or *unsigned bitfields*
`signed` `signed int`	$(-2^{N-1}, 2^{N-1})$	*N*-bit signed integer; size not larger than *int*
`unsigned` `unsigned int`	$[0, 2^N)$	*N*-bit unsigned integer; size not larger than *int*

Enumerations

You declare an enumeration with one or more *enumeration constants.* For example:

```
enum Hue {black, red, green, blue = 4, magenta};
```

This declaration defines an enumeration type (with tag **`Hue`**) that has the enumeration constants **`black`** (with value 0) **`red`** (with value 1), **`green`** (with value 2), **`blue`** (with value 4), and **`magenta`** (with value 5).

An enumeration is compatible with the type that the translator chooses to represent it, but the choice is implementation-defined. The translator can represent an enumeration as any integer type that promotes to *int*. A value you specify for an enumeration constant (such as **4** for **blue** above) must be an arithmetic constant expression and representable as type *int*. (See **CLASSES OF EXPRESSIONS** in ***Chapter 7: Expressions.***) If you write:

```
enum Hue {red, green, blue = 4} x;
int *p = &x;            DANGEROUS PRACTICE
```

not all translators treat **&x** as type *pointer to int*. (See ***Chapter 5: Declarations*** for additional information on declaring enumerations.)

Floating-Point Types

The translator predefines three floating-point types. All represent values that are signed approximations to real values, to some minimum specified precision, over some minimum specified range. Table 4.4 lists the properties of the three floating types.
No relationship exists between the representations of integer types and floating-point types.

Table 4.4: *Properties of floating-point types.*

Designation	Minimum Range	Restrictions on Representation
float	$[-10^{+38}, -10^{-38}]$ 0 $[10^{-38}, 10^{+38}]$	at least 6 decimal digits of precision
double	$[-10^{+38}, -10^{-38}]$ 0 $[10^{-38}, 10^{+38}]$	at least 10 decimal digits; range and precision at least that of *float*
long double	$[-10^{+38}, -10^{-38}]$ 0 $[10^{-38}, 10^{+38}]$	at least 10 decimal digits; range and precision at least that of *double*

DERIVING TYPES

You can derive types from other types by declaring:

- *pointers* to other types
- *structures* containing other object types
- *unions* containing other object types
- *arrays* of other object types
- *functions* that return object or incomplete types

You cannot call a function that returns an incomplete type other than *void*. Any other incomplete return type must be complete before you call the function.

Table 4.5 summarizes the constraints on deriving types.

Table 4.5: *Constraints on deriving types.*

Derived Type	Function Type	Object Type	Incomplete Type
pointer to	any	any except bitfield types	any
structure containing	—	any	—
union containing	—	any	—
array of	—	any except bitfield types	—
function returning	—	any except bitfield types or array types	any except incomplete array types

Pointer Types

A *pointer type* describes an object whose values are the storage addresses that the program uses to designate functions or objects of a given type. You can declare a pointer type that points to any other type except a bitfield type. For example:

```
char *pc;               pc is a pointer to char
void *pv;               pv is a pointer to void
void (*pf)(void);       pf is a pointer to a function
```

Several constraints exist on the representation of pointer types:

- Every pointer type can represent a *null pointer value* that compares equal to an integer zero, and does not equal the address of *any* function or object in the program.
- The types *pointer to char, pointer to signed char, pointer to unsigned char,* and *pointer to void* share the same representation.
- Any valid object pointer can safely be converted to *pointer to void* and back to the original type.
- All *pointer to function* types share the same representation (which need not be the same as for *pointer to void*).
- Otherwise, different pointer types can have different representations.

No relationship exists between the representations of pointer types and integer or floating-point types.

Structure Types

A *structure type* describes an object whose values are composed of *sequences* of *members* that have other object types. For example:

```
struct {
     char ch;           struct contains a char
     long lo;                followed by a long
     } st;                   st contains st.ch and st.lo
```

The members occupy successive locations in storage, so an object of structure type can represent the value of all its members at the same time. Every structure member list (enclosed in braces) within a given translation unit defines a different (incompatible) structure type.

Some implementations align objects of certain types on special storage boundaries. A Motorola 68000, for example, requires that a *long* object be aligned on an even storage boundary. (The byte with the lowest address, used to designate the entire object, has an address that is a multiple of 2.)

A structure type can contain a *hole* after each member to ensure that the member following is suitably aligned. A hole can occur after the last member of the structure type to ensure that an array of that structure type has each element of the array suitably aligned. In the Motorola 68000 example above, a one-byte (or larger) hole occurs after the member **ch**, but a hole probably does not occur after the member **lo**. Holes do not participate in representing the value of a structure.

Union Types

A *union type* describes an object whose values are composed of *alternations* of members that have other object types. For example:

```
union {
     char ch;               union contains a char
     long lo;                    followed by a long
     } un;                  un contains un.ch or un.lo
```

All members of a union type overlap in storage, so an object of union type can represent the value of only one of its members at any given time. Every union member list (enclosed in braces) within a translation unit defines a different (incompatible) union type.

Like a structure type, a union type can have a hole after each of its members. The holes are at least big enough to ensure that a union type occupies the same number of bytes (regardless of which member is currently valid) and to ensure that an array of that union type has each element of the array suitably aligned.

Array Types

An *array type* describes an object whose values are composed of *repetitions* of *elements* that have some other object type. For example:

```
char ac[10];          contains chars ac(0), ac(1), and so on
```

Elements of an array type occupy successive storage locations, beginning with element number zero, so an object of array type can represent multiple element values at the same time.

The number of elements in an array type is specified by its *repetition count.* In the example above, the repetition count is 10. An array type does not contain additional holes because all other types pack tightly when composed into arrays. The expression you write for a repetition count must be an arithmetic constant expression whose value is greater than zero. (See **CLASSES OF EXPRESSIONS** in ***Chapter 7: Expressions.***)

Function Types

A *function type* describes a function whose return value is either an object or an incomplete type other than an array type. The incomplete type *void* indicates that the function returns no result. A function type can also describe the number and types of arguments needed in an expression that calls the function. (See ***Chapter 6: Functions.***) For example:

```
double sinh(double x);     one double argument,
                               returns double result
void wrapup(void);         no argument or return value
```

A function type does not represent a value. Instead, it describes how an expression calls (passes control to) a body of executable code. When the function returns (passes control back) to the expression that calls it, it can provide a return value as the value of the function call subexpression.

INCOMPLETE TYPES

An *incomplete type* can be a structure type whose members you have not yet specified, a union type whose members you have not yet specified, an array type whose repetition count you have not yet specified, or the type *void.* You *complete* an incomplete type by specifying the missing information. Once completed, an incomplete type becomes an object type.

You create an *incomplete structure type* when you declare a structure type without specifying its members. For example:

```
struct complex *pc;        pc points to incomplete
                           structure type complex
```

You complete an incomplete structure type by declaring the same structure type later in the same scope with its members specified, as in:

```
struct complex {
     float re, im;
     };                    complex now completed
```

You create an *incomplete union type* when you declare a union type without specifying its members. For example:

```
union stuff *ps;           ps points to incomplete
                           union type stuff
```

You complete an incomplete union type by declaring the same union type later in the same scope with its members specified, as in:

```
union stuff {
     int in;
     float fl;
     };                    stuff now completed
```

You create an *incomplete array type* when you declare an object that has array type without specifying its repetition count. For example:

```
char a[];                  a has incomplete array type
```

You complete an incomplete array type by redeclaring the same name later in the same scope with the repetition count specified, as in:

```
char a[25];                a now has complete type
```

You can declare but you cannot define an object whose type is *void*. (See **CLASSES OF EXPRESSIONS** in ***Chapter 7: Expressions***.) You cannot complete the type *void*.

TYPE QUALIFIERS

You can *qualify* any object type or incomplete type with any combination of the two type qualifiers **`const`** and **`volatile`**. Each type qualifier designates a qualified version of some type. The qualified and unqualified versions of a type have the same representation:

- A *const* qualified type indicates that access to the designated object cannot alter the value stored in the object. All other object types can have their values altered.
- A *volatile* qualified type indicates that agencies unknown to the translator can access or alter the value stored in the object. The translator can assume that it has complete control of all objects that do not have *volatile* qualified types.

You write a type qualifier within a declaration either as part of the type part or as part of a pointer decoration. (See **DECLARATION SYNTAX** in ***Chapter 3: Syntax***.) All combinations of pointer decorations and type qualifiers are meaningful. A few examples are:

```
volatile int vi;                 vi is a volatile int
const int *pci;                  pci points to const int
int * const cpi;                 cpi is a const pointer to int
const int * const cpci;          cpci is a const pointer to const int
const int * volatile vpci;       vpci is a volatile pointer to const int
```

Moreover, all four combinations of type qualifiers are meaningful:

- You specify *no* type qualifiers for the "normal" objects in the program.
- You specify *const* qualified types for objects that the program does not alter (such as tables of constant values).
- You specify *volatile* qualified types for objects accessed or altered by signal handlers, by concurrently executing programs, or by special hardware (such as a memory-mapped I/O control register).
- You specify both *const* and *volatile* qualified types for objects that the program does not alter, but that other agencies can alter (such as a memory-mapped interval timer).

If you declare an object as having a *const* qualified type (such as **`cpi`** in the example above), then no expression within the program should attempt to alter the value stored in the object. The implementation can place the object in read-only memory (ROM) or replace references to its stored value with the known value.

A pointer to *const* qualified type can point to an object that does not have *const* qualified type. A pointer to a type that is not *const* qualified can point to an object that has *const* qualified type. You should not, however, alter the value stored in the object with such a pointer.

For example:

```
const int ci, *pci;
int i, *pi;
pci = &i;              permissible
pi = (int *)&ci;       type cast required
i = *pci + *pi;        permissible
*pci = 3;              INVALID: *pci is const
*pi = 3;               INVALID: ci is const
```

If you declare an object as having a *volatile* qualified type (such as **vi** in the example above), then no expression within the program should access or alter the value stored in the object via an lvalue that does not have a *volatile* qualified type. (Lvalues are described under **CLASSES OF EXPRESSIONS** in ***Chapter 7: Expressions.***)

A pointer to *volatile* qualified type can point to an object that does not have *volatile* qualified type. A pointer to a type that is not *volatile* qualified can point to an object that has *volatile* qualified type. You should not, however, access the object with such a pointer.

COMPATIBLE AND COMPOSITE TYPES

In many contexts, the translator must test whether two types are *compatible,* which occurs when one of the following conditions is met:

- Both types are the same.
- Both are pointer types, with the same type qualifiers, that point to compatible types.
- Both are array types whose elements have compatible types. If both specify repetition counts, the repetition counts are equal.
- Both are function types whose return types are compatible. If both specify types for their parameters, both have the same number of parameters (including ellipses) and the types of corresponding parameters are compatible. (See **FUNCTION DECLARATIONS** in ***Chapter 6: Functions.***) Otherwise, at least one does not specify types for its parameters. If the other specifies types for its parameters, it specifies only a fixed number of parameters and does not specify parameters of type *float* or of any integer types that change when promoted. (See **FUNCTION CALLS** in ***Chapter 6: Functions.***)
- Both are structure, union, or enumeration types that are declared in different translation units with the same member names. Structure members are declared in the same order. Structure and union members whose names match are declared with compatible types. Enumeration constants whose names match have the same values.

Some examples of compatible types are:

```
long            is compatible with  long
long            is compatible with  signed long
char a[]        is compatible with  char a[10]
int f(int i)    is compatible with  int f()
```

Two types are *assignment-compatible* if they form a valid combination of types for the *assignment* operator (=). (See **OPERATOR SUMMARY** in ***Chapter 7: Expressions.***)

The translator combines compatible types to form a *composite type.* The composite type is determined in one of the following ways:

- For two types that are the same, it is the common type.
- For two pointer types, it is a similarly qualified pointer to the composite type pointed to.
- For two array types, it is an array of elements with the composite of the two element types. If one of the array types specifies a repetition count, that type provides the repetition count for the composite type. Otherwise, the composite has no repetition count.
- For two function types, it is a function type that returns a composite of the two return types. If both specify types for their parameters, each parameter type in the composite type is the composite of the two corresponding parameter types. If only one specifies types for its parameters, it determines the parameter types in the composite type. Otherwise, the composite type specifies no types for its parameters.
- For two structure, union, or enumeration types, it is the type declared in the current translation unit.

For example, the following two types are compatible:

```
FILE *openit(char *)        and     FILE *openit()
```

They have the composite type:

```
FILE *openit(char *)
```

For a more complex example, the two types:

```
void (*apf[])(int x)        and     void (*apf[20])()
```

are compatible and have the composite type:

```
void (*apf[20])(int x)
```

Chapter 5: Declarations

A translation unit consists of one or more declarations, each of which can:

- give meaning to a name that you create for use over some portion of a translation unit
- allocate storage for an object and (possibly) define its initial contents
- define the behavior of a function
- specify a type

Declarations can contain other declarations in turn.

This chapter describes how to use declarations to construct a C program. It describes how to create names and how to use the same name for distinct purposes. It also shows how to write object initializers to specify the initial values stored in objects. (See ***Chapter 6: Functions*** for a description of how to specify the behavior of functions.)

DECLARATION CONTEXTS AND LEVELS

You can write declarations in different *contexts*. Figure 5.1 shows the syntax of an arbitrary declaration (other than a function definition). This section shows graphically how each context restricts the declarations that you can write, by eliminating from this syntax diagram those parts that are not permitted in a given context. This section also describes when you must write a name within the declarator part of a declaration and when you must not.

Figure 5.1: *Syntax of* **`declaration`**.

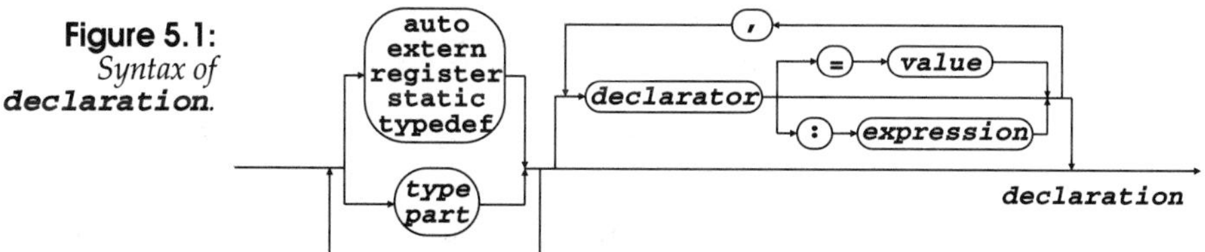

Figure 5.2 shows a sampler of all possible declaration contexts.

Figure 5.2: *Code sampler showing all declaration contexts.*

```
struct stack {                          outer declaration
     int top, a[100];                   member declaration
     } stk = {0};

void push(val)                          function definition
     int val;                           parameter declaration
     {
     extern void oflo(                  block declaration
          char *mesg);                  prototype declaration
     if (stk.top < sizeof a /
          sizeof (int))                 type-name declaration
          stk.a[stk.top++] = val;
     else
          oflo("stack overflow");
     }
```

Outer Declaration

You write an *outer declaration* as one of the declarations that make up a translation unit, as shown in Figure 5.3. An outer declaration is one that is not contained within another declaration or function definition.

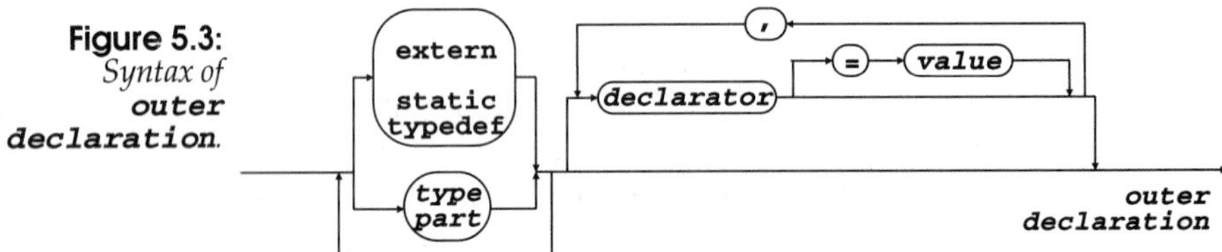

Figure 5.3: *Syntax of* **outer declaration**.

You can omit the declarator only for a structure, union, or enumeration declaration that declares a tag. You must write a name within the declarator of any other outer declarator.

Member Declaration

You write a *member declaration* to declare members of a structure or union, as part of another declaration, as shown in Figure 5.4.

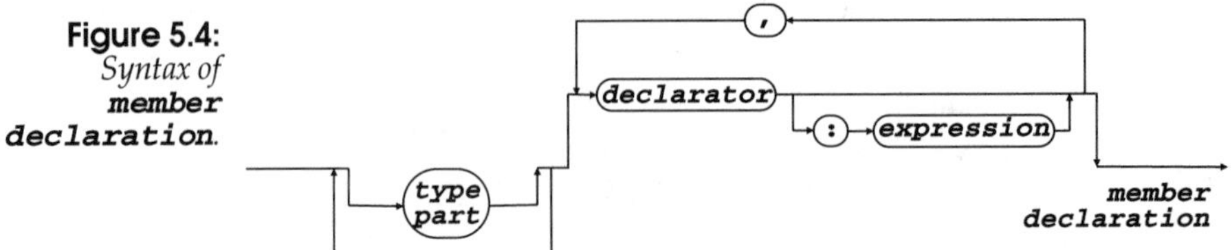

Figure 5.4: *Syntax of* **member declaration**.

A bitfield can be *unnamed*. If the declarator is for a bitfield that has zero size, do not write a name within the declarator. If the declarator is for a bitfield that has nonzero size, then you can optionally write a name; otherwise, you *must* write a name.

Function Definition

You write a *function definition* as one of the declarations that make up a translation unit, as shown in Figure 5.5. You cannot write a function definition within another declaration or function definition.

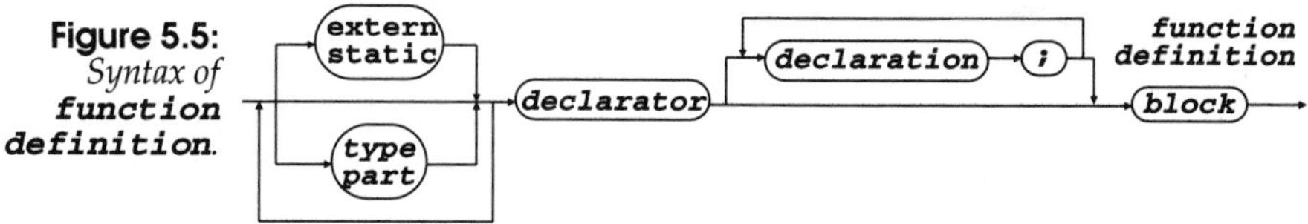

Figure 5.5: *Syntax of* **function definition**.

This is the only context where you can omit both the storage class and any type part. You must write a name within the declarator.

Parameter Declaration

You write a *parameter declaration* as part of a function definition whose function declarator contains a list of parameter names, as shown in Figure 5.6. You must write a parameter name within the declarator.

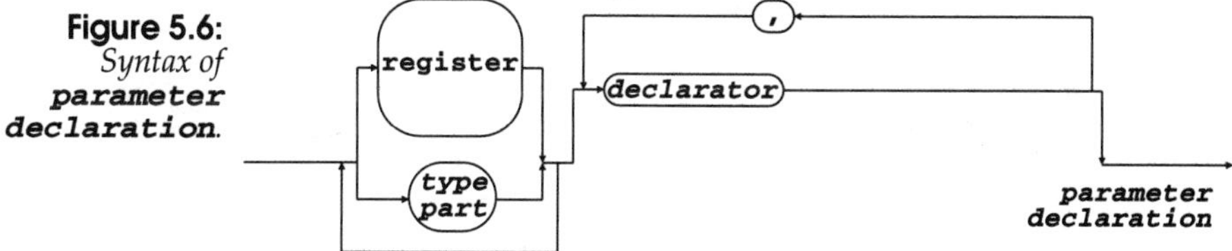

Figure 5.6: *Syntax of* **parameter declaration**.

Block Declaration

You write a *block declaration* as one of the declarations that begin a block within a function definition, as shown in Figure 5.7.

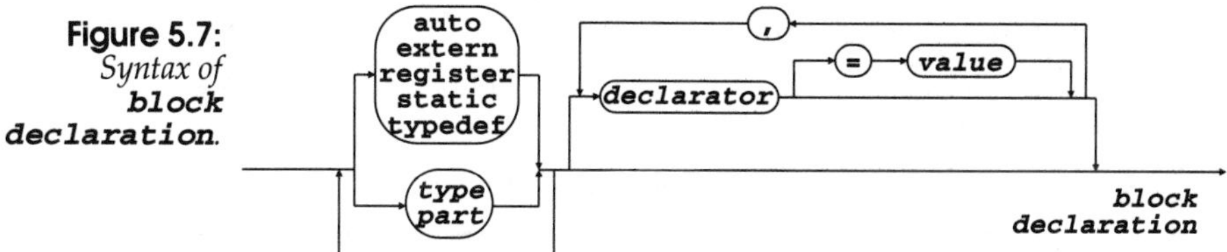

Figure 5.7: *Syntax of* **block declaration**.

You can omit the declarator only for a structure, union, or enumeration declaration that has a tag. Otherwise, you must write a name within the declarator.

Prototype Declaration

You write a *prototype declaration* within a declarator as part of a function decoration to declare a function parameter, as shown in Figure 5.8.

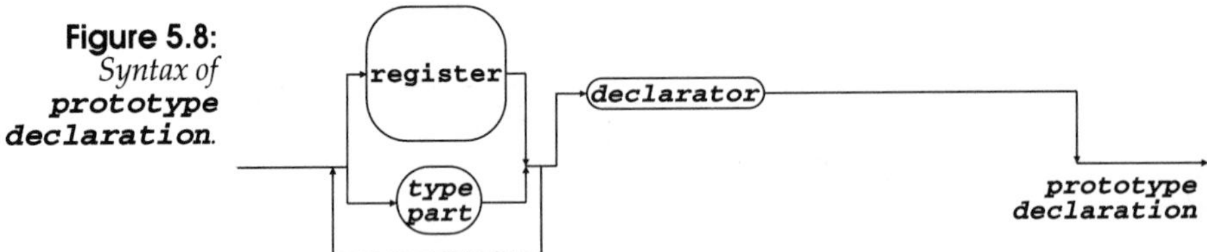

Figure 5.8: *Syntax of* **`prototype declaration`**.

If the prototype declaration declares a parameter for a function that you are defining (it is part of a function definition), then you must write a name within the declarator. Otherwise, you can omit the name.

Type-Name Declaration

You write a *type-name declaration* within an expression, either as a *type cast* operator or following the *sizeof* operator, as shown in Figure 5.9. Do not write a name within the declarator.

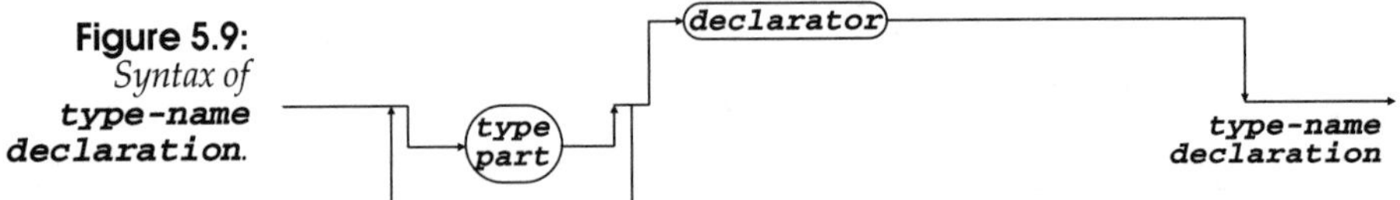

Figure 5.9: *Syntax of* **`type-name declaration`**.

Declaration Levels

You use member declarations and type-name declarations only to specify type information. You declare the functions and objects that make up the program in the remaining five contexts shown above. These contexts reside at three *declaration levels:*

- *File-level declarations* are the outer declarations and function definitions that make up the translation unit.
- *Parameter-level declarations* are parameter and prototype declarations that declare parameters for functions.
- *Block-level declarations* are block declarations.

How the translator interprets a declaration that you write depends on the level at which you write it. In particular, the meaning of a storage class keyword that you write (or the absence of a storage class keyword) differs considerably among the declaration levels. (See **OBJECT DECLARATIONS** later in this chapter.)

VISIBILITY AND NAME SPACES

You use names when you declare or define different entities in a program (possibly by including a standard header). The entities that have names are:

- *macros* — which the translator predefines or which the program defines with a *define* directive
- *keywords* — which the translator predefines
- *functions* and *objects* — which the program declares, and which either the Standard C library or the program defines
- *type definitions* and *enumeration constants* — which the program defines
- *enumeration tags, structure tags,* and *union tags* — which the program declares and can also define
- *goto labels* — which the program defines

The program can declare or define some of these entities by including standard headers. (See **LIBRARY ORGANIZATION** in ***Chapter 8: Library.***) The program can implicitly declare a function by calling the function within an expression. (See **FUNCTION DECLARATIONS** in ***Chapter 6: Functions.***)

Each entity is *visible* over some region of the program text. You refer to a visible entity by writing its name. A macro, for example, is visible from the *define* directive that defines it to any *undef* directive that removes the definition or to the end of the translation unit. An object that you declare within a block is visible from where you declare it to the end of the block (except where it is masked, as described below).

Name Spaces

You can sometimes *mask* an entity by giving another meaning to the same name. An object that you declare within an inner block, for example, can mask a declaration in a containing block (until the end of the inner block). You can use an existing name for a new entity only if its name occupies a different name space from the entity it masks. You can specify an open-ended set of name spaces.

The diagram in Figure 5.10 shows the relationship between various name spaces. Each box in this diagram is a separate name space. You can use a name only one way within a given name space. The diagram shows, for example, that within a block you cannot use the same name both as a structure tag and as a union tag.

```
union x {int i; float f;};
struct x {... };              INVALID: same name space
```

Each box in this diagram masks any boxes to its right. If the translator can interpret a name as designating an entity within a given box, then the same name in any box to its right is not visible. If you define a macro with-

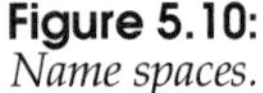

Figure 5.10: *Name spaces.*

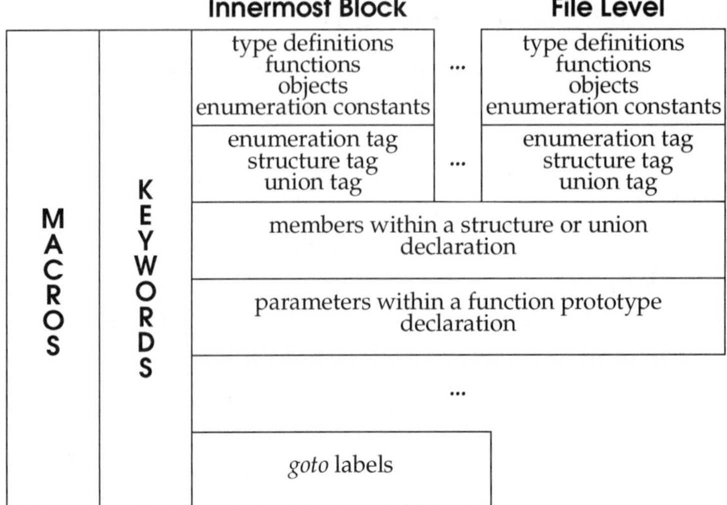

out parameters, for example, then the translator will always take the name as the name of the macro. The macro definition masks any other meaning.

```
extern int neg(int x);
#define neg(x)  (-(x))
y = neg(i + j);                  macro masks function
```

You introduce two new name spaces with every block that you write. One name space includes all functions, objects, type definitions, and enumeration constants that you declare or define within the block. The other name space includes all enumeration, structure, and union tags that you define within the block. You can also introduce a new structure or union tag within a block before you define it by writing a declaration without a declarator, as in:

```
{                                new block
struct x;                        new meaning for x
struct y {
    struct x *px;                px points to new x
```

A structure or union declaration with only a tag (and no definition or declarator) masks any tag name declared in a containing block.

The outermost block of a function definition includes in its name space all the parameters for the function, as object declarations. The name spaces for a block end with the end of the block.

You introduce a new *goto* label name space with every function definition you write. Each *goto* label name space ends with its function definition.

You introduce a new member name space with every structure or union whose content you define. You identify a member name space by the type of left operand that you write for a member selection operator, as in **x.y** or **p->y**. A member name space ends with the end of the block in which you declare it.

Scope

The *scope* of a name that you declare or define is the region of the program over which the name retains its declared or defined meaning. A name is visible over its scope except where it is masked:

- A file-level declaration is in scope from the point where it is complete to the end of the translation unit.
- A parameter-level declaration is in scope from the point where it is declared in the function definition to the end of the outermost block of the function definition. (If there is no function definition, the scope of a parameter-level declaration ends with the declaration.)
- A block-level declaration is in scope from the point where it is complete to the end of the block.

A macro name is in scope from the point where it is defined (by a *define* directive) to the point where its definition is removed (by an *undef* directive, if any). You cannot mask a macro name.

LINKAGE AND MULTIPLE DECLARATIONS

You can sometimes use the same name to refer to the same entity in multiple declarations. For functions and objects, you write declarations that specify various kinds of *linkage* for the name you declare. By using linkage, you can write multiple declarations:

- for the same name in the same name space
- for the same name in different name spaces

In either of these two cases, you can have the declarations refer to the same function or object.

You can use the same enumeration, structure, or union tag in multiple declarations to refer to a common type. Similarly, you can use a type definition to define an arbitrary type in one declaration and use that type in other declarations.

Linkage

A declaration specifies the *linkage* of a name. Linkage determines whether the same name declared in different declarations refers to the same function or object. There are three kinds of linkage:

- A name with *external linkage* designates the same function or object as does any other declaration for the same name with external linkage. The two declarations can be in the same translation unit or in different translation units. Different names that you write with external linkage must differ (other than in case) within the first six characters.
- A name with *internal linkage* designates the same function or object as does any other declaration for the same name with internal linkage in the same translation unit.

- A name with *no linkage* designates a unique object or a type definition; do not declare the same name again in the same name space.

The names of functions always have either external or internal linkage.

The rules for determining linkage are given in **OBJECT DECLARATIONS** and **FUNCTION DECLARATIONS** later in this chapter. Do not declare the same name with both internal linkage and external linkage in the same translation unit.

Whenever two declarations designate the same function or object, the types specified in the two declarations must be compatible. If two such declarations are in the same name space, the resulting type for the second declaration is the composite type. (See **COMPATIBLE AND COMPOSITE TYPES** in *Chapter 4: Types.*)

For example, a valid combination of declarations is:

```
extern int a[];                 external linkage
extern int a[10];               type is compatible
```

Tags

You use enumeration, structure, and union tags to designate the same integer, structure, or union type in multiple declarations. You provide a definition for the type (enclosed in braces) in no more than one of the declarations. You can use a structure or union tag (but not an enumeration tag) in a declaration before you define the type, to designate a structure or union of unknown content. (See **INCOMPLETE TYPES** in *Chapter 4: Types.*) When you later provide a definition for the incomplete structure or union type, it must be in the same name space. (See **VISIBILITY AND NAME SPACES** earlier in this chapter.)

For example:

```
struct node {                   begin definition of node
    int type, value;
    struct node *L, *R;         valid: although node incomplete
    } *root = NULL;             node now complete
```

Here, a declaration that refers to the structure whose tag is `node` appears before the structure type is complete. This is the only way to declare a structure that refers to itself in its definition.

Type Definitions

You use type definitions to designate the same arbitrary type in multiple declarations. A type definition is not a new type; it is a synonym for the type you specify when you write the type definition.

For example:

```
typedef int I, AI[], *PI;
extern int i, ai[10], *pi;
extern I i;                     valid: compatible type
extern AI ai;                   valid: compatible type
extern PI pi;                   valid: compatible type
```

You can write any type in a type definition. You cannot, however, use a type definition in a function definition if the parameter list for the function being defined is specified by the type definition.

For example:

```
typedef void VOID;            valid type definition
typedef VOID VF(int x);       valid type definition
VF *pf;                       valid use of type definition
VF f {                        INVALID use of type definition
```

The parameter list for a function must appear explicitly as a function decoration in the declarator part of a function definition, as in:

```
VOID f(int x) {               valid use of type definition
```

A type definition behaves exactly like its synonym when the translator compares types. (The type definition and its synonym are compatible.)

OBJECT DECLARATIONS

You declare the objects that the program manipulates at file level, at parameter level (within a function definition), or at block level. (See **DECLARATION CONTEXTS AND LEVELS** earlier in this chapter.) The storage class keyword you write (if any) determines several properties of an object declaration. The same storage class can have different meanings at the three declaration levels.

The properties you specify by writing a given storage class at a given declaration level are *linkage, duration, form of initialization,* and *definition status.* An object declaration can specify that a name has:

- *external linkage*
- *internal linkage*
- *no linkage*

Some declarations accept the *previous linkage* of a declaration that is visible at file level for the same name (with external or internal linkage). If such a declaration is not visible, then the previous linkage is taken to be external linkage.

An object declaration can specify that the declared object has one of two *durations:*

- An object with *static duration* exists from program startup to program termination. It assumes its initial value prior to program startup.
- An object with *dynamic duration* exists from the time that control enters the block in which you declare the object to the time that control leaves the block. If you specify an initializer, then the initializer is evaluated and its value is stored in the object when control enters the block. (A *goto* or *switch* statement that transfers control to a *case, default,* or *goto* label within the block allocates storage for objects with dynamic duration but it does not store any initial values.) A function that calls itself recursively, either directly or indirectly, allocates a separate version of an object with dynamic duration for each activation of the block that declares the object.

Table 5.1: *Object declarations in various contexts.*

Storage Class	File-Level Declaration	Parameter-Level Declaration	Block-Level Declaration
none	external linkage static duration static initializer tentative definition	no linkage dynamic duration no initializer definition	no linkage dynamic duration dynamic initializer definition
`auto`	—	—	no linkage dynamic duration dynamic initializer definition
`extern`	previous linkage static duration static initializer not a definition	—	previous linkage static duration no initializer not a definition
`register`	—	no linkage dynamic duration no initializer definition	no linkage dynamic duration dynamic initializer definition
`static`	internal linkage static duration static initializer tentative definition	—	no linkage static duration static initializer definition
`typedef`	no linkage no duration no initializer type definition	—	no linkage no duration no initializer type definition

A type definition for an object type has *no duration* because duration has no meaning in this case.

An object declaration can permit one of two *forms of initialization:*

- A *static initializer* contains only expressions that the translator can evaluate prior to program startup. (See **CLASSES OF EXPRESSIONS** in ***Chapter 7: Expressions.***)
- A *dynamic initializer* can contain an expression that the program evaluates when it executes, called an *rvalue expression.* (See **CLASSES OF EXPRESSIONS** in ***Chapter 7: Expressions.***) If you write a list of expressions (separated by commas and enclosed in braces) to initialize an object of array, structure, or union type, then each expression must be a valid static initializer, even within a dynamic initializer. (See **OBJECT INITIALIZERS** later in this chapter.)

You must write *no initializer* in some cases.

Each of the four kinds of *definition status* of a declaration determines whether the declaration causes storage for an object to be allocated:

- If an object declaration is a *definition,* then it causes storage to be allocated for the object.

- If an object declaration is a *tentative definition* and you write no definition for the same object later in the translation unit, then the translator allocates storage for the object at the end of the translation unit. The initial value in this case is all zeros.
- If an object declaration is a *type definition,* then it only defines a type. (No object exists.)
- If an object declaration is *not a definition* and you do not write an initializer, then the declaration does not allocate storage for the object. If you write any expression that refers to the object, then you must provide a definition (in the same or another translation unit) that designates the same object.

Table 5.1 summarizes the effect of each storage class at each declaration level on object declarations. The table specifies the definition status assuming that you do not write an initializer. In all cases, if you write an initializer (where permitted), then the declaration allocates storage for the object. (It is a definition.) For example, the following two declarations both name the same object:

```
static int abc;          internal linkage, tentative definition
extern int abc;          previous linkage, no definition
```

FUNCTION DECLARATIONS

You declare the functions that a program calls at file level or at block level. The translator alters any declaration you write at parameter level with type *function returning T* to type *pointer to function returning T,* which is an object type. (See **DECLARATION CONTEXTS AND LEVELS** and **OBJECT DECLARATIONS** earlier in this chapter.)

The storage class keyword you write (if any) determines several properties of a function declaration. A storage class can have different meanings at the different declaration levels. The properties that you specify by writing a given storage class at a given declaration level are *linkage* and *definition status.*

A function declaration can specify that a name has:

- *internal linkage*
- *no linkage*

Some declarations accept the *previous linkage* of a declaration that is visible at file level for the same name (with external or internal linkage). If such a declaration is not visible, then the previous linkage is taken to be *external linkage.*

The *definition status* of a declaration determines whether you can write a function definition in that context. You have one of three possibilities:

- You *can define* a function.
- You *cannot define* a function.
- You provide a *type definition.*

Table 5.2 summarizes the effect of each storage class, at each declaration level, on function declarations.

For example, the following declarations both name the same function:

```
static int f(void);          internal linkage
extern int f(void);          previous linkage
```

Table 5.2: *Function declarations in various contexts.*

Storage Class	File-Level Declaration	Parameter-Level Declaration	Block-Level Declaration
none	previous linkage can define	(becomes *pointer to function*)	previous linkage cannot define
`auto`	—	—	—
`extern`	previous linkage can define	—	previous linkage cannot define
`register`	—	(becomes *pointer to function*)	—
`static`	internal linkage can define	—	—
`typedef`	no linkage type definition	—	no linkage type definition

READING DECLARATIONS

Reading a declaration is not always easy. Proceed with caution any time:

- you omit the name
- you write parentheses in the declarator
- you give a new meaning to a name that is visible as a type definition

This section provides some simple guidelines for writing and reading complex declarations.

When you write a declaration, avoid redundant parentheses. In particular, never write parentheses around a name, as in **`int (x)`**, because it is easy for you or others to misread the parenthesized name as a parameter list, and the type changes if you omit the name.

You *must* omit the name when you write a *type cast* operator. You *can* omit the name in a declarator when you write a function parameter declaration that is not part of a function definition. If you omit the name in the example above, you get **`int ()`**, which specifies type *function returning int,* not type *int.*

Avoid writing a declaration that masks a type definition. If you must mask a type definition, write at least one type part in the masking declaration that is not a type qualifier. The translator assumes that a name visible as a type definition is always a type part if that is a valid interpretation of the source text, even if another interpretation is also valid.

For example:

```
typedef char Small;
int g(short Small);            valid: Small has new meaning
int f(Small)                   Small taken as type definition
    short Small;               INVALID: not a parameter name
```

To read a declaration, you must first replace the name if it has been omitted. You determine where to write the name by reading the declaration from left to right until you encounter:

- the end of the declaration
- a right parenthesis
- a left bracket
- a left parenthesis followed by either a type part or a right parenthesis

You write the name immediately to the left of this point.

For example:

```
int          becomes  int x
void (*)()   becomes  void (*x)()
char []      becomes  char x[]
long ()      becomes  long x()
```

You read a complex declaration by first locating the name (using the previous rules). Then you:

1. Read the array or function decorations from left to right, beginning with the name, until you come to the end of the declarator or to a right parenthesis.
2. Read the pointer decorations from right to left, beginning back at the name, until you come to the beginning of the declarator, to a type part, or to a left parenthesis.
3. If you encounter a left parenthesis, repeat the first two steps (treating the parenthesized declarator as if it were the name).
4. Read the type specified by the type parts.

The following diagram can also help:

d7 d6 (d4 d3 NAME d1 d2) d5

Read the decorations in increasing numeric order, beginning with **d1** and ending with the type parts (**d7**). It is often sufficient simply to remember that, in the absence of parentheses (or within a pair of grouping parentheses), you read the pointer decorations as the last part of the type.

For example:

```
int *fpi(void)       is   function returning pointer to int
int (*pfi)(void)     is   pointer to function returning int

unsigned int *(* const *name[5][10])(void)
                     is   array with 5 elements of
                          array with 10 elements of
                          pointer to
                          pointer which is constant to
                          function (no parameters) returning
                          pointer to
                          unsigned int
```

OBJECT INITIALIZERS

You can specify an initial value for an object by writing an *initializer*. (See **OBJECT DECLARATIONS** earlier in this chapter.) The type of the object and the declaration context constrain how you write an initializer.

You initialize an object with static duration by writing a *static initializer*. A static initializer for an object with scalar type consists of a single expression (possibly enclosed in braces) that the translator can evaluate prior to program startup. (See **CLASSES OF EXPRESSIONS** in ***Chapter 7: Expressions.***) A static initializer for an object with array, structure, or union type consists of a list of one or more initializers separated by commas and enclosed in braces.

For example:

```
extern char *first = NULL;
static short February[4] = {29, 28, 28, 28};
```

You initialize an object with dynamic duration by writing a *dynamic initializer*. For other than array types, any rvalue expression that is assignment-compatible with the type of the object can serve as a dynamic initializer. You can also write a dynamic initializer in the same form as a static initializer.

For example:

```
auto int bias = {RAND_MAX/2};        static form initializer
auto int val = rand() < bias;        dynamic form initializer
```

The initializers that you write within a list separated by commas are *inner initializers*. You write an inner initializer the same way you write a static initializer, except that you can omit the outermost braces:

- For an object of structure type, the list of inner initializers you write initializes each member of the structure in turn, beginning with the first. The translator skips unnamed bitfields, which you cannot initialize.
- For an object of union type, you can initialize only the first member of the union.
- For an object of array type, the list of inner initializers you write initializes each element of the array in turn, beginning with element number zero. The last array subscript varies most rapidly.

Some examples are:

```
struct complex {
    float real, imag;
    } neg_one = {-1, 0};             values for real and imag
union {
    struct complex *p;
    float value;
    } val_ptr = {&neg_one};          initializes pointer member
int a23[2][3] = {{00, 01, 02},       all braces present
                 {10, 11, 12}};          on inner initializers
int a32[3][2] = {00, 01,             braces omitted
                 10, 11,                 on inner initializers
                 20, 21};
```

Table 5.3: *Object initializers in various contexts.*

Type	Dynamic Initializer	Static Initializer	Inner Initializer
arithmetic	{ arithmetic rvalue }	{ arithmetic constant expression }	{ arithmetic constant expression }
	arithmetic rvalue	arithmetic constant expression	arithmetic constant expression
pointer	{ assignment-compatible rvalue }	{ address constant expression }	{ address constant expression }
	assignment-compatible rvalue	address constant expression	address constant expression
structure	{ inner initializer list for members }	{ inner initializer list for members }	{ inner initializer list for members }
	compatible structure rvalue		inner initializer list for members
union	{ inner initializer for first member }	{ inner initializer for first member }	{ inner initializer for first member }
	compatible union rvalue		inner initializer for first member
array	{ inner initializer list for elements }	{ inner initializer list for elements }	{ inner initializer list for elements }
			inner initializer list for elements
array of character	`{ "..." }` `"..."`	`{ "..." }` `"..."`	`{ "..." }` `"..."`
array of **`wchar_t`**	`{ L"..." }` `L"..."`	`{ L"..." }` `L"..."`	`{ L"..." }` `L".."`

If you do not provide as many initializers as there are members or elements to initialize, the translator initializes any remaining members or elements to the value zero. Do not provide excess initializers. You can initialize an object of incomplete array type, in which case the number of element initializers you write determines the repetition count and completes the array type.

For example:

```
double matrix[10][10] = {1.0};          rest set to 0
int ro[] = {1, 5, 10, 50, 100, 500};    6 elements
```

You can initialize an array of any character type by writing a string literal or an array of **wchar_t** by writing a wide character string literal, as shorthand for a sequence of character constants. The translator retains the terminating null character only when you initialize an object of incomplete array type. (An object of complete array type is padded as needed with trailing zero initializers.)

For example:

```
char fail[6] = "fail";      same as {'f','a','i','l',0,0}
char bad[] = "bad";         same as {'b','a','d','\0'}
wchar_t hai[3] = L"hai";    same as {L'h',L'a',L'i'}
```

But note:

```
wchar_t hai[3] = {L'h',L'a',L'i','\0'};         INVALID
```

Table 5.3 summarizes the various constraints on initializer expressions or initializer lists, depending on context and the type of the object. This table shows you, for example, that you can write an arbitrary arithmetic rvalue expression as the initializer for an object with arithmetic type and dynamic duration. You can write an arithmetic constant expression, with or without braces, anywhere you initialize an object with arithmetic type. (An arithmetic constant expression is a special case of an arithmetic rvalue expression. See **CLASSES OF EXPRESSIONS** in ***Chapter 7: Expressions***.)

The table also shows you that you can initialize the elements of an object of array type, in any context, by writing a list of initializers in braces. You can omit the braces only for a string literal initializer or for a list you write as an inner initializer for some containing initializer.

Chapter 6: Functions

You write functions to specify all the actions that a program performs when it executes. The type of a function tells you the type of result it returns (if any). It can also tell you the types of any arguments that the function expects when you call it from within an expression.

This chapter shows how to declare a function. It describes all the statements (listed alphabetically) you use to specify the actions that the function performs. And it shows what happens when you call a function.

FUNCTION DECLARATIONS

When you declare a function, you specify the type of result it returns. If the function does not return a value, then you declare it to be a *function returning void.* Otherwise, a function can return any object or incomplete type except an array type or a bitfield type. (The type must be complete before any call to the function.)

You can also declare the types of the arguments that the function expects. You write a list of one or more declarations separated by commas and enclosed within the parentheses of the function decoration. If the function does not expect any arguments, you write only the keyword **void**.

For example:

```
void reset(void);               no arguments, no return
double base_val(void);          no arguments, double return
```

If the function expects a fixed number of arguments, you declare a corresponding *parameter* for each of them. You list the parameter declarations in the same order that the arguments appear in a call to the function. You can omit the names of any of the parameters if you are not also defining the function.

```
void seed(int val);             one int argument
int max(int, int);              two int arguments
```

The translator converts a parameter declared with type *array of T* to type *pointer to T.* It converts a parameter declared with type *function returning T* to type *pointer to function returning T.* Otherwise, each parameter must have another object type.

```
int scanx(char a[]);            changed to char *a
void callit(int f(void));       changed to int (*f)(void)
```

If the function expects a varying number of arguments, you end the list of parameters with an ellipsis (`...`). You must write at least one parameter declaration before the ellipsis.

```
char *copy(char *s, ...);    one or more arguments
```

Here, the function **copy** has a mandatory argument of type *pointer to char*. It can also accept zero or more additional arguments whose number and types are unspecified.

All the function declarations shown above that provide type information about the arguments within the function decoration are called *function prototypes.*

You can also declare a function and not provide information about the number or types of its arguments. Do not write declarations within the parentheses of the function decoration.

```
double bessel();             no argument information
```

Here, the function **bessel** has some fixed, but unspecified, number of arguments, whose types are also unspecified.

You can declare a function *implicitly* from within an expression. If the left operand of a function call operator is a name with no visible declaration as a function, object, enumeration constant, or type definition, then the translator declares it in the current name space as a *function returning int* without argument information. The name has external linkage. It is much better, however, to declare all functions explicitly before you call them.

```
    y = min(a, b);           implies extern int min();
```

The translator uses argument type information to check and to convert argument expressions that you write when you call the function. The behavior is as if the argument value is assigned to the object corresponding to the parameter. When you specify no type information for an argument, the translator determines its type from the type of the argument expression. (See **FUNCTION CALLS** later in this chapter.)

FUNCTION DEFINITIONS

You define a function by writing a *function definition,* a special form of declaration that ends with a *block,* as shown in Figure 6.1. Within the block you write any declarations visible only within the function (block-level declarations), and the sequence of statements that specifies the actions that the function performs when you execute it. Any statement can be another block, containing additional declarations and statements.

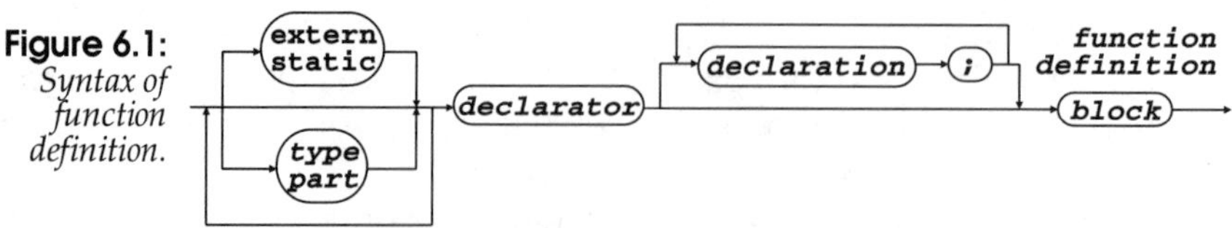

Figure 6.1: *Syntax of function definition.*

The declarator part of a function definition must contain a name for the function. The name must have a function type. The declarator must also contain a function decoration that names the parameters for the function. In a function prototype, you cannot omit any of the parameter names. Some examples are:

```
int min(int a, int b)
    {
    return a < b ? a : b;
    }

void swap(char *x, char *y)
    {
    char t;
    t = *x, *x = *y, *y = t;
    }
```

Here, the function definitions for both **min** and **swap** also serve as function prototypes. Wherever these names are visible later in the translation unit, the translator uses the argument type information to check and convert argument expressions on any calls to these functions.

You can also define a function and not provide argument information. (Do not use this capability in programs that you write: It is retained in Standard C to support only programs written in older C dialects.)

You define a function without arguments by writing a function decoration with empty parentheses.

For example:

```
void clear_error()              no arguments, no information
    {errno = 0; }
```

You define a function with arguments that provides no argument information for subsequent checking and conversion during function calls by writing a list of parameter names within the function decoration. You declare the parameters in a sequence of zero or more parameter declarations before the block part of the function definition.

```
long lmax(a, b)
    long a, b;
    {return a < b ? b : a; }
```

You can declare the parameters in any order. You declare each parameter no more than once. If you do not declare a parameter, the translator takes its type as *int*. To avoid an ambiguity, do not write a parameter name that is visible as a type name.

A function that you define without parameter information is compatible with a function prototype that specifies a compatible return type, the same (fixed) number of arguments, a parameter of promoted type for each parameter in the definition that has integer type, a parameter of type *double* for each parameter in the definition that has type *float*, and a parameter of compatible type for each parameter in the definition that is not an integer type or type *float*. (See **COMPATIBLE AND COMPOSITE TYPES** in ***Chapter 4: Types***.)

STATEMENTS

You express the actions that a function performs by writing *statements* within the block part of a function definition. Statements evaluate expressions and determine flow of control through a function. This section describes each statement and how it determines flow of control.

When you call a function, control passes to the first statement within the block part of a function definition. Except for the *jump* statements (*break, continue, goto,* and *return*), each statement within a block passes control (after it has completed its execution) to the next statement within the block. Some statements can execute a contained statement repeatedly, and some can execute a contained statement only when a certain condition is true, but all these statements pass control to the next statement within the block, if any. If a next statement is not within the block, control passes to the statement following the block.

Because no statement follows the block part of a function definition, the translator inserts a *return* statement (without an expression) at the end of that block. A *return* statement returns control to the expression that invoked the function.

You can write a sequence of declarations at the beginning of each block. When control enters the block, the program allocates any objects that you declare within the block with dynamic duration. The program allocates these objects even if control enters the block via a jump to some form of label (*case, default,* or *goto*) within the block.

A dynamic initializer behaves just like an *expression* statement that assigns the initializer to the object that you declare. Any dynamic initializers that you specify within a block form a sequence of statements that the translator prefixes to the sequence of statements within the block. If control enters the block via a jump to some form of label within the block, these initializers are not executed.

In the descriptions that follow, a syntax diagram shows how to write each statement. A verbal description tells what the statement does, and then a *flowchart* illustrates the flow of control through the statement:

- Control enters the statement from the previous statement along the arrow leading in from the left margin.
- Control passes to the next statement along an arrow leading out to the right margin.

A *jump* statement causes control to pass to another designated target.

Expression Contexts

Expressions appear in three different contexts within statements:

- a *test context*
- a *value context*
- a *side-effects context*

test context In a test context, the value of an expression causes control to flow one way within the statement if the computed value is nonzero or another way if the computed value is zero. You can write only an expression that has a scalar rvalue result, because only scalars can be compared with zero. A test-context expression appears within a flowchart inside a diamond that has one arrow entering and two arrows leaving it.

value context In a value context, the program makes use of the value of an expression. A *return* statement, for example, returns the value of any expression you write as the value of the function. You can write only an expression with a result that the translator can convert to an rvalue whose type is assignment-compatible with the type required by the context. A value-context expression appears within a flowchart inside a rectangle with one arrow entering it and one arrow leaving it. (It does not alter the flow of control.)

side-effects context In a side-effects context, the program evaluates an expression only for its side effects, such as altering the value stored in an object or writing to a file. (See **CLASSES OF EXPRESSIONS** in ***Chapter 7: Expressions.***) You can write only a *void* expression (an arbitrary expression that computes no useful value or discards any value that it computes) or an expression that the translator can convert to a *void* result. (See **CLASS CONVERSIONS** in ***Chapter 7: Expressions.***) A side-effects context expression appears within a flowchart inside a rectangle with one arrow entering it and one arrow leaving it. (It does not alter the flow of control.)

Block A *block,* shown in Figure 6.2, lets you write a series of declarations followed by a series of statements in a context where the translator permits only a single statement. You also use it to limit the visibility or duration of declarations used only within the block.

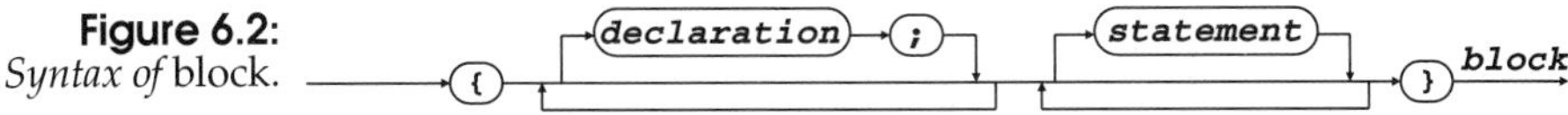

Figure 6.2: *Syntax of* block.

Figure 6.3 shows the flowchart for a typical block, using the notation:

```
{ decl-1; decl-2; ... decl-n;
  stat-1; stat-2; ... stat-n; }
```

Figure 6.3: *Flowchart for a representative* block.

decl-1 → decl-2 → ... → stat-n

For example:

```
if ((c = getchar()) != EOF)
    {
    putchar(c);
    ++nc;
    }
```

Break Statement

A *break* statement, shown in Figure 6.4, transfers control to the statement following the innermost *do*, *for*, *switch*, or *while* statement that contains the *break* statement. You can write a *break* statement only within one of these statements.

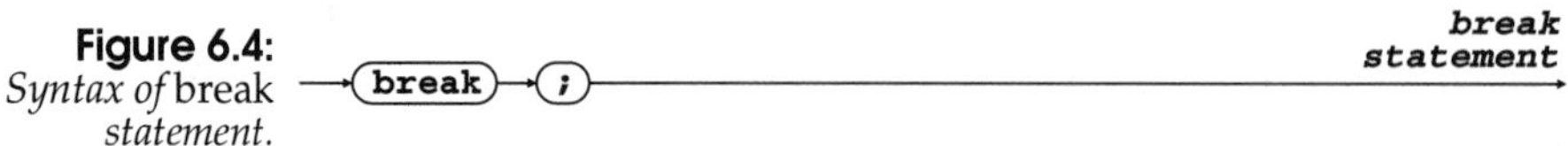

Figure 6.4: *Syntax of* break *statement.*

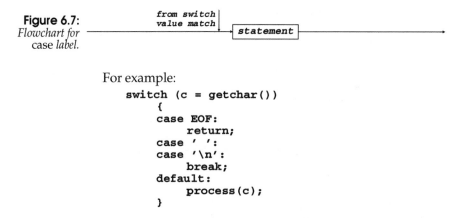

Figure 6.5 shows the flowchart for a *break* statement.

break

Figure 6.5: *Flowchart for* break *statement.*

For example:

```
for (s = first; s[0]; ++s)
if (s[0] == escape && s[1] == wanted)
     break;                  leave the for statement
```

Case Label

A *case* label, shown in Figure 6.6, serves as a target within a *switch* statement. It has no other effect on the flow of control, nor does it perform any action. The expression is in a value context and must be an integer constant expression.

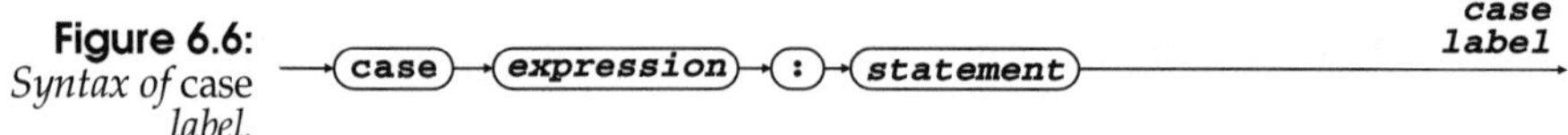

Figure 6.6: *Syntax of* case *label.*

Figure 6.7 shows the flowchart for a *case* label.

from switch
value match
statement

Figure 6.7: *Flowchart for* case *label.*

For example:

```
switch (c = getchar())
     {
     case EOF:
          return;
     case ' ':
     case '\n':
          break;
     default:
          process(c);
     }
```

Continue Statement

A *continue* statement, shown in Figure 6.8, transfers control out of the statement controlled by the innermost *do*, *for*, or *while* statement that contains the *continue* statement. It begins the next iteration of the loop. You can write a *continue* statement only within one of these statements.

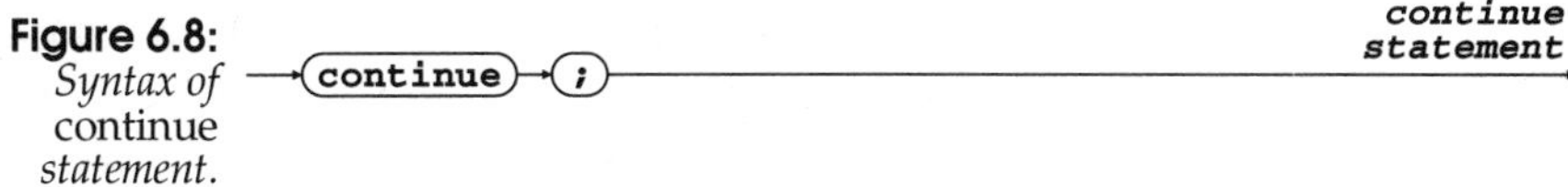

Figure 6.8: *Syntax of* continue *statement.*

Figure 6.9 shows the flowchart for a continue statement.

Figure 6.9: *Flowchart for* continue *statement.*

For example:

```
for (p = head; p; p = p->next)
        {
        if (p->type != wanted)
             continue;
        process(p);
        }
```

Default Label

A *default* label, shown in Figure 6.10, serves as a target within a *switch* statement. Otherwise, it has no effect on the flow of control, nor does it perform any action.

Figure 6.10: *Syntax of* default *label.*

Figure 6.11 shows the flowchart for a *default* label.

Figure 6.11: *Flowchart for* default *label.*

For example:

```
switch (lo = strtol(s, NULL, 10))
        {
        case LONG_MIN:
        case LONG_MAX:
             if (errno == ERANGE)
                  oflo = YES;
        default:
             return (lo);
        }
```

Do Statement

A *do* statement, shown in Figure 6.12, executes a statement one or more times, while the test-context expression has a nonzero value.

Figure 6.12: *Syntax of* do *statement.*

Figure 6.13 shows the flowchart for a *do* statement, using the notation:

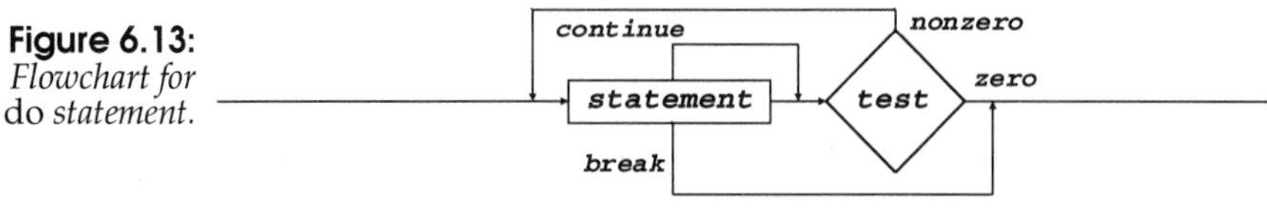

Figure 6.13: *Flowchart for* do *statement.*

```
do
    statement
    while (test);
```

If the program executes a *break* statement within the controlled statement, control transfers to the statement following the *do* statement. A *break* statement for this *do* statement can be contained within another statement (inside the controlled statement) but not within an inner *do, for, switch,* or *while* statement.

If the program executes a *continue* statement within the controlled statement, control transfers to the test-context expression in the *do* statement. A *continue* statement for this *do* statement can be contained within another statement (inside the controlled statement) but not within an inner *do, for,* or *while* statement.

For example:

```
do
    putchar(' ');
    while (++col % cols_per_tab);
```

Expression Statement

An *expression* statement, shown in Figure 6.14, evaluates an expression in a side-effects context.

Figure 6.14: *Syntax of* expression *statement.*

Figure 6.15 shows the flowchart for an expression statement.

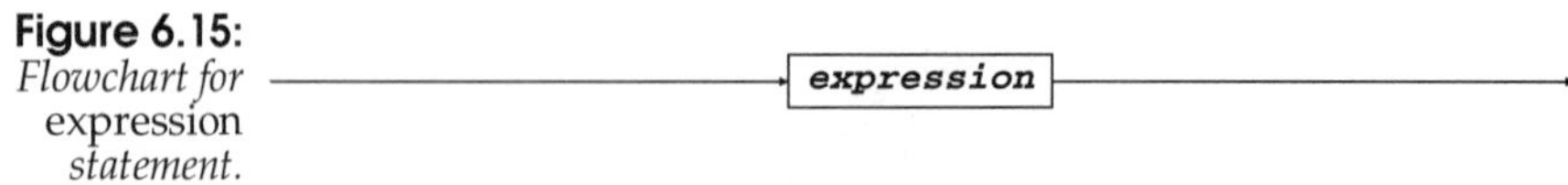

Figure 6.15: *Flowchart for* expression *statement.*

For example:

```
printf("hello\n");        call a function
y = m * x + b;            store a value
++count;                  alter a stored value
```

For Statement

A *for* statement, shown in Figure 6.16, executes a statement zero or more times, while the optional test-context expression has a nonzero value. You can also write two side-effects context expressions in a *for* statement.

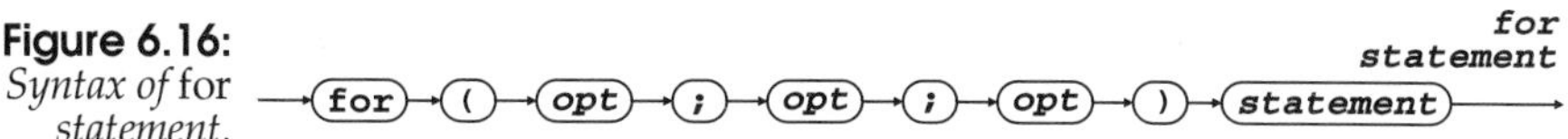

Figure 6.16: *Syntax of* for *statement.*

The program executes the optional expression, called `se-1` below, before it first evaluates the test-context expression. (This is typically a loop initializer of some form.) The program executes the optional expression, called `se-2` below, after it executes the controlled statement each time. (This is typically an expression that prepares for the next iteration of the loop.) If you write no test-context expression, the translator uses the expression `1`, and therefore executes the statement indefinitely.

Figure 6.17 shows the flowchart for a *for* statement, using the notation:

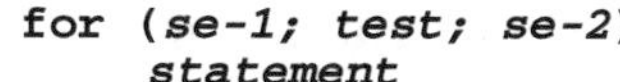

```
for (se-1; test; se-2)
    statement
```

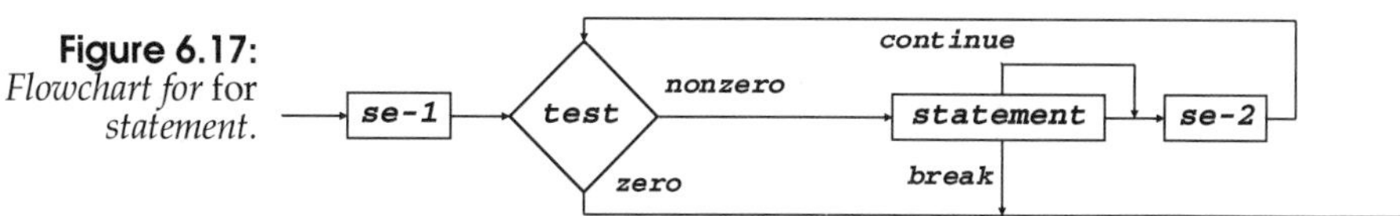

Figure 6.17: *Flowchart for* for *statement.*

If the program executes a *break* statement within the controlled statement, control transfers to the statement following the *for* statement. A *break* statement for this *for* statement can be contained within another statement (inside the controlled statement) but not within an inner *do, for, switch,* or *while* statement.

If the program executes a *continue* statement within the controlled statement, control transfers to the expression that the program executes after it executes the controlled statement (*se-2* above). A *continue* statement for this *for* statement can be contained within another statement (inside the controlled statement) but not within an inner *do, for,* or *while* statement.

For example:

```
for (i = 0; i < sizeof a / sizeof a[0]; ++i)
    process(a[i]);             for each array element
for (p = head; p; p = p->next)
    process(p);                for each linked list item
for (; ; )                  forever
    do_x(get_x());
```

Goto Label

A *goto* label, shown in Figure 6.18, serves as the target for a *goto* statement. It has no other effect on the flow of control, nor does it perform any action. Do not write two *goto* labels within the same function that have the same name.

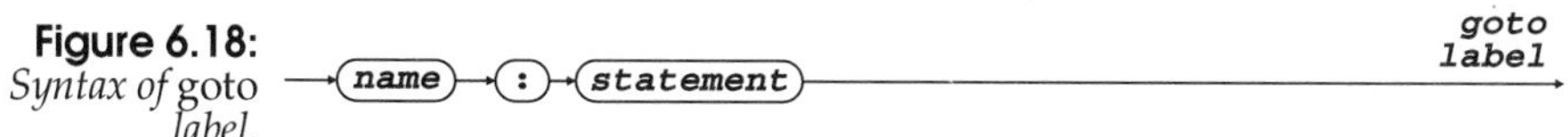

Figure 6.18: *Syntax of* goto *label.*

Figure 6.19 shows the flowchart for the *goto* label.

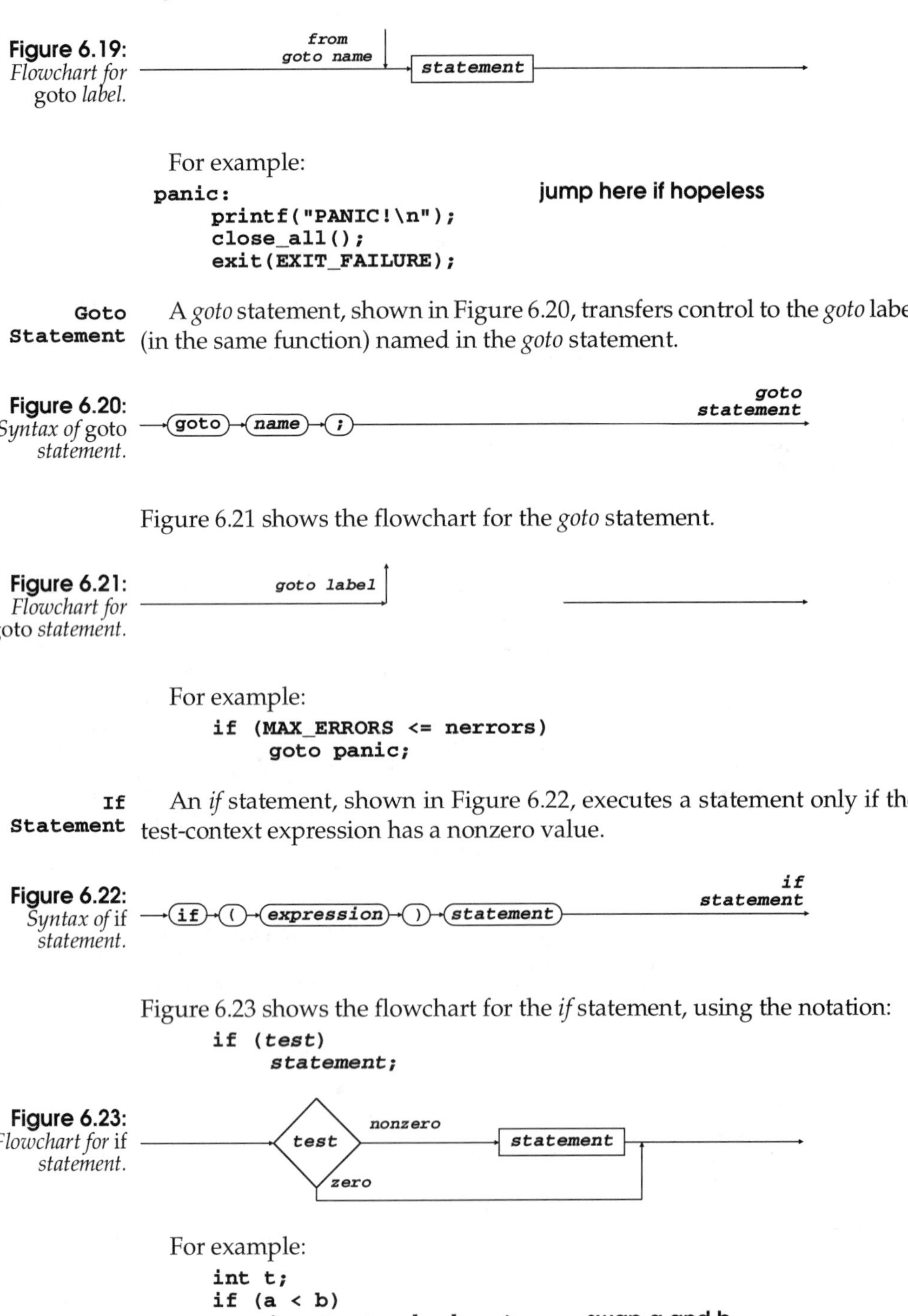

Figure 6.19: *Flowchart for* goto *label.*

For example:

```
panic:                                  jump here if hopeless
    printf("PANIC!\n");
    close_all();
    exit(EXIT_FAILURE);
```

Goto Statement A *goto* statement, shown in Figure 6.20, transfers control to the *goto* label (in the same function) named in the *goto* statement.

Figure 6.20: *Syntax of* goto *statement.*

Figure 6.21 shows the flowchart for the *goto* statement.

Figure 6.21: *Flowchart for* goto *statement.*

For example:

```
if (MAX_ERRORS <= nerrors)
    goto panic;
```

If Statement An *if* statement, shown in Figure 6.22, executes a statement only if the test-context expression has a nonzero value.

Figure 6.22: *Syntax of* if *statement.*

Figure 6.23 shows the flowchart for the *if* statement, using the notation:

```
if (test)
    statement;
```

Figure 6.23: *Flowchart for* if *statement.*

For example:

```
int t;
if (a < b)
    t = a, a = b, b = t;        swap a and b
```

If-Else Statement An *if-else* statement, shown in Figure 6.24, executes one of two statements, depending on whether the test-context expression has a nonzero value.

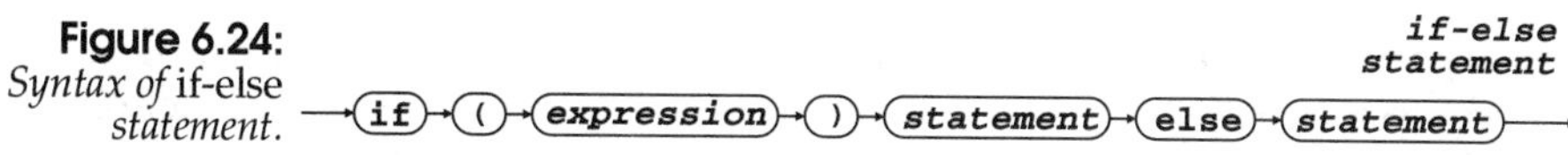

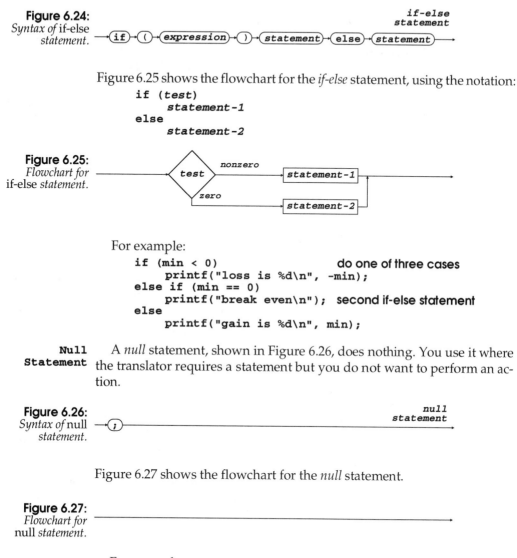

Figure 6.24: *Syntax of* if-else *statement.*

Figure 6.25 shows the flowchart for the *if-else* statement, using the notation:

```
if (test)
    statement-1
else
    statement-2
```

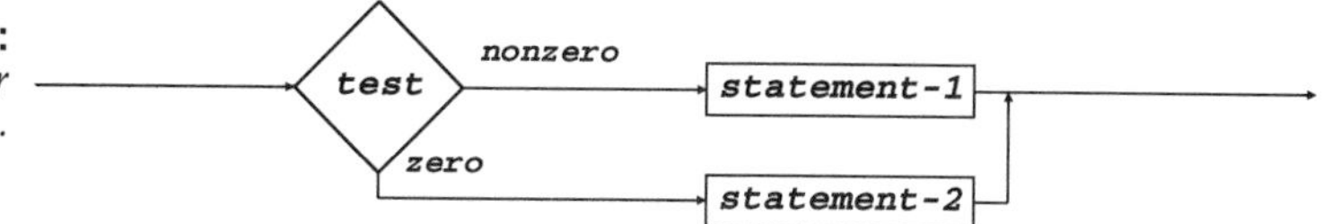

Figure 6.25: *Flowchart for* if-else *statement.*

For example:

```
if (min < 0)                          do one of three cases
    printf("loss is %d\n", -min);
else if (min == 0)
    printf("break even\n");  second if-else statement
else
    printf("gain is %d\n", min);
```

Null Statement A *null* statement, shown in Figure 6.26, does nothing. You use it where the translator requires a statement but you do not want to perform an action.

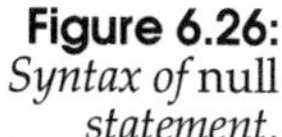
Figure 6.26: *Syntax of* null *statement.*

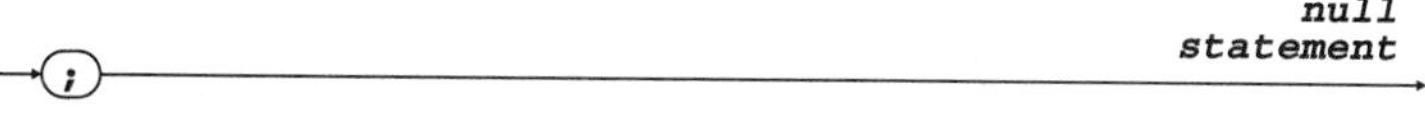

Figure 6.27 shows the flowchart for the *null* statement.

Figure 6.27: *Flowchart for* null *statement.*

For example:

```
if (done)
        while (getchar() != EOF) read and skip input
            ;                    nothing else to do
```

Return Statement A *return* statement, shown in Figure 6.28, terminates execution of the function and transfers control to the expression that called the function. If you write the optional expression (a value-context expression) within the *return* statement, the rvalue result must be assignment-compatible with the

Figure 6.28: *Syntax of* return *statement.*

```
→(return)→(opt)→(;)───────────────────────→ return statement
```

type returned by the function. The program converts the value of the expression to the type returned and returns it as the value of the function call. If you do not write an expression within the *return* statement, the program must execute that *return* only for a function call that occurs in a side-effects context.

Figure 6.29 shows the flowchart for the *return* statement, using the notation:

```
return expression;
```

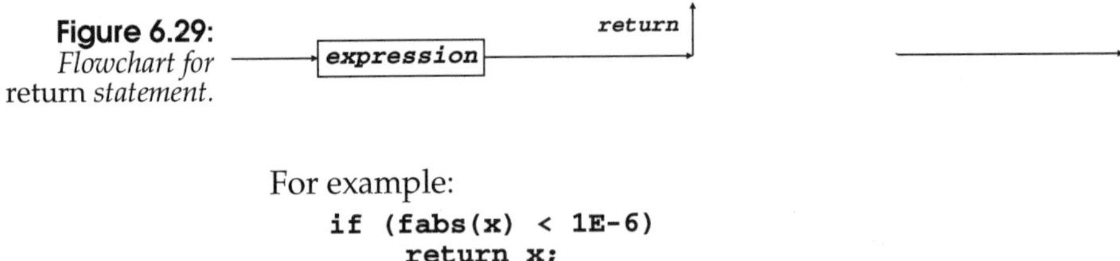

Figure 6.29: *Flowchart for* return *statement.*

For example:

```
if (fabs(x) < 1E-6)
    return x;
```

Switch Statement A *switch* statement, shown in Figure 6.30, jumps to a place within a controlled statement, depending on the value of an integer expression. The controlled statement is almost invariably a block. The expression is in a value context.

Figure 6.30: *Syntax of* switch *statement.*

The program evaluates the expression and then compares the value with each of the *case* labels contained in the controlled statement. A *case* label can be contained within another statement (inside the controlled statement) but not within an inner *switch* statement.

Each *case* label contains an integer constant expression whose value is converted to the promoted type of the expression in the *switch* statement before it is compared to the value of that expression. Do not write two *case* labels whose expressions have the same converted value within the same *switch* statement.

If the value of a *case* label expression equals the value of the *switch* statement expression, control transfers to the *case* label. Otherwise, control transfers to a *default* label contained within the *switch* statement.

A *default* label can be contained within another statement (inside the controlled statement) but not within an inner *switch* statement. You can write no more than one *default* label within a *switch.*

If you do not write a *default* label, and the value of the *switch* statement expression does not match any of the *case* label expressions, control transfers to the statement following the *switch* statement.

If the program executes a *break* statement within the controlled statement, control transfers to the statement following the *switch* statement. A *break* statement for this *switch* statement can be contained within another statement (inside the controlled statement) but not within an inner *do, for, switch,* or *while* statement.

A *switch* statement takes many forms. Figure 6.31 shows the flowchart for the *switch* statement, using the representative example:

```
switch (expr)
     {
     case val-1:
          stat-1;
          break;
     case val-2:
          stat-2;                    falls through to next
     default:
          stat-n
     }
```

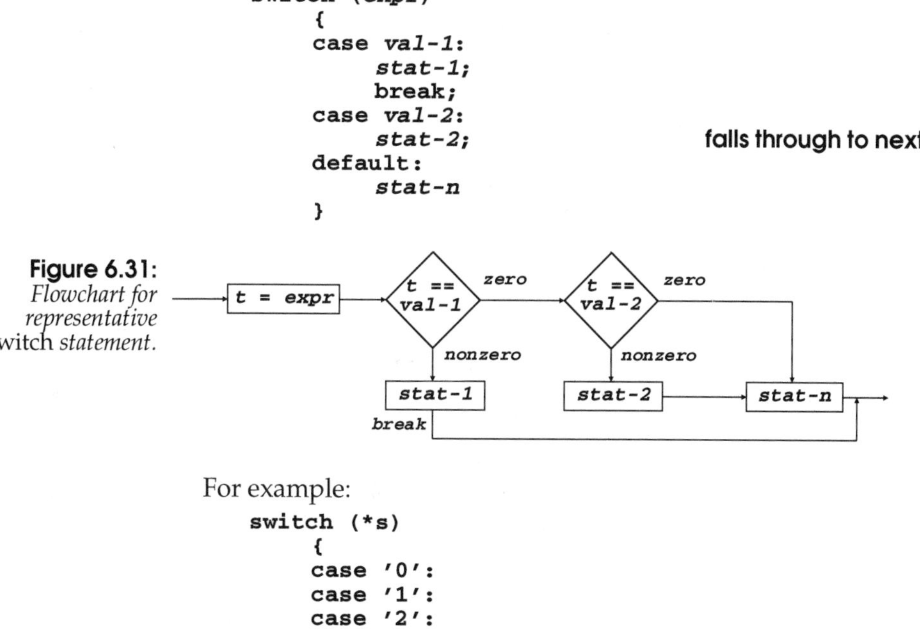

Figure 6.31: *Flowchart for representative* switch *statement.*

For example:

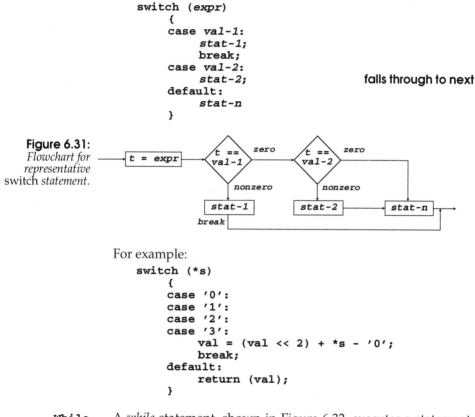

```
switch (*s)
     {
     case '0':
     case '1':
     case '2':
     case '3':
          val = (val << 2) + *s - '0';
          break;
     default:
          return (val);
     }
```

While Statement

A *while* statement, shown in Figure 6.32, executes a statement zero or more times, while the test-context expression has a nonzero value.

Figure 6.32: *Syntax of* while *statement.*

Figure 6.33 shows the flowchart for the *while* statement, using the notation:

```
while (test)
     statement
```

If the program executes a *break* statement within the controlled statement, control transfers to the statement following the *while* statement. A *break* statement for this *while* statement can be contained within another

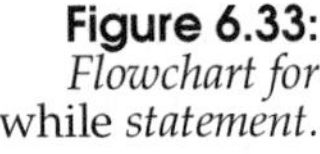

Figure 6.33: *Flowchart for* while *statement.*

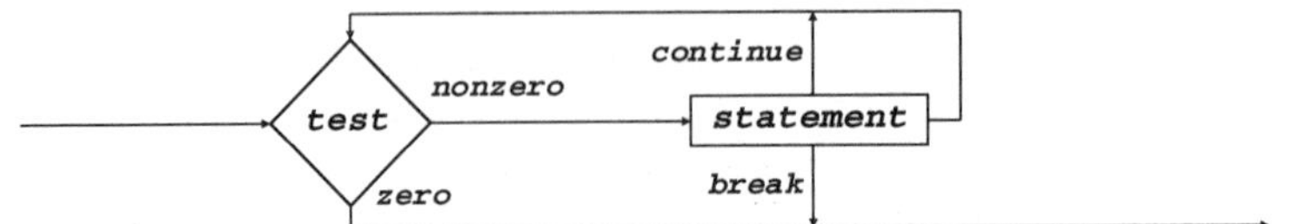

statement (inside the controlled statement) but not within an inner *do, for, switch,* or *while* statement.

If the program executes a *continue* statement within the controlled statement, control transfers to the test-context expression in the *while* statement. A *continue* statement for this *while* statement can be contained within another statement (inside the controlled statement) but not within an inner *do, for,* or *while* statement.

For example:

```
while ((c = getchar()) != EOF)
     process(c);
```

FUNCTION CALLS

You call a function by writing a function call operator within an expression. When the program evaluates the expression, it suspends execution of the statement containing the expression and transfers control to the first statement in the block that defines the actions of the called function. Objects with dynamic duration remain in existence for the block containing the function call. A function can call itself, or call another function that calls it, recursively. The program allocates a separate set of objects with dynamic duration for each activation of a function.

Before the called function gets control, the program stores the value of each argument expression in a newly allocated object associated with the corresponding parameter. You access the object corresponding to the named parameter by writing the parameter name. Unless you declare the parameter to have a *const* type, you can also alter the value stored in its object. You can access the values stored in the unnamed arguments to a function with a varying number of arguments by using the macros defined in the standard header **<stdarg.h>**. (See *Chapter 19:* **<stdarg.h>**.) When the function returns control to its caller, it deallocates the objects created to hold argument values.

When a function executes a *return* statement, it returns control to its caller. You call a *function returning void,* or any function that executes a *return* statement without an expression (either explicit or implicit), only from a side-effects context. Any other function call is an rvalue expression whose type is the type returned by the function and whose value is the value of the expression in the *return* statement.

When you call a function with a fixed number of arguments, write exactly as many arguments as the function has parameters. When you call a function with a varying number of arguments, write at least as many arguments as the function has parameters.

The type of the function can provide information about the type of an argument if it corresponds to one of the declared parameters in a function prototype. In this instance, the argument expression must be assignment-compatible with its corresponding parameter. Its value is converted as if by assignment before it is stored in the parameter object. (See **COMPATIBLE AND COMPOSITE TYPES** in *Chapter 4: Types*.)

For example:

```
double fun(double);
y = fun(0);              integer 0 converted to double
```

The type of the function can also fail to provide any information about an argument, if the function declaration is not a function prototype or if the argument is one of the unnamed arguments in a varying-length argument list. In this instance, the argument expression must be an rvalue. Hence:

- An integer argument type is promoted.
- An lvalue of type *array of T* becomes an rvalue of type *pointer to T*.
- A function designator of type *function returning T* becomes an rvalue of type *pointer to function returning T*.

In addition, an argument of type *float* is converted to *double*.

For example:

```
char ch;
float f(), a[10];
f(  a,                   array becomes pointer to float
    f,                   function becomes pointer to function
    ch,                  char becomes int or unsigned int
    a[2] );              float becomes double
```

A function call you write for a function that does not have argument information behaves the same as one for a function prototype that specifies:

- the same return type as the actual function
- the same (fixed) number of arguments as the actual function
- a parameter of promoted type for each argument expression in the function call that has integer type
- a parameter of type *double* for each argument expression in the function call that has type *float*
- a parameter of compatible type for each argument expression in the function call that is not an integer type or type *float*

All declarations for the same function must be compatible. While these rules permit you to write compatible function declarations with and without argument information, you should write only function prototypes.

Chapter 7: Expressions

You write expressions to determine values, to alter values stored in objects, and to call functions that perform input and output. In fact, you express all computations in the program by writing expressions.

The translator must evaluate some of the expressions you write to determine properties of the program. The translator or the target environment must evaluate other expressions prior to program startup to determine the initial values stored in objects with static duration. The program evaluates the remaining expressions when it executes.

This chapter describes the different classes of expressions and the restrictions on each class. It presents the common rules for writing all expressions, determining their types, and computing their values. It also discusses the constraints on the flow of control through an expression. (See **STATEMENTS** in ***Chapter 6: Functions*** for a description of how flow of control passes between expressions.)

EXPRESSION SUBCONTEXTS

Within a statement or declaration, every full expression that you write inhabits one of three contexts (See **EXPRESSION CONTEXTS** in ***Chapter 6: Functions***.) The three contexts are:

- a *test context*
- a *value context*
- a *side-effects context*

More generally, however, every full expression or subexpression that you write inhabits one of four *expression subcontexts,* depending on its goal:

- an *rvalue subcontext,* which includes test and value contexts
- an *lvalue subcontext*
- a *function-designator subcontext*
- a *side-effects subcontext*

An rvalue subcontext specifies a value that has an object type other than an array type. You create an rvalue subcontext wherever you need to specify a test or value to the translator, determine an initial value prior to program startup, or compute a value when the program executes.

An lvalue subcontext designates an object, but its expression can have either an object type or an incomplete type. You create an lvalue subcontext wherever you need to access the value stored in an object, alter the stored value, or determine the address of the object. (If the type is incomplete, you can determine only the address of the object.)

A function-designator subcontext designates a function. Hence, its expression has a function type. You create a function-designator subcontext wherever you need to call a function or determine its address.

A side-effects subcontext specifies no value and designates no object or function. Hence, its expression can have type *void.* You create a side-effects subcontext when you need to cause only side effects.

For example, consider the following code sequence:

```
void f(int);
int x;
f(x = 3);
```

In the last line:

- `f` is in a function-designator subcontext
- `x` is in an lvalue subcontext
- `3` and `x = 3` are both in rvalue subcontexts
- `f(x = 3)` is in a side-effects subcontext

CLASSES OF EXPRESSIONS

Every expression that you write belongs to one of several *expression classes,* depending upon its form. Four of these classes are closely associated with the four expression contexts:

- An *rvalue expression* has an object type other than an array type.
- An *lvalue expression* designates an object and has an object type or an incomplete type.
- A *function-designator expression* has a function type.
- A *void expression* has type *void.*

The first two of these classes have a number of subclasses. For instance, an arbitrary rvalue expression can be evaluated only by the program when it executes. One connotation of the term "rvalue expression" is that you cannot write such an expression where the translator must be able to determine its value before the program executes. Four subclasses of rvalue expressions, however, have a value that the translator or the target environment can determine prior to program startup:

- an *address constant expression*
- an *arithmetic constant expression*
- an *integer constant expression*
- a *#if expression*

An address constant expression specifies a value that has a pointer type and that the translator or target environment can determine prior to program startup. Therefore, the expression must not cause side effects. You must not write subexpressions with type *void*. (You cannot write a *function call, assigning* operator, or *comma* operator. See **OPERATOR SUMMARY** later in this chapter.) You write address constant expressions to specify the initial values stored in objects of pointer type with static duration.

For example:

```
extern int first;
static int *pf = &first;        &first is address constant
```

An arithmetic constant expression specifies a value that has an arithmetic type and that the translator or target environment can determine prior to program startup. Therefore, the expression must not cause side effects. You must write only subexpressions that have arithmetic type. (You cannot write a *function call, assigning* operator, or *comma* operator except as part of the operand of a *sizeof* operator. See **OPERATOR SUMMARY** later in this chapter.) You write arithmetic constant expressions to specify the initial values stored in objects of arithmetic type with static duration.

For example:

```
extern int counter = 0;
static int flt_bits = 6 / 0.30103 + 0.5;
static int ret_bytes = sizeof f();
```

An integer constant expression specifies a value that has an integer type and that the translator can determine at the point in the program where you write the expression. The same restrictions apply as for arithmetic constant expressions. In addition, you must write only subexpressions that have integer type. You can, however, write a floating-point constant as the operand of an integer *type cast* operator. You write integer constant expressions to specify:

- the value associated with a *case* label
- the value of an enumeration constant
- the repetition count in an array decoration within a declarator
- the number of bits in a bitfield declarator

For example:

```
extern int a[20], a_copy[sizeof a / sizeof a[0]];
enum {red = 1, green = 4, blue = 16} color;
```

A *#if* expression specifies a value that can be determined by an *if* or *elif* directive. After preprocessing replaces all names within the expression, the same restrictions apply as for integer constant expressions. (See **CONDITIONAL DIRECTIVES** in ***Chapter 2: Preprocessing.***)

For example:

```
#if __STDC__ && 32767 < INT_MAX
```

Lvalue expressions fall into one of four subclasses:

- an *accessible lvalue expression*

- a *modifiable lvalue expression*
- an *array lvalue expression*
- an *incomplete non-array lvalue expression*

An accessible lvalue expression designates an object that has an object type other than an array type. Hence, you can access the value stored in the object.

For example:

```
static const struct complex imag = {0, 1};
return imag;                        imag is accessible lvalue
```

A modifiable lvalue expression designates an object that has an object type other than an array type or a *const* type. Hence, you can alter the value stored in the object.

For example:

```
static int next_no = 0;
return ++next_no;                   next_no is modifiable lvalue
```

An array lvalue expression designates an object that has an array type. The type can be incomplete. You often write expressions that implicitly convert an array lvalue expression to an rvalue expression of a pointer type. (See **CLASS CONVERSIONS** later in this chapter.) You can also take the address of an array lvalue expression. For example:

```
static int bmask[] = {1, 8, 2, 4};
int (*pb)[] = &bmask;               &bmask is pointer to array
y = arg & bmask[i];                 bmask is array lvalue
scan_it(bmask);                     bmask becomes pointer to int
```

An incomplete non-array lvalue expression designates an object that has type *void* or an incomplete structure or union type. You can only take the address of such an expression. For example:

```
extern struct who_knows rom;
static struct who_knows *rom_base = &rom;
```

CLASS CONVERSIONS

Many of the expression subclasses are proper subsets of other subclasses. In other cases, the translator can convert an expression of one class to another when the context demands it. Figure 7.1 illustrates all classes and subclasses of expressions and how they relate. Each box denotes a different class or subclass. It contains a subset of all expressions that you can write. An unlabeled arrow connects each subset to its containing set.

For example, an integer constant expression is a subset of all arithmetic constant expressions, which in turn is a subset of all rvalue expressions. An incomplete non-array lvalue expression is not a subset of any other. A label on an arrow tells you that a conversion occurs if you write an expression of one class where the context requires a result of another class. For example, an rvalue expression that you write in a side-effects subcontext becomes a *void* result by dropping the value associated with the rvalue. (See **STATEMENTS** in ***Chapter 6: Functions***.)

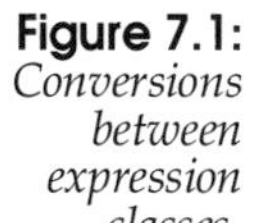

Figure 7.1: *Conversions between expression classes.*

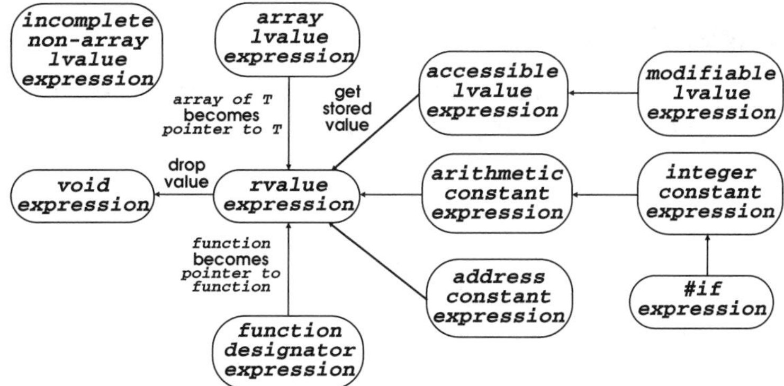

The translator can make four conversions to satisfy context:

- from rvalue expression to *void* expression
- from accessible lvalue expression to rvalue expression
- from array lvalue expression to rvalue expression
- from function-designator expression to rvalue expression

If you write an rvalue expression in a side-effects subcontext, the translator discards the value of the expression and converts its type to *void.* For example:

```
int y;
y = 3;              rvalue y = 3 becomes void
```

If you write an accessible lvalue expression in an rvalue subcontext (such as a test or value context), the translator accesses the value stored in the object to determine the result. A qualified type (*const* or *volatile*) becomes its corresponding unqualified type. For example:

```
const int x;
int y;
y = x;              const int lvalue x becomes int rvalue
```

If you write an array lvalue expression in an rvalue subcontext, the translator converts the type *array of T* to *pointer to T.* The value of the expression is the address of the first element of the array. For example:

```
int a[10], *pi;
pi = a;             array a becomes pointer rvalue
```

If you write a function-designator expression in an rvalue subcontext, the translator converts the type *function returning T* to *pointer to function returning T.* The value of the expression is the address of the function. For example:

```
int f(void);
int (*pf)(void);
pf = f;             function f becomes pointer rvalue
```

TYPE CONVERSIONS

Within several contexts the translator converts the type of a scalar expression (or subexpression). The conversions are called:

- *promoting*
- *balancing*
- *assigning*
- *type casting*

This section describes each of these conversions and the context in which it occurs. It also shows how the translator determines the value of the converted type from the value of the original type.

Promoting

Except when it is the operand of the *sizeof* operator, an integer rvalue expression has one of four types:

- *int*
- *unsigned int*
- *long*
- *unsigned long*

When you write an expression in an rvalue context and the expression has an integer type that is not one of these types, the translator *promotes* its type. If all of the values representable in the original type are also representable as type *int*, then the promoted type is *int*. Otherwise, the promoted type is *unsigned int*.

Thus, for *signed char, short,* and any *signed bitfield* type, the promoted type is *int*. For each of the remaining integer types (*char, unsigned char, unsigned short,* any plain *bitfield* type, or any *unsigned bitfield* type), the effect of these rules is to favor promoting to *int* wherever possible, but to promote to *unsigned int* if necessary to preserve the original value in all possible cases.

For example:

```
signed char ch;
unsigned short us, f(char *, ...);
f("%i%x", ch,    ch becomes int
     us);        us becomes int or unsigned int
```

Balancing

When you write an infix operator that has two arithmetic rvalue operands, the translator frequently determines the type of the result by *balancing* the types of the two operands. To balance two types, the translator applies the following rules to the promoted types of the operands:

- Unless the two types are *unsigned int* and *long*, the balanced type is the promoted type (of the two) that occurs later in the sequence: *int, unsigned int, long, unsigned long, float, double,* and *long double.*
- If the two types are *unsigned int* and *long* and the type *long* can represent all values of type *unsigned int,* the balanced type is *long.*
- Otherwise, the balanced type is *unsigned long.*

Each of the operands is converted to the balanced type, the arithmetic operation occurs between the now identical types, and the result of the operation has the balanced type. For example:

```
int i;
long lo;
double d;
return ((i + lo)      i becomes long
          + d);       (i + lo) becomes double
```

Assigning and Type Casting

You store a value in an object by writing an expression that contains an *assigning* operator. The assigning operators are `=`, `*=`, `/=`, `%=`, `+=`, `-=`, `<<=`, `>>=`, `&=`, `^=`, and `|=`. (See **OPERATOR SUMMARY** later in this chapter for descriptions of the assigning operators.)

If the type of the value to be stored by an assigning operator is compatible with the type of the object, the program stores the value unmodified. Otherwise, the translator determines the appropriate conversion to perform before storing the new value.

You can also specify a type conversion by writing a *type cast* operator. You can specify any type conversion permitted for an assigning operator, plus several other conversions between scalar types. (See **OPERATOR SUMMARY** later in this chapter for a description of the *type cast* operator.)

The translator defines a number of conversions between scalar types that you can specify by assigning or type casting. It does not define all possible conversions, however:

- You can convert any arithmetic (integer or floating-point) type to any other arithmetic type. The conversion preserves the original value, wherever possible. Otherwise, the value changes with the representation as described later in this section.
- You can convert any pointer type to an integer type, but the result is always implementation-defined. You cannot convert a pointer type to a floating-point type.
- You can convert any integer type to any pointer type. The value zero yields a null pointer. Any nonzero value yields an implementation-defined result. You cannot convert a floating-point type to a pointer type.
- You can convert any object pointer or pointer to incomplete type to any other object pointer or pointer to incomplete type. The result is implementation-defined, however, unless the original pointer is suitably aligned for use as the resultant pointer. You can safely convert any such

pointer to a pointer to a character type (or a *pointer to void*, which has the same representation). You can use such a pointer to character to access the first byte of the object as a character. If you then convert that pointer to a type compatible with the original pointer, it will equal the original pointer and you can use the pointer to access the object. For example:

```
int i;
char *pc = (char *)&i;          valid type cast
*(int *)pc = 3;                 also valid

if (*pc == *(int *)pc)          also valid
    printf("int stores l.s. byte first\n");
```

- You can convert a pointer to any function type to a pointer to any other function type. If you then convert that pointer to a type compatible with the original pointer, it will equal the original pointer and you can use the pointer to call the function. For example:

```
extern int sum(int, int);
void (*pv)(void) = (void (*)(void)&sum;       valid

if (((int (*)(int, int))pv)(1, 2) == 3)       also valid
    printf("sum was called properly\n");
```

Table 7.1 summarizes all possible scalar conversions. Note that you can convert any scalar type to any other scalar type by specifying no more than two conversions. In many cases, however, at least one of the conversions is implementation-defined.

Table 7.1: *Permissible scalar conversions.*

To: \ From:	**Arithmetic Type**	**Pointer to Incomplete or Object**	**Pointer to Function**
Arithmetic Type	any	to integer only	to integer only
Pointer to Incomplete or Object	from integer only	any	—
Pointer to Function	from integer only	—	any

Changing Representations

When you convert between any two arithmetic types, what happens to the value depends on the number of bits used to represent the original and final types. Table 7.2 summarizes all possible conversions between arithmetic types. The table assumes that:

- A signed integer value X occupying N bits can represent all integers in the range $-2^{N-1} < X < 2^{N-1}$ (at least).
- An unsigned integer value X occupying N bits can represent all integers in the range $0 \le X < 2^N$ (and no others).

- A floating-point value X can be characterized as having N bits reserved for representing sign and magnitude, so it can exactly represent all integers in the range $-2^{N-1} < X < 2^{N-1}$ (at least).

The table shows what happens when you convert an M-bit representation with value X to an N-bit representation, for the three cases where M is less than, equal to, or greater than N. The abbreviations used in this table are:

- impl.-def. — implementation-defined
- m.s. — most significant
- *trunc(X)* — the integer part of X, truncated toward zero
- X % Y — the nonnegative remainder after dividing X by Y

Table 7.2: *Conversions between arithmetic types.*

Conversion	N < M	N = = M	N > M
signed integer to signed integer	discard m.s. $M–N$ bits (can overflow)	same value	same value
unsigned integer to signed integer	if $(X < 2^{N-1})$ same value; else impl.-def. (can overflow)	if $(X < 2^{N-1})$ same value; else impl.-def. (can overflow)	same value
floating-point to signed integer	if $(\|X\| < 2^{N-1})$ *trunc(X);* else impl.-def. (can overflow)	if $(\|X\| < 2^{N-1})$ *trunc(X);* else impl.-def. (can overflow)	if $(\|X\| < 2^{N-1})$ *trunc(X);* else impl.-def. (can overflow)
signed integer to unsigned integer	if $(0 \le X)$ $X \% 2^N$; else impl.-def.	if $(0 \le X)$ same value; else $X + 2^N$	if $(0 \le X)$ same value; else $X + 2^N$
unsigned integer to unsigned integer	$X \% 2^N$	same value	same value
floating-point to unsigned integer	if $(0 \le X < 2^N)$ *trunc(X);* else impl.-def. (can overflow)	if $(0 \le X < 2^N)$ *trunc(X);* else impl.-def. (can overflow)	if $(0 \le X < 2^N)$ *trunc(X);* else impl.-def. (can overflow)
signed integer to floating-point	keep sign, keep m.s. $N–1$ bits	same value	same value
unsigned integer to floating-point	+ sign, keep m.s. $N–1$ bits	+ sign, keep m.s. $N–1$ bits	same value
floating-point to floating-point	keep m.s. $N–1$ bits (can overflow)	same value	same value

Pointer Arithmetic

You can add an integer to a value of type pointer to object. If the value of the pointer is the address of an array element, then adding one to the value yields the address of the next array element. Thus, for a pointer **p** to any object:

(char *)(p + 1) **is identical to** **(char *)p + sizeof (*p)**

If the value of **p** is the address of the first element in an array object, then ***(p + n)** designates element number **n** (counting from zero). If the value of **p** is the address of the last element in an array object, then **(p + 1)** is a valid address, even though ***(p + 1)** is not an accessible lvalue. You can perform pointer arithmetic on **(p + 1)** just as you can on the address of any of the elements of the array. If you form any other address that does not designate an element of the array object (by adding an integer to a pointer), the result is undefined.

READING EXPRESSIONS

You compose an expression from one or more terms and zero or more operators, as shown in Figure 7.2.

Figure 7.2: *Syntax of expression.*

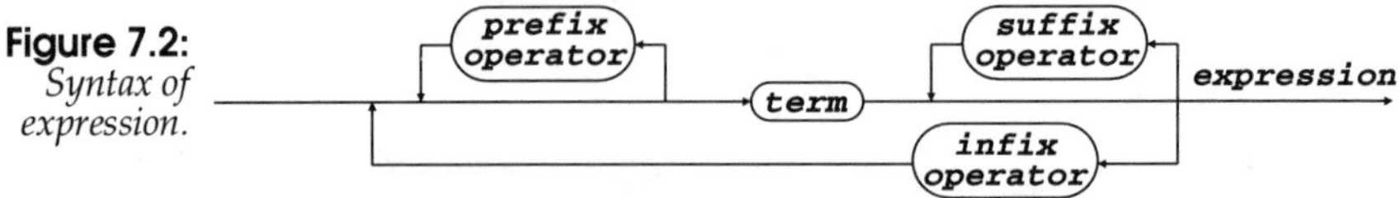

Each term has a well-defined type and class. If an expression consists of a single term without operators, then the type and class of the expression are the type and class of the term.

Each operator requires one, two, or three *operands.* An operand is a subexpression that can itself (generally) contain additional operators as well as terms. If you write an expression with one or more terms and a single operator, then the terms must be the operands of the operator. Each operator accepts operands with only certain combinations of types and classes. The types and classes of the operands determine the type and class of the expression containing the operator.

If you write an expression with one or more terms and two operators, then the translator must determine which terms to group with which operators. You can enclose any subexpression in parentheses to make clear that it groups as a single operand. Such parentheses have no other effect than to control grouping. If you do not write such parentheses, however, the translator applies a number of *precedence* rules to determine how the expression groups. Every expression you write groups in only one way.

This section describes how to determine the type and class of any term. Later sections in this chapter explain the rules for grouping operands in the presence of two or more operators, the effect of each operator, what operands it accepts, and what result it produces.

Figure 7.3:
Syntax of term.

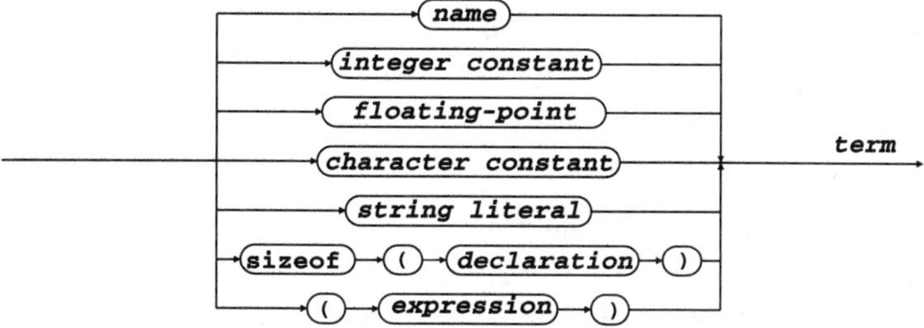

A term takes one of several forms, as shown in Figure 7.3.

name A *name* in this context be declared as one of three entities:

- a function
- an object (possibly with incomplete type)
- an enumeration constant

For a function, the name is a function-designator expression with the declared type. For an object, the name is an lvalue expression with the declared type. For an enumeration constant, the name is an rvalue expression with type *int*. (You can write a type definition or tag in an expression only as part of a type-name declaration enclosed in parentheses, to make a *type cast* operator or the operand of a *sizeof* operator.)

If no declaration is visible for one of these entities and if you write a left parenthesis immediately following the name, then the translator implicit declares the name in the current name space as a *function returning int* without any argument information. (See **FUNCTION DECLARATIONS** in ***Chapter 6: Functions.***)

integer constant An *integer constant* is an rvalue expression whose type depends on the value, the base, and any suffix you write. Each base and suffix determines a sequence of possible types. The translator selects the earliest type in the sequence that can represent the value of the particular integer constant.

For a *decimal integer constant,* the sequences are:

- no suffix — *int, long, unsigned long*
- `U` suffix — *unsigned int, unsigned long*
- `L` suffix — *long, unsigned long*
- `UL` suffix — *unsigned long*

For an *octal* or *hexadecimal integer constant,* the sequences are:

- no suffix — *int, unsigned int, long, unsigned long*
- `U` suffix — *unsigned int, unsigned long*
- `L` suffix — *long, unsigned long*
- `UL` suffix — *unsigned long*

For example, if type *int* has a 16-bit representation:

```
70        070      0x70        all type int
7000U     070U     0x7000      all type unsigned
70000     070L     0x700L      all type long
```

floating-point constant A *floating-point constant* is an rvalue expression whose type depends on any suffix you write:

- no suffix — *double*
- **F** suffix — *float*
- **L** suffix — *long double*

character constant A *character constant* is an rvalue expression whose type depends on the number of characters you specify and any prefix you write:

- no prefix — *int*
- **L** prefix — the type **wchar_t** promoted

If you specify more than one character in a character constant, the type and value are implementation-defined.

string literal A *string literal* is an lvalue expression whose type depends on the number of characters you specify and any prefix you write:

- no prefix — *array of char* with repetition count *N*
- **L** prefix — *array of* **wchar_t** with repetition count *N*

N is one more than the number of characters you specify when you write the string (for the terminating null character). For example:

```
"hello"          type is array of 6 char
L"hai"           type is array of 4 wchar_t
```

sizeof The term **sizeof (*declaration*)** is an rvalue expression of type **size_t**.

parentheses Any expression you write enclosed in parentheses is a term whose type and class are the type and class of the expression. Enclosing an expression in parentheses has no effect other than to control grouping.

GROUPING

In the absence of parentheses, the translator *groups* operators with operands in the following order:

1. The translator applies a *postfix operator,* shown in Figure 7.4, immediately following a term before it applies any other operator. It then applies any postfix operators to the right of that operator, grouping from left to right.

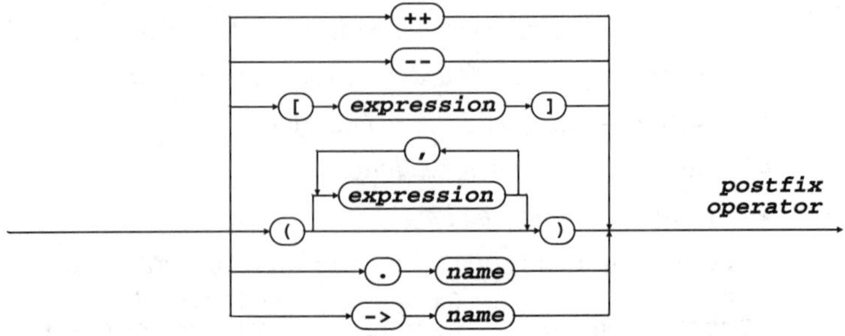

Figure 7.4: *Syntax of postfix operator.*

2. The translator applies a *prefix operator*, shown in Figure 7.5, immediately preceding a term and any postfix operators. It then applies any prefix operators to the left of that operator, grouping from right to left.

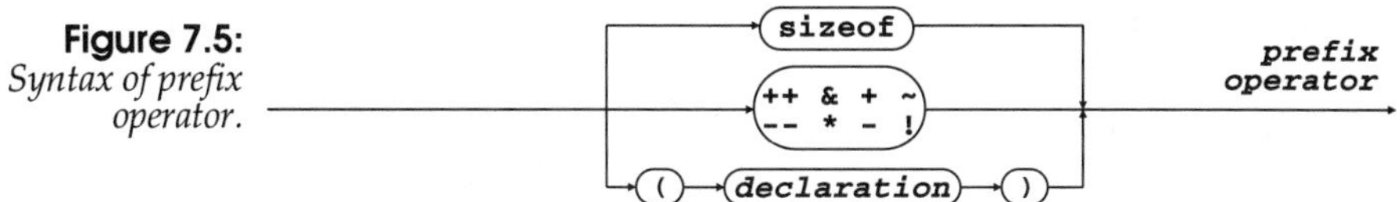

Figure 7.5: *Syntax of prefix operator.*

3. The translator applies *infix operators*, shown in Figure 7.6, in descending order of precedence. Operators at the same order of precedence group either from left to right or from right to left, as indicated for the particular precedence level.

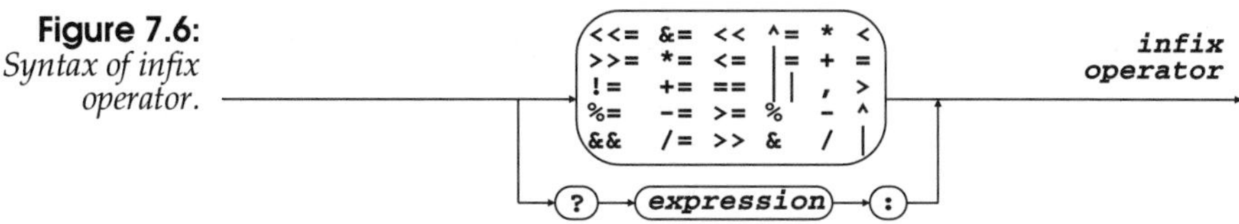

Figure 7.6: *Syntax of infix operator.*

The translator resolves two ambiguities by:

- always interpreting **`sizeof (`*`declaration`*`)`** as a term (never as the *sizeof* operator followed by a *type cast* operator)
- always interpreting a comma within a function call argument list as an argument expression separator (never as a *comma* operator within an argument expression).

In either case, you can use parentheses to obtain the alternate grouping.

Table 7.3, shows all operators grouped by precedence level in descending order. The table also shows how operators group within a given precedence level.

For example:

```
y = m * x + b   is   y = ((m * x) + b)
*p++ = -x->y    is   (*(p++)) = (-(x->y))
```

OPERATOR SUMMARY

This section describes every operator. It lists the operators alphabetically by name, showing how to write each one with operands **`X`**, **`Y`**, and **`Z`** (as needed). Following a description of what the operator does is a table of all permissible combinations of operand types and classes, with the type and class of the result for each combination.

Some expressions produce a result that has an integer type that varies among implementations. Each of these types has a type definition that you can include in the program by including the standard header **`<stddef.h>`**. (See *Chapter 20:* **`<stddef.h>`**.) The type definitions are:

Table 7.3: *Operator precedence and grouping.*

Operator	Notation	Grouping
postincrement	`X++`	from left to right
postdecrement	`X--`	
subscript	`X[Y]`	
function call	`X(Y)`	
select member	`X.Y`	
point at member	`X->Y`	
sizeof	`sizeof X`	from right to left
preincrement	`++X`	
predecrement	`--X`	
address of	`&X`	
indirection	`*X`	
plus	`+X`	
minus	`-X`	
bitwise NOT	`~X`	
logical NOT	`!X`	
type cast	`(`***declaration***`)X`	
multiply	`X*Y`	from left to right
divide	`X/Y`	
remainder	`X%Y`	
add	`X+Y`	from left to right
subtract	`X-Y`	
left shift	`X<<Y`	from left to right
right shift	`X>>Y`	
less than	`X<Y`	from left to right
less than or equal	`X<=Y`	
greater than	`X>Y`	
greater than or equal	`X>=Y`	
equals	`X==Y`	from left to right
not equals	`X!=Y`	
bitwise AND	`X&Y`	from left to right
bitwise exclusive OR	`X^Y`	from left to right
bitwise inclusive OR	`X|Y`	from left to right
logical AND	`X&&Y`	from left to right
logical OR	`X||Y`	from left to right
conditional	`Z?X:Y`	from right to left

(continued)

- **`ptrdiff_t`** (which is the type of the *subtract* operator when its operands are both pointers to objects)
- **`size_t`** (which is the type of the *sizeof* operator)
- **`wchar_t`** (which is the type of an element of a wide character string literal)

Continuing *Operator precedence and grouping.*

Operator	Notation	Grouping
assignment	`X=Y`	from right to left
multiply assign	`X*=Y`	
divide assign	`X/=Y`	
remainder assign	`X%=Y`	
add assign	`X+=Y`	
subtract assign	`X-=Y`	
left shift assign	`X<<=Y`	
right shift assign	`X>>=Y`	
bitwise AND assign	`X&=Y`	
bitwise exclusive OR assign	`X^=Y`	
bitwise inclusive OR assign	`X|=Y`	
comma	`X,Y`	from left to right

You do not have to include these type definitions in the program to use the *subtract* or *sizeof* operators, for example, or to write wide-character string literals.

If the result of an operation cannot be represented by a value of the result type, then an *exception* occurs:

overflow
- *Overflow* is an exception where the value is too large to be represented by an arithmetic type.

underflow
- *Underflow* is an exception where the value is too small to be represented by a floating-point type.

If any form of exception occurs, the program behavior is undefined.

A type described below as *Q qualified* can be:

- unqualified
- *const* qualified
- *volatile* qualified
- *const* and *volatile* qualified

(See **TYPE QUALIFIERS** in ***Chapter 4: Types***.)

For pointer arithmetic, every object is considered an array object (with perhaps only one element). If the array **`a`** has **`N`** elements, then **`a[N]`** is the element immediately beyond the array.

Add Assign **`X+=Y`**

You write **`X+=Y`** to access the value stored in the object designated by **`X`**, add the value of **`Y`** to the stored value, and store the new value back in the object.

Result	X	Y
type of **`X`** rvalue	arithmetic modifiable lvalue	arithmetic rvalue
type of **`X`** rvalue	pointer to object modifiable lvalue	integer rvalue

Add `X+Y`

You write **X+Y** to add the value of **Y** to the value of **X**. You can add an integer to a pointer value only if the result is the address of an element within (or just beyond) the same array object.

Result	X	Y
balanced type of **X** and **Y** rvalue	arithmetic rvalue	arithmetic rvalue
type of **X** rvalue	pointer to object rvalue	integer rvalue
type of **Y** rvalue	integer rvalue	pointer to object rvalue

Address of `&X`

You write **&X** to obtain the address of the function or object designated by **X**. You cannot obtain the address of an object declared with storage class **register**.

Result	X
pointer to *T* rvalue	any object type *T* except bitfield lvalue
pointer to *T* rvalue	incomplete type *T* lvalue
pointer to *T* rvalue	function type *T* function designator

Assignment `X=Y`

You write **X=Y** to store the value of **Y** in the object designated by **X**. If **Y** is an lvalue expression (that is converted to an rvalue expression to obtain its stored value), then the object it designates either must have no bytes in common with the object designated by **X** or must overlap exactly, and the objects must have compatible types.

Result	X	Y
type of **X** rvalue	arithmetic modifiable lvalue	arithmetic rvalue
type of **X** rvalue	pointer, structure, or union type *T* modifiable lvalue	type of **X** rvalue
type of **X** rvalue	pointer to qualified *T* modifiable lvalue	pointer to same or less qualified type compatible with *T* rvalue
type of **X** rvalue	pointer to *void* modifiable lvalue	pointer to object or incomplete type rvalue
type of **X** rvalue	pointer to object or incomplete type modifiable lvalue	pointer to *void* rvalue
type of **X** rvalue	any pointer type modifiable lvalue	integer zero rvalue

Bitwise AND Assign `X&=Y`

You write `X&=Y` to access the value stored in the object designated by `X`, form the bitwise AND of the value of `Y` with the stored value, and store the new value back in the object. (See the *Bitwise AND* operator following.)

Result	X	Y
type of `X`	integer	integer
rvalue	modifiable lvalue	rvalue

Bitwise AND `X&Y`

You write `X&Y` to form the bitwise AND of the values of `X` and `Y`. Each bit of the result is set if the corresponding bits in both `X` and `Y` are set.

Result	X	Y
balanced type of `X` and `Y`	integer	integer
rvalue	rvalue	rvalue

Bitwise Exclusive OR Assign `X^=Y`

You write `X^=Y` to access the value stored in the object designated by `X`, form the bitwise exclusive OR of the value of `Y` with the stored value, and store the new value back in the object. (See the *Bitwise exclusive OR* operator following.)

Result	X	Y
type of `X`	integer	integer
rvalue	modifiable lvalue	rvalue

Bitwise Exclusive OR `X^Y`

You write `X^Y` to form the bitwise exclusive OR of the values of `X` and `Y`. Each bit of the result is set if the corresponding bits in `X` and `Y` differ.

Result	X	Y
balanced type of `X` and `Y`	integer	integer
rvalue	rvalue	rvalue

Bitwise Inclusive OR Assign `X|=Y`

You write `X|=Y` to access the value stored in the object designated by `X`, form the bitwise inclusive OR of the value of `Y` with the stored value, and store the new value back in the object. (See the *Bitwise inclusive OR* operator following.)

Result	X	Y
type of `X`	integer	integer
rvalue	modifiable lvalue	rvalue

Bitwise Inclusive OR `X|Y`

You write `X|Y` to form the bitwise inclusive OR of the values of `X` and `Y`. Each bit of the result is set if either of the corresponding bits in `X` or `Y` is set.

Result	X	Y
balanced type of `X` and `Y`	integer	integer
rvalue	rvalue	rvalue

Bitwise NOT `~X`

You write `~X` to form the bitwise NOT of the value of `X`. Each bit of the result is set if the corresponding bit in `X` is not set.

Result	X
type of `X`	integer
rvalue	rvalue

Comma `X,Y`

You write **X,Y** to first evaluate **X** as a side-effects context expression and then to evaluate **Y**. There is a sequence point between the evaluation of the two operands.

Result	X	Y
type of **Y** rvalue	*void* expression	any rvalue

Conditional `Z?X:Y`

You write **Z?X:Y** to evaluate one of the operands **X** and **Y**, depending on the value of the test-context expression **Z**, which must be a scalar rvalue. If **Z** has a nonzero value, then only **X** is evaluated; otherwise, only **Y** is evaluated. The value of the expression is the value of the operand that is evaluated, converted to the result type. A sequence point occurs between the evaluation of **Z** and the evaluation of **X** or **Y**.

Result	X	Y
balanced type of **X** and **Y** rvalue	arithmetic rvalue	arithmetic rvalue
type of **X** rvalue	structure or union rvalue	type of **X** rvalue
type of **X** rvalue	pointer to *T* rvalue	integer zero rvalue
type of **Y** rvalue	integer zero rvalue	pointer to *T* rvalue
pointer to *Q* and *Q′* qualified composite of *T* and *T′* rvalue	pointer to *Q* qualified type *T* rvalue	pointer to *Q′* qualified compatible type *T′* rvalue
pointer to *Q* and *Q′* qualified *void* rvalue	pointer to *Q* qualified *void* rvalue	pointer to *Q′* qualified object or incomplete type rvalue
pointer to *Q* and *Q′* qualified *void* rvalue	pointer to *Q* qualified object or incomplete type rvalue	pointer to *Q′* qualified *void* rvalue
void expression	*void* expression	*void* expression

Divide Assign `X/=Y`

You write **X/=Y** to access the value stored in the object designated by **X**, divide that value by the value of **Y**, and store the new value back in the object. (See the *Divide* operator following.)

Result	X	Y
type of **X** rvalue	arithmetic modifiable lvalue	arithmetic rvalue

Divide `X/Y`

You write **X/Y** to divide the value of **X** by the value of **Y**. Do not divide by zero. For integer types, a positive quotient truncates toward zero.

Result	X	Y
balanced type of **X** and **Y** rvalue	arithmetic rvalue	arithmetic rvalue

Equals
X==Y

You write **X==Y** to test whether the value of **X** equals the value of **Y**. The result is an *int* rvalue whose value is 1 if the test is successful; otherwise, the value is zero. Each of the operands is converted to a common test type for the comparison. The table below shows the test type, rather than the result type.

Test	X	Y
balanced type of **X** and **Y** rvalue	arithmetic rvalue	arithmetic rvalue
type of **X** rvalue	pointer to *T* rvalue	integer zero rvalue
type of **Y** rvalue	integer zero rvalue	pointer to *T* rvalue
pointer to *Q* and *Q′* qualified composite of *T* and *T′* rvalue	pointer to *Q* qualified type *T* rvalue	pointer to *Q′* qualified compatible type *T′* rvalue
pointer to *Q* and *Q′* qualified *void* rvalue	pointer to *Q* qualified *void* rvalue	pointer to *Q′* qualified object or incomplete type rvalue
pointer to *Q* and *Q′* qualified *void* rvalue	pointer to *Q* qualified object or incomplete type rvalue	pointer to *Q′* qualified *void* rvalue

Function Call
X(Y)

You write **X(Y)** to call a function. The value of the expression (if any) is the value that the function returns. A sequence point occurs after the program evaluates **X** and **Y** and before it calls the function. (See **FUNCTION CALLS** in ***Chapter 6: Functions*** for how to call functions.)

Result	X	Y
object type *T* rvalue	function returning *T* function designator	zero or more argument rvalues
object type *T* rvalue	pointer to function returning *T* rvalue	zero or more argument rvalues
void expression	function returning *void* function designator	zero or more argument rvalues
void expression	pointer to function returning *void* rvalue	zero or more argument rvalues

Greater Than Or Equal
X>=Y

You write **X>=Y** to test whether the value of **X** is greater than or equal to the value of **Y**. The result is an *int* rvalue whose value is 1 if the test is successful; otherwise, the value is zero. Each of the operands is converted to a common test type for the comparison. You can compare two pointer values only if they are the addresses of elements within (or just beyond) the same array object. The table below shows the test type, rather than the result type.

Test	X	Y
balanced type of **x** and **y** rvalue	arithmetic rvalue	arithmetic rvalue
pointer to *Q* and *Q′* qualified composite of *T* and *T′* rvalue	pointer to *Q* qualified type *T* rvalue	pointer to *Q′* qualified compatible type *T′* rvalue

Greater Than **X>Y**

You write **x>y** to test whether the value of **x** is greater than the value of **y**. The result is an *int* rvalue whose value is 1 if the test is successful; otherwise, the value is zero. Each of the operands is converted to a common test type for the comparison. You can compare two pointer values only if they are the addresses of elements within (or just beyond) the same array object. The table below shows the test type, rather than the result type.

Test	X	Y
balanced type of **x** and **y** rvalue	arithmetic rvalue	arithmetic rvalue
pointer to *Q* and *Q′* qualified composite of *T* and *T′* rvalue	pointer to *Q* qualified type *T* rvalue	pointer to *Q′* qualified compatible type *T′* rvalue

Indirection ***X**

You write ***x** to use the value of the pointer **x** to designate an entity. The address of the entity is the value of the pointer.

Result	X
type *T* lvalue	pointer to object incomplete type *T* rvalue
type *T* function designator	pointer to function type *T* rvalue
void expression	pointer to *void* rvalue

Left Shift Assign **X<<=Y**

You write **x<<=y** to access the value stored in the object designated by **x**, shift that value to the left by the number of bit positions specified by the value of **y**, and store the new value back in the object. (See the *Left Shift* operator following.)

Result	X	Y
type of **x** rvalue	integer modifiable lvalue	integer rvalue

Left Shift **X<<Y**

You write **x<<y** to shift the value of **x** to the left by the number of bit positions specified by the value of **y**. For an *N*-bit representation for the (promoted) value of **x**, the value of **y** must be in the range [0, *N*). Zeros fill the vacated bit positions.

Result	X	Y
type of **x** rvalue	integer rvalue	integer rvalue

Less Than Or Equal
`X<=Y`

You write `X<=Y` to test whether the value of `X` is less than or equal to the value of `Y`. The result is an *int* rvalue whose value is 1 if the test is successful; otherwise, the value is zero. Each of the operands is converted to a common test type for the comparison. You can compare two pointer values only if they are the addresses of elements within (or just beyond) the same array object. The table below shows the test type, rather than the result type.

Test	X	Y
balanced type of `X` and `Y` rvalue	arithmetic rvalue	arithmetic rvalue
pointer to Q and Q' qualified composite of T and T' rvalue	pointer to Q qualified type T rvalue	pointer to Q' qualified compatible type T' rvalue

Less Than
`X<Y`

You write `X<Y` to test whether the value of `X` is less than the value of `Y`. The result is an *int* rvalue whose value is 1 if the test is successful; otherwise, the value is zero. Each of the operands is converted to a common test type for the comparison. You can compare two pointer values only if they are the addresses of elements within (or just beyond) the same array object. The table below shows the test type, rather than the result type.

Test	X	Y
balanced type of `X` and `Y` rvalue	arithmetic rvalue	arithmetic rvalue
pointer to Q and Q' qualified composite of T and T' rvalue	pointer to Q qualified type T rvalue	pointer to Q' qualified compatible type T' rvalue

Logical AND
`X&&Y`

You write `X&&Y` to test whether both of the operands `X` and `Y` are nonzero. If `X` is zero, then only `X` is evaluated and the value of the expression is zero; otherwise, `Y` is evaluated and the value of the expression is 1 if `Y` is nonzero or zero if `Y` is zero. A sequence point occurs between the evaluation of `X` and the evaluation of `Y`.

Result	X	Y
int rvalue	scalar rvalue	scalar rvalue

Logical NOT
`!X`

You write `!X` to test whether `X` is zero. If `X` is zero, the value of the expression is 1; otherwise, the value is zero.

Result	X
int rvalue	scalar rvalue

Logical OR
`X||Y`

You write `X||Y` to test whether either of the operands `X` or `Y` is nonzero. If `X` has a nonzero value, then only `X` is evaluated and the value of the expression is 1; otherwise, `Y` is evaluated and the value of the expression is

1 if **Y** is nonzero or zero if **Y** is zero. A sequence point occurs between the evaluation of **X** and the evaluation of **Y**.

Result	X	Y
int rvalue	scalar rvalue	scalar rvalue

Minus X-Y You write **-X** to negate the value of **X**.

Result	X
type of **X** rvalue	arithmetic rvalue

Multiply Assign X*=Y You write **X*=Y** to access the value stored in the object designated by **X**, multiply that value by the value of **Y**, and store the new value back in the object.

Result	X	Y
type of **X** rvalue	arithmetic modifiable lvalue	arithmetic rvalue

Multiply X*Y You write **X*Y** to multiply the value of **X** by the value of **Y**.

Result	X	Y
balanced type of **X** and **Y** rvalue	arithmetic rvalue	arithmetic rvalue

Not Equals X!=Y You write **X!=Y** to test whether the value of **X** does not equal the value of **Y**. The result is an *int* rvalue whose value is 1 if the test is successful; otherwise, the value is zero. Each of the operands is converted to a common test type for the comparison. The table below shows the test type, rather than the result type.

Test	X	Y
balanced type of **X** and **Y** rvalue	arithmetic rvalue	arithmetic rvalue
type of **X** rvalue	pointer to *T* rvalue	integer zero rvalue
type of **Y** rvalue	integer zero rvalue	pointer to *T* rvalue
pointer to *Q* and *Q′* qualified composite of *T* and *T′* rvalue	pointer to *Q* qualified type *T* rvalue	pointer to *Q′* qualified compatible type *T′* rvalue
pointer to *Q* and *Q′* qualified *void* rvalue	pointer to *Q* qualified *void* rvalue	pointer to *Q′* qualified object or incomplete type rvalue
pointer to *Q* and *Q′* qualified *void* rvalue	pointer to *Q* qualified object or incomplete type rvalue	pointer to *Q′* qualified *void* rvalue

Plus
+X

You write **+X** to leave the value of **X** unchanged. (You use this operator primarily to emphasize that a term is not negated.)

Result	X
type of **X** rvalue	arithmetic rvalue

Point at
X->Y

You write **X->Y** to select the member whose name is **Y** from the structure or union whose address is the value of **X**.

Result	X	Y
type of member **Y** lvalue	pointer to structure or union rvalue	member name within structure or union

Postdecrement
X--

You write **X--** to access the value stored in the object designated by **X**, subtract 1 from the value, and store the new value back in the object. The value of the expression is the *original* value stored in the object.

Result	X
type *T* rvalue	scalar type *T* modifiable lvalue

Postincrement
X++

You write **X++** to access the value stored in the object designated by **X**, add 1 to the value, and store the new value back in the object. The value of the expression is the *original* value stored in the object.

Result	X
type *T* rvalue	scalar type *T* modifiable lvalue

Predecrement
--X

You write **--X** to access the value stored in the object designated by **X**, subtract 1 from the value, and store the new value back in the object. The value of the expression is the *final* value stored in the object.

Result	X
type *T* rvalue	scalar type *T* modifiable lvalue

Preincrement
++X

You write **++X** to access the value stored in the object designated by **X**, add 1 to the value, and store the new value back in the object. The value of the expression is the *final* value stored in the object.

Result	X
type *T* rvalue	scalar type *T* modifiable lvalue

Remainder Assign
X%=Y

You write **X%=Y** to access the value stored in the object designated by **X**, divide that value by the value of **Y**, and store the remainder back in the object. (See the *remainder* operator following.)

Result	X	Y
type of **X** rvalue	integer modifiable lvalue	integer rvalue

Remainder `X%Y`

You write **X%Y** to compute the remainder of the value of **X** divided by the value of **Y**. Do not divide by zero. Barring overflow or division by zero, it is always true that:

```
X = (X / Y) * Y + (X % Y)
```

Result	X	Y
balanced type of **X** and **Y** rvalue	integer rvalue	integer rvalue

Right Shift Assign `X>>=Y`

You write **X>>=Y** to access the value stored in the object designated by **X**, shift that value to the right by the number of bit positions specified by the value of **Y**, and store the new value back in the object. (See the *Right Shift* operator following.)

Result	X	Y
type of **X** rvalue	integer modifiable lvalue	integer rvalue

Right Shift `X>>Y`

You write **X>>Y** to shift the value of **X** to the right by the number of bit positions specified by the value of **Y**. For an *N*-bit representation for the value of **X**, the (promoted) value of **Y** must be in the range [0, *N*). If **X** is nonnegative, then zeros fill the vacated bit positions; otherwise, the result is implementation-defined.

Result	X	Y
balanced type of **X** and **Y** rvalue	integer rvalue	integer rvalue

Select `X.Y`

You write **X.Y** to select the member **Y** from the structure or union **X**. The result is an lvalue expression only if **X** is an lvalue expression.

Result	X	Y
type of member **Y** lvalue	structure or union lvalue	member name within the structure or union
type of member **Y** rvalue	structure or union rvalue	member name within the structure or union

Sizeof `sizeof X`

You write **sizeof X** to determine the size in bytes of an object whose type is the type of **X**. Do not write a function-designator expression for **X**. The translator uses the expression you write for **X** only to determine a type; it is not evaluated. The operand **X** is otherwise not considered a part of the expression containing the *sizeof* operator. Therefore, prohibitions on what can be in an expression (such as an arithmetic constant expression) do not apply to any part of **X**.

Result	X
size_t rvalue	object type lvalue
size_t rvalue	object type rvalue

Subscript `X[Y]`

You write **X[Y]** to designate an array element. The operator is identical in effect to ***((X)+(Y))**. Typically, **X** is an array lvalue expression (which becomes a pointer rvalue expression) or an rvalue expression of some pointer type whose value is the address of an array element. In this case, **Y** is an integer rvalue. The designated array element is `Y` elements away from the element designated by `X`. Because of the symmetry of the two operands, however, you can write them in either order.

Result	X	Y
object type *T* lvalue	pointer to *T* rvalue	integer rvalue
object type *T* lvalue	integer rvalue	pointer to *T* rvalue

Subtract Assign `X-=Y`

You write `X-=Y` to access the value stored in the object designated by `X`, subtract the value of `Y` from the value, and store the new value back in the object. (See the *subtract* operator following.)

Result	X	Y
type of `X` rvalue	arithmetic modifiable lvalue	arithmetic rvalue
type of `X` rvalue	pointer to object modifiable lvalue	integer rvalue

Subtract `X-Y`

You write `X-Y` to subtract the value of `Y` from the value of `X`. You can subtract two pointer values only if they are the addresses of elements within (or just beyond) the same array object. The result tells you how many elements lie between the two addresses.

Result	X	Y
balanced type of `X` and `Y` rvalue	arithmetic rvalue	arithmetic rvalue
type of `X` rvalue	pointer to object rvalue	integer rvalue
`ptrdiff_t` rvalue	pointer to *Q* qualified object type *T* rvalue	pointer to *Q′* qualified compatible type *T′* rvalue

Type Cast `(decl)X`

You write `(decl)X` to convert the value of `X` to the scalar (or *void*) type *T* that you specify in the type-name declaration `decl` enclosed in parentheses. The table below shows valid combinations of declared type and operand type. (See **TYPE CONVERSIONS** earlier in this chapter.)

Result	Type *T*	X
type *T* rvalue	integer	scalar rvalue
type *T* rvalue	floating-point	arithmetic rvalue
type *T* rvalue	pointer to any type	integer rvalue
type *T* rvalue	pointer to object or incomplete type	pointer to object or incomplete type rvalue
type *T* rvalue	pointer to function	pointer to function rvalue
void expression	*void*	scalar rvalue or *void* expression

ORDER OF EVALUATION

When the program evaluates an expression, it has considerable latitude in choosing the *order* in which it evaluates subexpressions. For example, the translator can alter:

```
y = *p++;
```

either to:

```
temp = p; p += 1; y = *temp;
```

or to:

```
y = *p; p += 1;
```

As another example, the program can evaluate the expression **f() + g()** by calling the functions in either order.

side effects The order of evaluation is important in understanding when *side effects* occur. A side effect is a change in the state of the program that occurs when evaluating an expression. Side effects occur when the program:

- stores a value in an object
- accesses a value from an object of *volatile* qualified type
- alters the state of a file

sequence point A *sequence point* is a point in the program at which you can determine which side effects have occurred and which have yet to take place. Each of the expressions you write as part of a statement, for example, has a sequence point at the end of it. You can be sure that for:

```
y = 37;
x += y;
```

the program stores the value 37 in **y** before it accesses the value stored in **y** to add it to the value stored in **x**.

Sequence points can also occur within expressions. The *comma, conditional, function call, logical AND,* and *logical OR* operators each contain a sequence point. For example, you can write:

```
if ((c = getchar()) != EOF && isprint(c))
```

and know that the program evaluates **isprint(c)** only after a new value is stored in **c** from the call to **getchar**.

Between two sequence points, you must access the value stored in an object whose contents you are altering only to determine the new value to store, and store a value in an object no more than once.

For example:

```
val = 10 * val + (c - '0');        well defined
i = ++i + 2;                   NOT well defined
```

An expression can contain sequence points and still not have a definite order of evaluation. In the example above, the expression **f() + g()** contains a sequence point before each function call, but the *add* operator imposes no ordering on the evaluation of its operands.

PART II

The Standard C Library

Chapter 8: Library

The program can call on a large number of functions from the Standard C *library.* These functions perform essential services such as input and output. They also provide efficient implementations of frequently used operations. Numerous macro and type definitions accompany these functions to help you to make better use of the library.

This chapter tells how to use the library. It describes what happens at program startup and at program termination. It describes how to read and write data between the program and data files and how to use the formatting functions to simplify input and output. The chapters that follow summarize all functions, macros, and types defined in the library, giving a brief description of each entity.

LIBRARY ORGANIZATION

All library entities are declared or defined in one or more *standard headers.* The 18 standard headers are:

`<assert.h>`	`<locale.h>`	`<stdio.h>`
`<ctype.h>`	`<math.h>`	`<stdlib.h>`
`<errno.h>`	`<setjmp.h>`	`<string.h>`
`<float.h>`	`<signal.h>`	`<time.h>`
`<iso646.h>`	`<stdarg.h>`	`<wchar.h>`
`<limits.h>`	`<stddef.h>`	`<wctype.h>`

Amendment 1 The headers `<iso646.h>`, `<wchar.h>`, and `<wctype.h>` are added with Amendment 1.

A *freestanding implementation* of Standard C provides only a subset of these standard headers:

`<float.h>` `<limits.h>` `<stdarg.h>` `<stddef.h>`

Each freestanding implementation defines:

- how it starts the program
- what happens when the program terminates
- what library functions (if any) it provides

This book describes what is common to every *hosted implementation* of Standard C. A hosted implementation provides the full library described in this chapter, including all standard headers and functions.

You include the contents of a standard header by naming it in an *include* directive. For example:

```
#include <stdio.h>      /* include I/O facilities */
```

You can include the standard headers in any order, a standard header more than once, or two or more standard headers that define the same macro or the same type.

Do not include a standard header within a declaration. Do not define macros that have the same names as keywords before you include a standard header.

A standard header never includes another standard header. A standard header declares or defines only the entities described for it in the chapters that follow in this book.

masking macros Every function in the library is declared in a standard header. The standard header can also provide a macro, with the same name as the function, that masks the function declaration and achieves the same effect. The macro typically expands to an expression that executes faster than a call to the function of the same name. The macro can, however, cause confusion when you are tracing or debugging the program. So you can use a standard header in two ways to declare or define a library function. To take advantage of any macro version, include the standard header so that each apparent call to the function can be replaced by a macro expansion.

For example:

```
#include <ctype.h>
char *skip_space(char *p)
     {
     while (isspace(*p))         can be a macro
          ++p;
     return (p);
     }
```

To ensure that the program calls the actual library function, include the standard header and remove any macro definition with an *undef* directive.

For example:

```
#include <ctype.h>
#undef isspace                   remove any macro definition
int f(char *p) {
     while (isspace(*p))         must be a function
          ++p;
```

You can use many functions in the library without including a standard header (although this practice is not recommended). If you do not need defined macros or types to declare and call the function, you can simply declare the function as it appears in this chapter. Again, you have two choices. You can declare the function explicitly.

For example:

```
     double sin(double x);       declared in <math.h>
     y = rho * sin(theta);
```

Or you can declare the function implicitly if it is a function returning *int* with a fixed number of arguments, as in:

```
     n = atoi(str);              declared in <stdlib.h>
```

If the function has a varying number of arguments, such as **printf** (declared in **<stdio.h>**), you must declare it explicitly: Either include the standard header that declares it or write an explicit declaration.

LIBRARY CONVENTIONS

A library macro that masks a function declaration expands to an expression that evaluates each of its arguments once (and only once). Arguments that have side effects evaluate the same way whether the expression executes the macro expansion or calls the function. Macros for the functions **getc** and **putc** (declared in **<stdio.h>**) are explicit exceptions to this rule. Their **stream** arguments can be evaluated more than once. Avoid argument expressions that have side effects with these macros.

A library function that alters a value stored in memory assumes that the function accesses no other objects that overlap with the object whose stored value it alters. You cannot depend on consistent behavior from a library function that accesses and alters the same storage via different arguments. The function **memmove** (declared in **<string.h>**) is an explicit exception to this rule. Its arguments can point at objects that overlap.

Some library functions operate on *strings*. You designate a string by an rvalue expression that has type *pointer to char* (or by an array lvalue expression that converts to an rvalue expression with such a type). Its value is the address of the first byte in an object of type *array of char*. The first successive element of the array that has a null character stored in it marks the end of the string.

- A *filename* is a string whose contents meet the requirements of the target environment for naming files.
- A *multibyte string* is composed of zero or more multibyte characters, followed by a null character. (See **MULTIBYTE CHARACTERS** in ***Chapter 1: Characters***.)
- A *wide-character string* is composed of zero or more wide characters (stored in an array of **wchar_t**), followed by a null wide character (with a zero value).

If an argument to a library function has a pointer type, then the value of the argument expression must be a valid address for an object of its type. This is true even if the library function has no need to access an object by using the pointer argument. An explicit exception is when the description of the library function spells out what happens when you use a null pointer.

Some examples are:

```
strcpy(s1, NULL)         is INVALID
memcpy(s1, NULL, 0)      is UNSAFE
realloc(NULL, 50)        is the same as malloc(50)
```

PROGRAM STARTUP AND TERMINATION

The target environment controls the execution of the program (in contrast to the translator part of the implementation, which prepares the parts of the program for execution). The target environment passes control to the program at *program startup* by calling the function **main** that you define as part of the program. *Program arguments* are strings that the target environment provides, such as text from the command line that you type to invoke the program. If the program does not need to access *program arguments*, you can define **main** as:

```
extern int main(void)
    { body of main }
```

If the program uses program arguments, you define **main** as:

```
extern int main(int argc, char **argv)
    { body of main }
```

- **argc** is a value (always greater than zero) that specifies the number of program arguments.
- **argv[0]** designates the first element of an array of strings. **argv[argc]** designates the last element of the array, whose stored value is a null pointer.

For example, if you invoke a program by typing:

```
echo hello
```

a target environment can call **main** with:

- The value 2 for **argc**.
- The address of an array object containing **"echo"** stored in **argv[0]**.
- The address of an array object containing **"hello"** stored in **argv[1]**.
- A null pointer stored in **argv[2]**.

argv[0] is the name used to invoke the program. The target environment can replace this name with a null string (**""**). The program can alter the values stored in **argc**, in **argv**, and in the array objects whose addresses are stored in **argv**.

Before the target environment calls **main**, it stores the initial values you specify in all objects that have static duration. It also opens three files, controlled by the text-stream objects designated by the macros:

- **stdin** (for standard input)
- **stdout** (for standard output)
- **stderr** (for standard error output)

(See **FILES AND STREAMS** later in this chapter.)

If **main** returns to its caller, the target environment calls **exit** with the value returned from **main** as the status argument to **exit**. If the *return* statement that the program executes has no expression, the status argument is undefined. This is the case if the program executes the implied *return* statement at the end of the function definition.

You can also call **exit** directly from any expression within the program. In both cases, **exit** calls all functions registered with **atexit** in reverse order of registry and then begins *program termination.* At program termination, the target environment closes all open files, removes any temporary files that you created by calling **tmpfile**, and then returns control to the invoker, using the status argument value to determine the termination status to report for the program.

The program can also *abort,* by calling **abort**, for example. Each implementation defines whether it closes files, whether it removes temporary files, and what termination status it reports when a program aborts.

FILES AND STREAMS

A program communicates with the target environment by reading and writing *files* (ordered sequences of bytes). A file can be, for example, a data set that you can read and write repeatedly (such as a disk file), a stream of bytes generated by a program (such as a pipeline), or a stream of bytes received from or sent to a peripheral device (such as your keyboard or display). The latter two are *interactive files;* they are the principal means by which to interact with the program.

You manipulate all these kinds of files in much the same way — by calling library functions. You include the standard header **<stdio.h>** to declare most of these functions.

Before you can perform many of the operations on a file, the file must be *opened.* Opening a file associates it with a *stream.* The library maintains the state of each stream in an object of type **FILE**.

The target environment opens three files prior to program startup. (See **PROGRAM STARTUP AND TERMINATION** earlier in this chapter.) You can open a file by calling the library function **fopen** with two arguments. The first argument is a *filename,* a multibyte string that the target environment uses to identify which file you want to read or write. The second argument is a string that specifies:

- whether you intend to read data from the file or write data to it or both
- whether you intend to generate new contents for the file (or create a file that did not previously exist) or leave the existing contents in place
- whether writes to a file can alter existing contents or should only append bytes at the end of the file
- whether you want to manipulate a *text stream* or a *binary stream*

Amendment 1 Once the file is successfully opened, you can then determine whether the stream is *byte oriented* (a *byte stream*) or *wide oriented* (a *wide stream*). Wide oriented streams are supported only with Amendment 1. A stream is initially *unbound.* Calling certain functions to operate on the stream make it byte oriented, while certain other functions make it wide oriented. Once established, a stream maintains its orientation until it is closed by a call to **fclose** or **freopen**.

Text and Binary Streams

A *text stream* consists of one or more *lines* of text that can be written to a text-oriented display so that they can be read. When reading from a text stream, the program reads an ***NL*** (*newline*) at the end of each line. When writing to a text stream, the program writes an ***NL*** to signal the end of a line. To match differing conventions among target environments for representing text in files, the library functions can alter the number and representations of characters you transmit between the program and a text stream.

For maximum portability, the program should not write:

- empty files
- ***space*** characters at the end of a line
- partial lines (by omitting the ***NL*** at the end of a file)
- characters other than the printable characters, ***NL***, and ***HT***

If you follow these rules, the sequence of characters you read from a text stream (either as single-byte or multibyte characters) will match the sequence of characters you wrote to the text stream when you created the file. Otherwise, the library functions can remove a file you create if the file is empty when you close it. Or they can alter or delete characters you write to the file.

A *binary stream* consists of one or more bytes of arbitrary information. You can write the value stored in an arbitrary object to a (byte-oriented) binary stream and read exactly what was stored in the object when you wrote it. The library functions do not alter the bytes you transmit between the program and a binary stream. They can, however, append an arbitrary number of null bytes to the file that you write with a binary stream. The program must deal with these additional null bytes at the end of any binary stream.

Byte and Wide Streams

A byte stream treats a file as a sequence of bytes. Within the program, the stream looks like the same sequence of bytes, except for the possible alterations described above.

Amendment 1 By contrast, a wide stream treats a file as a sequence of generalized multibyte characters, which can have a broad range of encoding rules. (Text and binary files are still read and written as described above.) Within the program, the stream looks like the corresponding sequence of wide characters. Conversions between the two representations occur within the Standard C library. The conversion rules can, in principle, be altered by a call to **setlocale** (declared in **<locale.h>**) that alters the category **LC_CTYPE**. Each wide stream determines its conversion rules at the time it becomes wide oriented, and retains these rules even if the category **LC_CTYPE** subsequently changes.

Controlling Streams

Amendment 1 **fopen** returns the address of an object of type **FILE**. You use this address as the **stream** argument to several library functions to perform various operations on an open file. For a byte stream, all input takes place as if each character is read by calling **fgetc**, and all output takes place as if each character is written by calling **fputc**. For a wide stream (with Amendment 1), all input takes place as if each character is read by calling **fgetwc**, and all output takes place as if each character is written by calling **fputwc**. You can *close* a file by calling **fclose**, after which the address of the **FILE** object is invalid.

A **FILE** object stores the state of a stream, including:

- an *error indicator* (set nonzero by a function that encounters a read or write error)
- an *end-of-file indicator* (set nonzero by a function that encounters the end of the file while reading)
- a *file-position indicator* (that specifies the next byte in the stream to read or write, if the file can support positioning requests)
- **Amendment 1** a *stream state* (that specifies whether the stream will accept reads and/or writes and, with Amendment 1, whether the stream is unbound, byte oriented, or wide oriented)
- **Amendment 1** a *parse state* (that remembers the state of any partly assembled or generated generalized multibyte character, as well as any shift state for the generalized multibyte sequence, in the file)
- a *file buffer* (that specifies the address and size of an array object that library functions can use to improve the performance of read and write operations to the stream)

Do not alter any value stored in a **FILE** object or in a file buffer that you specify for use with that object. You cannot copy a **FILE** object and portably use the address of the copy as a **stream** argument to a library function.

Figure 8.1 summarizes the valid state transitions for a stream. Each of the circles denotes a stable state. Each of the arcs denotes a transition that can occur as the result of a function call that operates on the stream. Five groups of functions can cause state transitions.

Functions in the first three groups are declared in **<stdio.h>**:

- The *byte read functions,* which include:

```
fgetc      fgets      fread      fscanf
getc       getchar    gets       scanf
ungetc
```

- The *byte write functions,* which include:

```
fprintf    fputc      fputs      fwrite
printf     putc       putchar    puts
vfprintf   vprintf
```

- The *position functions,* which include:

```
fflush     fseek      fsetpos    rewind
```

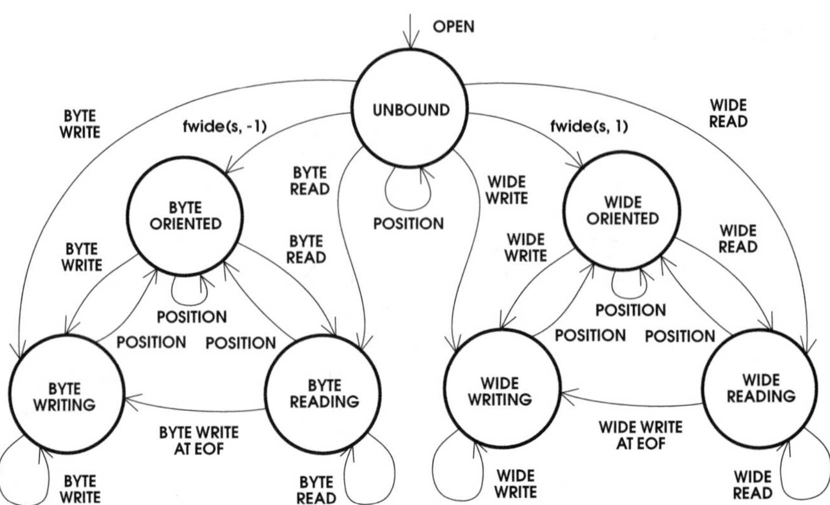

Figure 8.1: *States of a stream.*

Amendment 1 Functions in the remaining two groups are declared in **<wchar.h>**:

- The *wide read functions*, which include:

```
fgetwc      fgetws      fwscanf     getwc
getwchar    ungetwc     wscanf
```

- The *wide write functions*, which include:

```
fwprintf    fputwc      fputws      putwc
putwchar    vfwprintf   vwprinf     wprintf
```

For the stream **s**, the call **fwide(s, 0)** is always valid and never causes a change of state. Any other call to **fwide** (declared in **<wchar.h>**), or to any of the five groups of functions described above, causes the state transition shown in the state diagram. If no such transition is shown, the function call is invalid.

Amendment 1 The state diagram shows how to establish the orientation of a stream:

- The call **fwide(s, -1)**, or to a byte read or byte write function, establishes the stream as byte oriented.
- The call **fwide(s, 1)**, or to a wide read or wide write function, establishes the stream as wide oriented.

The state diagram also shows that you must call one of the position functions between most write and read operations:

- You cannot call a read function if the last operation on the stream was a write.
- You cannot call a write function if the last operation on the stream was a read, unless that read operation set the end-of-file indicator.

Finally, the state diagram shows that a position operation never *decreases* the number of valid function calls that can follow.

FORMATTED INPUT/OUTPUT

Several library functions help you convert data values between encoded internal representations and text sequences that you can read and write. You provide a *format string* as the value of the **format** argument to each of these functions. The functions fall into four categories. The first two categories are functions that perform byte-oriented stream operations:

- The *byte print functions* (declared in **<stdio.h>**) convert internal representations to sequences of type *char,* and help you compose such sequences for display:

fprintf	**printf**	**sprintf**
vfprintf	**vprintf**	**vsprintf**

- The *byte scan functions* (declared in **<stdio.h>** convert sequences of type *char* to internal representations, and help you scan such sequences that you read:

fscanf	**scanf**	**sscanf**

For these byte-oriented function, a format string is a multibyte string that begins and ends in the initial shift state. The remaining two categories are functions that perform wide-oriented stream operations:

Amendment 1
- The *wide print functions* (declared in **<wchar.h>**) convert internal representations to sequences of type **wchar_t**, and help you compose such sequences for display:

fwprintf	**wprintf**	**wsprintf**
vfwprintf	**vwprintf**	**vwsprintf**

Amendment 1
- The *wide scan functions* (declared in **<wchar.h>** convert sequences of type **wchar_t** to internal representations, and help you scan such sequences that you read:

fwscanf	**wscanf**	**wsscanf**

For a wide-oriented function, a format string is a wide-character string. In the descriptions that follow, a wide character **wc** from a format string or a stream is compared to a specific (byte) character **c** as if by evaluating the expression **wctob(wc) == c**, where **wctob** is declared in **<wchar.h>**.

In any case, a format string consists of zero or more *conversion specifications,* interspersed with literal text and white space. Here, white space is a sequence of one or more ***white space*** characters **c** for which the call **isspace(c)** returns nonzero. (The characters defined as ***white space*** can change when you change the **LC_CTYPE** locale category.) Figure 8.2 shows the syntax of a format string.

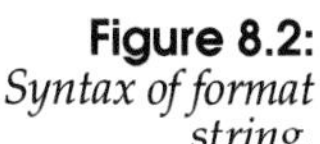

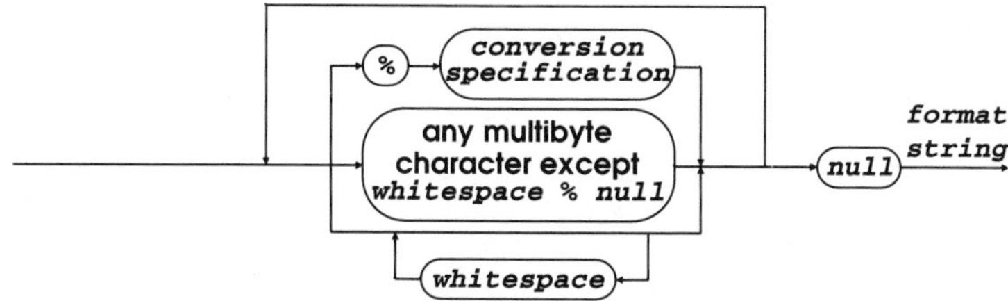

Figure 8.2: *Syntax of format string.*

A print or scan function scans the format string once from beginning to end to determine what conversions to perform. Every print or scan function accepts a varying number of arguments, either directly or under control of an argument of type **va_list**. Some conversion specifications in the format string use the next argument in the list. A print or scan function uses each successive argument no more than once. Trailing arguments can be left unused.

In the description that follows:

- *integer conversions* are the conversion specifiers that end in **d**, **i**, **o**, **u**, **x**, or **X**
- *floating-point conversions* are the conversion specifiers that end in **e**, **E**, **f**, **g**, or **G**

Print Functions

For the print functions, literal text or white space in a format string generates characters that match the characters in the format string. A conversion specification typically generates characters by converting the next argument value to a corresponding text sequence. Figure 8.3 shows the syntax for print conversion specifications.

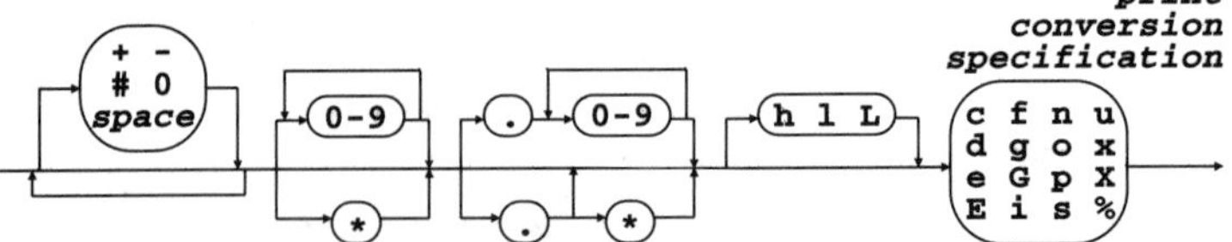

Figure 8.3: *Syntax of print conversion specification.*

Following the percent character (**%**) in the format string, you can write zero or more *flags*:

- **-** — to left-justify a conversion
- **+** — to generate a plus sign for signed values that are positive
- ***space*** — to generate a ***space*** for signed values that have neither a plus nor a minus sign
- **#** — to prefix **0** on an **o** conversion, to prefix **0x** on an **x** conversion, to prefix **0X** on an **X** conversion, or to generate a decimal point and fraction digits that are otherwise suppressed on a floating-point conversion
- **0** — to pad a conversion with leading zeros after any sign or prefix, in the absence of a minus (**-**) flag or a specified precision

field width Following any flags, you can write a *field width* that specifies the minimum number of characters to generate for the conversion. Unless altered by a flag, the default behavior is to pad a short conversion on the left with ***space*** characters. If you write an asterisk (*****) instead of a decimal number for a field width, then a print function takes the value of the next argument (which must be of type *int*) as the field width. If the argument value is negative, it supplies a **-** flag and its magnitude is the field width.

precision Following any field width, you can write a decimal point (`.`) followed by a *precision* that specifies one of the following: the minimum number of digits to generate on an integer conversion; the number of fraction digits to generate on an `e`, `E`, or `f` conversion; the maximum number of significant digits to generate on a `g` or `G` conversion; or the maximum number of characters to generate from a string on an `s` conversion.

If you write an `*` instead of a decimal number for a precision, a print function takes the value of the next argument (which must be of type *int*) as the precision. If the argument value is negative, the default precision applies. If you do not write either an `*` or a decimal number following the decimal point, the precision is zero.

conversion specifier Following any precision, you must write a one-character *conversion specifier*, possibly preceded by a one-character *conversion qualifier*. Each combination determines the type required of the next argument (if any) and how the library functions alter the argument value before converting it to a text sequence. The integer and floating-point conversions also determine what base to use for the text representation. If a conversion specifier requires a precision *p* and you do not provide one in the format, then the conversion specifier chooses a default value for the precision. Table 8.1 lists all defined combinations and their properties.

The conversion specifier determines any behavior not summarized in this table. In the following descriptions, *p* is the precision. Examples follow each of the conversion specifications. A single conversion can generate up to 509 characters.

%c You write `c` to generate a single character from the converted value. For a wide-oriented stream, conversion of the character `x` occurs as if by calling `btowc(x)` (declared in `<wchar.h>`).

```
printf("%c", 'a')                   generates a
printf("<%3c|%-3c>", 'a', 'b')      generates <  a|b  >
wprintf(L"%c", 'a')                 generates (wide) btowc(a)
```

%lc Amendment 1 You write `lc` to generate a single character from the converted value. Conversion of the character `x` occurs as if it is followed by a null character in an array of two elements of type `wchar_t` converted by the conversion specification `ls`, described below.

```
printf("%lc", L'a')                 generates a
wprintf(L"lc", L'a')                generates (wide) L'a'
```

%d %i %o %u %x %X You write `d`, `i`, `o`, `u`, `x`, or `X` to generate a possibly signed integer representation. `d` or `i` specifies signed decimal representation, `o` unsigned octal, `u` unsigned decimal, `x` unsigned hexadecimal using the digits `0-9` and `a-f`, and `X` unsigned hexadecimal using the digits `0-9` and `A-F`. The conversion generates at least *p* digits to represent the converted value. If *p* is zero, a converted value of zero generates no digits.

```
printf("%d %o %x", 31, 31, 31)      generates 31 37 1f
printf("%hu", 0xffff)               generates 65535
printf("%#X %+d", 31, 31)           generates 0X1F +31
```

Table 8.1: *Print conversion specifiers.*

Specifier	Argument Type	Converted Value	Base	Default Precision
`c`	`int x`	`(unsigned char)x`		
`lc`	`wint_t x`	`wchar_t a[2] = {x}`		
`d`	`int x`	`(int)x`	10	1
`hd`	`int x`	`(short)x`	10	1
`ld`	`long x`	`(long)x`	10	1
`e`	`double x`	`(double)x`	10	6
`Le`	`long double x`	`(long double)x`	10	6
`E`	`double x`	`(double)x`	10	6
`LE`	`long double x`	`(long double)x`	10	6
`f`	`double x`	`(double)x`	10	6
`Lf`	`long double x`	`(long double)x`	10	6
`g`	`double x`	`(double)x`	10	6
`Lg`	`long double x`	`(long double)x`	10	6
`G`	`double x`	`(double)x`	10	6
`LG`	`long double x`	`(long double)x`	10	6
`i`	`int x`	`(int)x`	10	1
`hi`	`int x`	`(short)x`	10	1
`li`	`long x`	`(long)x`	10	1
`n`	`int *x`			
`hn`	`short *x`			
`ln`	`long *x`			
`o`	`int x`	`(unsigned int)x`	8	1
`ho`	`int x`	`(unsigned short)x`	8	1
`lo`	`long x`	`(unsigned long)x`	8	1
`p`	`void *x`	`(void *)x`		
`s`	`char x[]`	`x[0]...`		large
`ls`	`wchar_t x[]`	`x[0]...`		large
`u`	`int x`	`(unsigned int)x`	10	1
`hu`	`int x`	`(unsigned short)x`	10	1
`lu`	`long x`	`(unsigned long)x`	10	1
`x`	`int x`	`(unsigned int)x`	16	1
`hx`	`int x`	`(unsigned short)x`	16	1
`lx`	`long x`	`(unsigned long)x`	16	1
`X`	`int x`	`(unsigned int)x`	16	1
`hX`	`int x`	`(unsigned short)x`	16	1
`lX`	`long x`	`(unsigned long)x`	16	1
`%`	none	`'%'`		

`%e %E` You write **`e`** or **`E`** to generate a signed fractional representation with an exponent. The generated text takes the form ± *d.dddE± dd,* where *d* is a decimal digit, the dot (.) is the decimal point for the current locale, and *E* is either **`e`** (for **`e`** conversion) or **`E`** (for **`E`** conversion). The generated text has one integer digit, a decimal point if *p* is nonzero or if you specify the **`#`** flag, *p* fraction digits, and at least two exponent digits. The result is rounded. The value zero has a zero exponent.

```
printf("%e", 31.4)        generates 3.140000e+01
printf("%.2E", 31.4)      generates 3.14E+01
```

`%f` You write **`f`** to generate a signed fractional representation with no exponent. The generated text takes the form ± *d.ddd,* where *d* is a decimal digit and the dot (.) is the decimal point for the current locale. The generated text has at least one integer digit, a decimal point if *p* is nonzero or if you specify the **`#`** flag, and *p* fraction digits. The result is rounded.

```
printf("%f", 31.4)                  generates 31.400000
printf("%.0f %#f", 31.0, 31.0)      generates 31 31.
```

%g %G You write **g** or **G** to generate a signed fractional representation with or without an exponent, as appropriate. For **g** conversion, the generated text takes the same form as either **e** or **f**. For **G** conversion, it takes the same form as either **E** or **f**. The precision *p* specifies the number of significant digits generated. (If *p* is 0, it is changed to 1.) If **e** conversion would yield an exponent in the range [–4, *p*), then **f** conversion occurs instead. The generated text has no trailing zeros in any fraction and has a decimal point only if there are nonzero fraction digits, unless you specify the **#** flag.

```
printf("%.6g", 31.4)              generates 31.4
printf("%.1g", 31.4)              generates 3.14e+01
```

%n You write **n** to store the number of characters generated (up to this point in the format) in the object of type *int* whose address is the value of the next successive argument.

```
printf("abc%n", &x)               stores 3
```

%p You write **p** to generate an external representation of a *pointer to void*. The conversion is implementation-defined.

```
printf("%p", (void *)&x)          generates, e.g. F4C0
```

%s You write **s** to generate a sequence of characters from the values stored in the argument string. For a wide stream, conversion occurs as if by repeatedly calling **mbrtowc** (declared in **<wchar.h>**), beginning in the initial shift state. The conversion generates no more than *p* characters, up to but not including the terminating null character.

```
printf("%s", "hello")             generates hello
printf("%.2s", "hello")           generates he
wprintf(L"%s", "hello")           generates (wide) hello
```

%ls
Amendment 1 You write **ls** to generate a sequence of characters from the values stored in the argument string. For a byte stream, conversion occurs as if by repeatedly calling **mbrtowc** (declared in **<wchar.h>**), beginning in the initial shift state, so long as complete multibyte characters can be generated. The conversion generates no more than *p* characters, up to but not including the terminating null character.

```
printf("%ls", L"hello")           generates hello
wprintf(L"%.2s", L"hello")        generates (wide) he
```

%% You write **%** to generate the percent character (**%**).

```
printf("%%")                      generates %
```

Scan Functions

For the scan functions, literal text in a format string must match the next characters to scan in the input text. White space in a format string must match the longest possible sequence of the next zero or more white-space characters in the input. Except for the conversion specifier **n** (which consumes no input), each conversion specification determines a pattern that one or more of the next characters in the input must match. And except for the conversion specifiers **c**, **n**, and **[**, every match begins by skipping any white-space characters in the input.

A scan function returns when:

- it reaches the terminating null in the format string
- it cannot obtain additional input characters to scan (input failure)
- a conversion fails (matching failure)

A scan function returns **EOF** (defined in **<stdio.h>**) if an input failure occurs before any conversion. Otherwise it returns the number of converted values stored. If one or more characters form a valid prefix but the conversion fails, the valid prefix is consumed before the scan function returns. Thus:

```
scanf("%i", &i)     consumes 0X from the field 0XZ
scanf("%f", &f)     consumes 3.2E from the field 3.2EZ
```

A conversion specification typically converts the matched input characters to a corresponding encoded value. The next argument value must be the address of an object. The conversion converts the encoded representation (as necessary) and stores its value in the object. Figure 8.4 shows the syntax for scan conversion specifications.

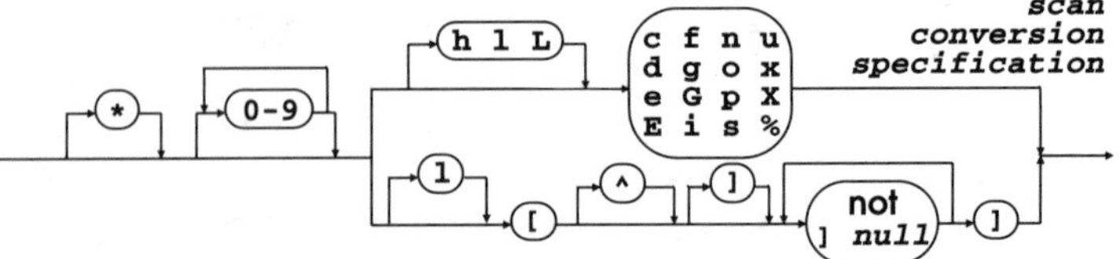

Figure 8.4: *Syntax of scan conversion specification.*

***** Following the percent character (%), you can write an asterisk (*) to indicate that the conversion should not store the converted value in an object.

field width Following any *, you can write a nonzero *field width* that specifies the maximum number of input characters to match for the conversion (not counting any white space that the pattern can first skip).

conversion specifier Following any field width, you must write a *conversion specifier*, either a one-character code or a *scan set*, possibly preceded by a one-character *conversion qualifier*. Each conversion specifier determines the type required of the next argument (if any) and how the scan functions interpret the text sequence and converts it to an encoded value. The integer and floating-point conversions also determine what library function to call to perform the conversion and what base to assume for the text representation. (The base is the **base** argument to the functions **strtol** and **strtoul**.) Table 8.2 lists all defined combinations and their properties.

The conversion specifier (or scan set) determines any behavior not summarized in this table. In the examples that follow each conversion specification, the function **sscanf** matches the underlined characters.

%c You write **c** to store the matched input characters in an array object. If you specify no field width *w*, then *w* has the value one. The match does not skip leading white space. Any sequence of *w* characters matches the conversion pattern. For a wide stream, conversion occurs as if by repeatedly calling **wcrtomb** (declared in **<wchar.h>**), beginning in the initial shift state.

Table 8.2: *Scan conversion specifiers.*

Specifier	Argument Type	Conversion Function	Base
`c`	`char x[]`		
`lc`	`wchar_t x[]`		
`d`	`int *x`	`strtol`	10
`hd`	`short *x`	`strtol`	10
`ld`	`long *x`	`strtol`	10
`e`	`float *x`	`strtod`	10
`le`	`double *x`	`strtod`	10
`Le`	`long double *x`	`strtod`	10
`E`	`float *x`	`strtod`	10
`lE`	`double *x`	`strtod`	10
`LE`	`long double *x`	`strtod`	10
`f`	`float *x`	`strtod`	10
`lf`	`double *x`	`strtod`	10
`Lf`	`long double *x`	`strtod`	10
`g`	`float *x`	`strtod`	10
`lg`	`double *x`	`strtod`	10
`Lg`	`long double *x`	`strtod`	10
`G`	`float *x`	`strtod`	10
`lG`	`double *x`	`strtod`	10
`LG`	`long double *x`	`strtod`	10
`i`	`int *x`	`strtol`	0
`hi`	`short *x`	`strtol`	0
`li`	`long *x`	`strtol`	0
`n`	`int *x`		
`hn`	`short *x`		
`ln`	`long *x`		
`o`	`unsigned int *x`	`strtoul`	8
`ho`	`unsigned short *x`	`strtoul`	8
`lo`	`unsigned long *x`	`strtoul`	8
`p`	`void **x`		
`s`	`char x[]`		
`ls`	`wchar_t x[]`		
`u`	`unsigned int *x`	`strtoul`	10
`hu`	`unsigned short *x`	`strtoul`	10
`lu`	`unsigned long *x`	`strtoul`	10
`x`	`unsigned int *x`	`strtoul`	16
`hx`	`unsigned short *x`	`strtoul`	16
`lx`	`unsigned long *x`	`strtoul`	16
`X`	`unsigned int *x`	`strtoul`	16
`hX`	`unsigned short *x`	`strtoul`	16
`lX`	`unsigned long *x`	`strtoul`	16
`[...]`	`char x[]`		
`l[...]`	`wchar_t x[]`		
`%`	none		

```
sscanf("129E-2", "%c", &c)            stores '1'
sscanf("129E-2", "%2c", &c[0])        stores '1', '2'
swscanf(L"129E-2", L"%c", &c)         stores '1'
```

`%lc` **Amendment 1** You write `lc` to store the matched input characters in an array object. If you specify no field width *w*, then *w* has the value one. The match does not skip leading white space. Any sequence of *w* characters matches the conversion pattern. For a byte stream, conversion occurs as if by repeatedly calling `mbrtowc` (declared in `<wchar.h>`), beginning in the initial shift state.

```
sscanf("129E-2", "%lc", &c)           stores L'1'
sscanf("129E-2", "%2lc", &c)          stores L'1', L'2'
swscanf(L"129E-2", L"%lc", &c)        stores L'1'
```

You write **d**, **i**, **o**, **u**, **x**, or **X** to convert the matched input characters as a signed integer and store the result in an integer object.

```
sscanf("129E-2", "%o%d%x", &i, &j, &k)    stores 10, 9, 14
```

%e %E %f %g %G You write **e**, **E**, **f**, **g**, or **G** to convert the matched input characters as a signed fraction, with an optional exponent, and store the result in a floating-point object.

```
sscanf("129E-2", "%e", &f)                stores 1.29
```

%n You write **n** to store the number of characters currently matched (up to this point in the format) in an integer object. The match does not skip leading white space and does not match any input characters.

```
sscanf("129E-2", "12%n", &i)              stores 2
```

%p You write **p** to convert the matched input characters as an external representation of a *pointer to void* and store the result in an object of type *pointer to void*. The input characters must match the form generated by the print functions with the **%p** conversion specification.

```
sscanf("129E-2", "%p", &p)                stores, e.g. 0x129e
```

%s You write **s** to store the matched input characters in an array object, followed by a terminating null character. If you do not specify a field width *w*, then *w* has a large value. Any sequence of up to *w* non white-space characters matches the conversion pattern. For a wide stream, conversion occurs as if by repeatedly calling **wcrtomb** (declared in **<wchar.h>**), beginning in the initial shift state.

```
sscanf("129E-2", "%s", &s[0])             stores "129E-2"
swscanf(L"129E-2", L"%s", &s[0])          stores "129E-2"
```

%ls **Amendment 1** You write **ls** to store the matched input characters in an array object, followed by a terminating null character. If you do not specify a field width *w*, then *w* has a large value. Any sequence of up to *w* non white-space characters matches the conversion pattern. For a byte stream, conversion occurs as if by repeatedly calling **mbrtowc** (declared in **<wchar.h>**), beginning in the initial shift state.

```
sscanf("129E-2", "%ls", &s[0])            stores L"129E-2"
swscanf(L"129E-2", L"%ls", &s[0])         stores L"129E-2"
```

scan set [...] You write **[** to store the matched input characters in an array object, followed by a terminating null character. If you do not specify a field width *w*, then *w* has a large value. The match does not skip leading white space. A sequence of up to *w* characters matches the conversion pattern by the following rules. You follow the left bracket (**[**) in the format with a sequence of zero or more *match* characters, terminated by a right bracket (**]**).

If you do not write a caret (**^**) immediately after the **[**, then each input character must match *one* of the match characters. Otherwise, each input character must not match *any* of the match characters, which begin with the character following the **^**. If you write a **]** immediately after the **[** or **[^**, then the **]** is the first match character, not the terminating **]**. If you write a minus (**-**) as other than the first or last match character, an implementation can give it special meaning. You cannot specify a null match character.

For a wide stream, conversion occurs as if by repeatedly calling **wcrtomb** (declared in **<wchar.h>**), beginning in the initial shift state.

```
sscanf("129E-2", "[54321]", &s[0])    stores "12"
swscanf(L"129E-2", L"[54321]", &s[0])    stores "12"
```

scan set
l[...]
Amendment 1

You write `l[` to store the matched input characters in an array object, followed by a terminating null character. If you do not specify a field width *w*, then *w* has a large value. The match does not skip leading white space. A sequence of up to *w* characters matches the conversion pattern by the following rules. You follow the left bracket (`[`) in the format with a sequence of zero or more *match* characters, terminated by a right bracket (`]`).

If you do not write a caret (`^`) immediately after the `[`, then each input character must match *one* of the match characters. Otherwise, each input character must not match *any* of the match characters, which begin with the character following the `^`. If you write a `]` immediately after the `[` or `[^`, then the `]` is the first match character, not the terminating `]`. If you write a minus (`-`) as other than the first or last match character, an implementation can give it special meaning. You cannot specify the null character as a match character.

For a byte stream, conversion occurs as if by repeatedly calling **mbrtowc** (declared in **<wchar.h>**), beginning in the initial shift state.

```
sscanf("129E-2", "l[54321]", &s[0])  stores L"12"
swscanf(L"129E-2", L"l[54321]", &s[0])  stores L"12"
```

%%

You write `%` to match the percent character (`%`). The function does not store a value.

```
sscanf("%  0XA", "%% %i")               stores 10
```

LIBRARY SUMMARY

The following chapters summarize the contents of each of the standard headers. They list the standard headers in alphabetical order. For each standard header, the names of macros, type definitions, and functions follow in alphabetical order, each followed by a brief description.

You can declare a function, without including its standard header, by reproducing the declaration shown in this book within the program. (See **LIBRARY ORGANIZATION** earlier in this chapter.) You cannot, however, define a macro or type definition without including its standard header because each of these varies among implementations.

You can use this summary in various ways:

- If you know the name of the entity about which you want information as well as its standard header, you can look it up directly.
- If you know only the name of the entity, find its standard header in **PREDEFINED NAMES** in *Appendix B: Names*.
- If you are not looking for a particular name, scan all the descriptions for a standard header that deals with the library facility about which you want information.

The standard headers are:

<assert.h> — for enforcing assertions when functions execute
<ctype.h> — for classifying characters
<errno.h> — for testing error codes reported by library functions
<float.h> — for testing floating-point type properties
<iso646.h> — for programming in ISO 646 variant character sets
<limits.h> — for testing integer type properties
<locale.h> — for adapting to different cultural conventions
<math.h> — for computing common mathematical functions
<setjmp.h> — for executing nonlocal *goto* statements
<signal.h> — for controlling various exceptional conditions
<stdarg.h> — for accessing argument lists of varying length
<stddef.h> — for defining several useful types and macros
<stdio.h> — for performing input and output
<stdlib.h> — for performing a variety of operations
<string.h> — for manipulating strings
<time.h> — for converting between various time and date formats
<wchar.h> — for manipulating wide streams and strings
<wctype.h> — for classifying wide characters

Chapter 9: <assert.h>

Include the standard header **<assert.h>** to define the macro **assert**, which is useful for diagnosing logic errors in the program. You can eliminate the testing code produced by the macro **assert** without removing the macro references from the program by defining the macro **NDEBUG** in the program before you include **<assert.h>**. Each time the program includes this header, it redetermines the definition of the macro **assert**.

assert

```
#undef assert
#if defined NDEBUG
 #define assert(test)  (void)0 •
#else
 #define assert(test)  <void expression>
#endif
```

If the *int* expression **test** equals zero, the macro writes to **stderr** a diagnostic message that includes:

- the text of **test**
- the source filename (the predefined macro **__FILE__**)
- the source line number (the predefined macro **__LINE__**)

It then calls **abort**.

You can write the macro **assert** in the program in any side-effect context. (See **STATEMENTS** in *Chapter 6: Functions*.)

Chapter 10: <ctype.h>

Include the standard header **<ctype.h>** to declare several functions that are useful for classifying and mapping codes from the target character set. Every function that has a parameter of type *int* can accept the value of the macro **EOF** or any value representable as type *unsigned char*. Thus, the argument can be the value returned by any of the functions:

```
fgetc     fputc     getc       getchar
putc      putchar   ungetc
```

(declared in **<stdio.h>**), or by:

```
tolower   toupper
```

(declared in **<ctype.h>**). You must not call these functions with other argument values.

Other library functions use these functions. The function **scanf**, for example, uses the function **isspace** to determine valid white space within an input field.

The character classification functions are strongly interrelated. Many are defined in terms of other functions. For characters in the basic C character set, Figure 10.1 shows the dependencies between these functions.The diagram tells you that the function **isprint** returns nonzero for ***space*** or for any character for which the function **isgraph** returns nonzero. The function **isgraph**, in turn, returns nonzero for any character for which either the function **isalnum** or the function **ispunct** returns nonzero. The

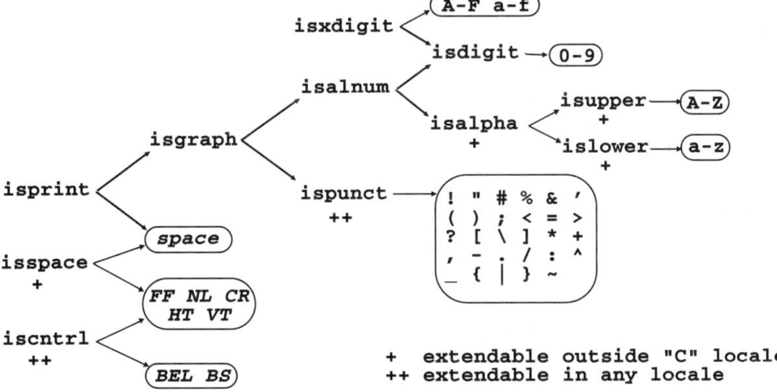

Figure 10.1: *Character classes for the basic C character set.*

function **isdigit**, on the other hand, returns nonzero only for the digits **0-9**.

An implementation can define additional characters that return nonzero for some of these functions. Any character set can contain additional characters that return nonzero for:

- **ispunct** (provided the characters cause **isalnum** to return zero)
- **iscntrl** (provided the characters cause **isprint** to return zero)

The diagram indicates with **++** those functions that can define additional characters in any character set.

Moreover, locales other than the **"C"** locale can define additional characters that return nonzero for:

- **isalpha**, **isupper**, and **islower** (provided the characters cause **iscntrl**, **isdigit**, **ispunct**, and **isspace** to return zero)
- **isspace** (provided the characters cause **isprint** to return zero)

The diagram indicates with **+** those functions that can define additional characters in locales other than the **"C"** locale.

Note that an implementation can define locales other than the **"C"** locale in which a character can cause **isalpha** (and hence **isalnum**) to return nonzero, yet still cause **isupper** and **islower** to return zero.

isalnum **int isalnum(int c);**

The function returns nonzero if **c** is any of:

a b c d e f g h i j k l m n o p q r s t u v w x y z
A B C D E F G H I J K L M N O P Q R S T U V W X Y Z
0 1 2 3 4 5 6 7 8 9

or any other locale-specific alphabetic character.

isalpha **int isalpha(int c);**

The function returns nonzero if **c** is any of:

a b c d e f g h i j k l m n o p q r s t u v w x y z
A B C D E F G H I J K L M N O P Q R S T U V W X Y Z

or any other locale-specific alphabetic character.

iscntrl **int iscntrl(int c);**

The function returns nonzero if **c** is any of:

BEL BS CR FF HT NL VT

or any other implementation-defined control character.

isdigit **int isdigit(int c);**

The function returns nonzero if **c** is any of:

0 1 2 3 4 5 6 7 8 9

isgraph **int isgraph(int c);**

The function returns nonzero if **c** is any character for which either **isalnum** or **ispunct** returns nonzero.

islower `int islower(int c);`

The function returns nonzero if **c** is any of:

a b c d e f g h i j k l m n o p q r s t u v w x y z

or any other locale-specific lowercase character.

isprint `int isprint(int c);`

The function returns nonzero if **c** is ***space*** or a character for which **isgraph** returns nonzero.

ispunct `int ispunct(int c);`

The function returns nonzero if **c** is any of:

! " # % & ' ( ) ; < = > ? [\ ] * + , - . / : ^ _ { | } ~

or any other implementation-defined punctuation character.

isspace `int isspace(int c);`

The function returns nonzero if **c** is any of:

CR FF HT NL VT space

or any other locale-specific space character.

isupper `int isupper(int c);`

The function returns nonzero if **c** is any of:

A B C D E F G H I J K L M N O P Q R S T U V W X Y Z

or any other locale-specific uppercase character.

isxdigit `int isxdigit(int c);`

The function returns nonzero if **c** is any of

a b c d e f
A B C D E F
0 1 2 3 4 5 6 7 8 9

tolower `int tolower(int c);`

The function returns the corresponding lowercase letter if one exists and if **isupper(c)**; otherwise, it returns **c**.

toupper `int toupper(int c);`

The function returns the corresponding uppercase letter if one exists and if **islower(c)**; otherwise, it returns **c**.

Chapter 11: <errno.h>

Include the standard header **<errno.h>** to test the value stored in **errno** by certain library functions. At program startup, the value stored in **errno** is zero. Library functions store only values greater than zero in **errno**. Any library function can alter the value stored in **errno**. This book documents only those cases where a library function is required to store a value in **errno**.

To test whether a function stores a value in **errno**, the program should store the value zero in **errno** immediately before it calls that library function. An implementation can define additional macros in this standard header that you can test for equality with the value stored in **errno**. All these additional macros have names that begin with **E**.

EDOM **#define EDOM** <#if expression>

The macro yields the value stored in **errno** on a domain error.

EILSEQ **#define EILSEQ** <#if expression>

The macro yields the value stored in **errno** on an invalid multibyte sequence.

ERANGE **#define ERANGE** <#if expression>

The macro yields the value stored in **errno** on a range error.

errno **#define errno** <*int* modifiable lvalue>

The macro designates an object that is assigned a value greater than zero on certain library errors.

Chapter 12: <float.h>

Include the standard header **<float.h>** to determine various properties of floating-point type representations. The standard header **<float.h>** is available even in a freestanding implementation.

You can test only the value of the macro **FLT_RADIX** in an *if* directive. (**FLT_RADIX** is a *#if* expression.) All other macros defined in this header expand to expressions whose values can be determined only when the program executes. (These macros are *rvalue expressions.*) Some target environments can change the rounding and error-reporting properties of floating-point type representations while the program is running.

DBL_DIG **#define DBL_DIG** <integer rvalue ≥ 10>

The macro yields the precision in decimal digits for type *double.*

DBL_EPSILON **#define DBL_EPSILON** <*double* rvalue ≤ 10^{-9}>

The macro yields the smallest x of type *double* such that $1.0 + x \neq 1.0$.

DBL_MANT_DIG **#define DBL_MANT_DIG** <*integer* rvalue>

The macro yields the number of mantissa digits, base **FLT_RADIX**, for type *double.*

DBL_MAX **#define DBL_MAX** <*double* rvalue ≥ 10^{37}>

The macro yields the largest finite representable value of type *double.*

DBL_MAX_10_EXP **#define DBL_MAX_10_EXP** <integer rvalue ≥ 37>

The macro yields the maximum integer x, such that 10^x is a finite representable value of type *double.*

DBL_MAX_EXP **#define DBL_MAX_EXP** <integer rvalue>

The macro yields the maximum integer x, such that **FLT_RADIX**$^{x-1}$ is a finite representable value of type *double.*

DBL_MIN **#define DBL_MIN** <*double* rvalue ≤ 10^{-37}>

The macro yields the smallest normalized, finite representable value of type *double.*

DBL_MIN_10_EXP `#define DBL_MIN_10_EXP` **<*integer* rvalue ≤ –37>**

The macro yields the minimum integer x such that 10^x is a normalized, finite representable value of type *double.*

DBL_MIN_EXP `#define DBL_MIN_EXP` **<integer rvalue>**

The macro yields the minimum integer x such that **FLT_RADIX**$^{x-1}$ is a normalized, finite representable value of type *double.*

FLT_DIG `#define FLT_DIG` **<integer rvalue ≥ 6>**

The macro yields the precision in decimal digits for type *float.*

FLT_EPSILON `#define FLT_EPSILON` **<*float* rvalue ≤ 10^{-5}>**

The macro yields the smallest x of type *float* such that $1.0 + x \neq 1.0$.

FLT_MANT_DIG `#define FLT_MANT_DIG` **<integer rvalue>**

The macro yields the number of mantissa digits, base **FLT_RADIX**, for type *float.*

FLT_MAX `#define FLT_MAX` **<*float* rvalue ≥ 10^{37}>**

The macro yields the largest finite representable value of type *float.*

FLT_MAX_10_EXP `#define FLT_MAX_10_EXP` **<integer rvalue ≥ 37>**

The macro yields the maximum integer x, such that 10^x is a finite representable value of type *float.*

FLT_MAX_EXP `#define FLT_MAX_EXP` **<integer rvalue>**

The macro yields the maximum integer x, such that **FLT_RADIX**$^{x-1}$ is a finite representable value of type *float.*

FLT_MIN `#define FLT_MIN` **<*float* rvalue ≤ 10^{-37}>**

The macro yields the smallest normalized, finite representable value of type *float.*

FLT_MIN_10_EXP `#define FLT_MIN_10_EXP` **<*integer* rvalue ≤ –37>**

The macro yields the minimum integer x, such that 10^x is a normalized, finite representable value of type *float.*

FLT_MIN_EXP `#define FLT_MIN_EXP` **<integer rvalue>**

The macro yields the minimum integer x, such that **FLT_RADIX**$^{x-1}$ is a normalized, finite representable value of type *float.*

FLT_RADIX `#define FLT_RADIX` **<#if expression ≥ 2>**

The macro yields the radix of all floating-point representations.

FLT_ROUNDS `#define FLT_ROUNDS` <integer rvalue>

The macro yields a value that describes the current rounding mode for floating-point operations. Note that the target environment can change the rounding mode while the program executes. How it does so, however, is not specified. The values are:

- –1 if the mode is indeterminate
- 0 if rounding is toward zero
- 1 if rounding is to nearest representable value
- 2 if rounding is toward +∞
- 3 if rounding is toward –∞

An implementation can define additional values for this macro.

LDBL_DIG `#define LDBL_DIG` <integer rvalue ≥ 10>

The macro yields the precision in decimal digits for type *long double.*

LDBL_EPSILON `#define LDBL_EPSILON` <*long double* rvalue ≤ 10^{-9}>

The macro yields the smallest *x* of type *long double* such that $1.0 + x \neq 1.0$.

LDBL_MANT_DIG `#define LDBL_MANT_DIG` <integer rvalue>

The macro yields the number of mantissa digits, base **FLT_RADIX**, for type *long double.*

LDBL_MAX `#define LDBL_MAX` <*long double* rvalue ≥ 10^{37}>

The macro yields the largest finite representable value of type *long double.*

LDBL_MAX_10_EXP `#define LDBL_MAX_10_EXP` <integer rvalue ≥ 37>

The macro yields the maximum integer *x,* such that 10^x is a finite representable value of type *long double.*

LDBL_MAX_EXP `#define LDBL_MAX_EXP` <integer rvalue>

The macro yields the maximum integer *x,* such that $\texttt{FLT\_RADIX}^{x-1}$ is a finite representable value of type *long double.*

LDBL_MIN `#define LDBL_MIN` <*long double* rvalue ≤ 10^{-37}>

The macro yields the smallest normalized, finite representable value of type *long double.*

LDBL_MIN_10_EXP `#define LDBL_MIN_10_EXP` <integer rvalue ≤ –37>

The macro yields the minimum integer *x,* such that 10^x is a normalized, finite representable value of type *long double.*

LDBL_MIN_EXP `#define LDBL_MIN_EXP` <integer rvalue>

The macro yields the minimum integer *x,* such that $\texttt{FLT\_RADIX}^{x-1}$ is a normalized, finite representable value of type *long double.*

Chapter 13: `<iso646.h>`

Amendment 1 (entire header) Include the standard header `<iso646.h>` to provide readable alternatives to certain operators or punctuators. The standard header `<iso646.h>` is available even in a freestanding implementation.

and `#define and &&`

The macro yields the operator `&&`.

and_eq `#define and_eq &=`

The macro yields the operator `&=`.

bitand `#define bitand &`

The macro yields the operator `&`.

bitor `#define bitor |`

The macro yields the operator `|`.

compl `#define compl ~`

The macro yields the operator `~`.

not `#define not !`

The macro yields the operator `!`.

not_eq `#define not_eq !=`

The macro yields the operator `!=`.

or `#define or ||`

The macro yields the operator `||`.

or_eq `#define or_eq |=`

The macro yields the operator `|=`.

xor `#define xor ^`

The macro yields the operator `^`.

xor_eq `#define xor_eq ^=`

The macro yields the operator `^=`.

Chapter 14: `<limits.h>`

Include the standard header **`<limits.h>`** to determine various properties of the integer type representations. The standard header **`<limits.h>`** is available even in a freestanding implementation.

You can test the values of all these macros in an *if* directive. (The macros are *#if* expressions.)

CHAR_BIT **#define CHAR_BIT <#if expression ≥ 8>**

The macro yields the maximum value for the number of bits used to represent an object of type *char*.

CHAR_MAX **#define CHAR_MAX <#if expression ≥ 127>**

The macro yields the maximum value for type *char*. Its value is:

- **SCHAR_MAX** if *char* represents negative values
- **UCHAR_MAX** otherwise

CHAR_MIN **#define CHAR_MIN <#if expression ≤ 0>**

The macro yields the minimum value for type *char*. Its value is:

- **SCHAR_MIN** if *char* represents negative values
- zero otherwise

INT_MAX **#define INT_MAX <#if expression ≥ 32,767>**

The macro yields the maximum value for type *int*.

INT_MIN **#define INT_MIN <#if expression ≤ –32,767>**

The macro yields the minimum value for type *int*.

LONG_MAX **#define LONG_MAX <#if expression ≥ 2,147,483,647>**

The macro yields the maximum value for type *long*.

LONG_MIN **#define LONG_MIN <#if expression ≤ –2,147,483,647>**

The macro yields the minimum value for type *long*.

MB_LEN_MAX **#define MB_LEN_MAX <#if expression ≥ 1>**

The macro yields the maximum number of characters that constitute a multibyte character in any supported locale.

SCHAR_MAX **#define SCHAR_MAX <#if expression ≥ 127>**

The macro yields the maximum value for type *signed char*.

SCHAR_MIN **#define SCHAR_MIN <#if expression ≤ –127>**

The macro yields the minimum value for type *signed char*.

SHRT_MAX **#define SHRT_MAX <#if expression ≥ 32,767>**

The macro yields the maximum value for type *short*.

SHRT_MIN **#define SHRT_MIN <#if expression ≤ –32,767>**

The macro yields the minimum value for type *short*.

UCHAR_MAX **#define UCHAR_MAX <#if expression ≥ 255>**

The macro yields the maximum value for type *unsigned char*.

UINT_MAX **#define UINT_MAX <#if expression ≥ 65,535>**

The macro yields the maximum value for type *unsigned int*.

ULONG_MAX **#define ULONG_MAX <#if expression ≥ 4,294,967,295>**

The macro yields the maximum value for type *unsigned long*.

USHRT_MAX **#define USHRT_MAX <#if expression ≥ 65,535>**

The macro yields the maximum value for type *unsigned short*.

Chapter 15: <locale.h>

Include the standard header **<locale.h>** to alter or access properties of the current locale. An implementation can define additional macros in this standard header with names that begin with **LC_**. You can use any of these macro names as the **category** argument to **setlocale**.

LC_ALL **#define LC_ALL** <integer constant expression>

The macro yields the **category** argument value that affects all categories.

LC_COLLATE **#define LC_COLLATE** <integer constant expression>

The macro yields the **category** argument value that affects the collation functions **strcoll** and **strxfrm**.

LC_CTYPE **#define LC_CTYPE** <integer constant expression>

The macro yields the **category** argument value that affects character classification functions and multibyte functions.

LC_MONETARY **#define LC_MONETARY** <integer constant expression>

The macro yields the **category** argument value that affects monetary information returned by **localeconv**.

LC_NUMERIC **#define LC_NUMERIC** <integer constant expression>

The macro yields the **category** argument value that affects numeric information returned by **localeconv**, including the decimal point used by numeric conversion, read, and write functions.

LC_TIME **#define LC_TIME** <integer constant expression>

The macro yields the **category** argument value that affects the time conversion function **strftime**.

NULL **#define NULL** <either 0, 0L, or (void *)0>

The macro yields a null pointer constant that is usable as an address constant expression.

lconv

```
struct lconv {
    char *currency_symbol;       ""         LC_MONETARY
    char *decimal_point;         "."        LC_NUMERIC
    char *grouping;              ""         LC_NUMERIC
    char *int_curr_symbol;       ""         LC_MONETARY
    char *mon_decimal_point;     ""         LC_MONETARY
    char *mon_grouping;          ""         LC_MONETARY
    char *mon_thousands_sep;     ""         LC_MONETARY
    char *negative_sign;         ""         LC_MONETARY
    char *positive_sign;         ""         LC_MONETARY
    char *thousands_sep;         ""         LC_NUMERIC
    char frac_digits;            CHAR_MAX   LC_MONETARY
    char int_frac_digits;        CHAR_MAX   LC_MONETARY
    char n_cs_precedes;          CHAR_MAX   LC_MONETARY
    char n_sep_by_space;         CHAR_MAX   LC_MONETARY
    char n_sign_posn;            CHAR_MAX   LC_MONETARY
    char p_cs_precedes;          CHAR_MAX   LC_MONETARY
    char p_sep_by_space;         CHAR_MAX   LC_MONETARY
    char p_sign_posn;            CHAR_MAX   LC_MONETARY
    };
```

struct lconv contains members that describe how to format numeric and monetary values. Functions in the Standard C library use only the field **decimal_point**. The information is otherwise advisory:

- Members of type *pointer to char* all point to strings.
- Members of type *char* have nonnegative values.
- A *char* value of **CHAR_MAX** indicates that a meaningful value is not available in the current locale.

The members shown above can occur in arbitrary order and can be interspersed with additional members. The comment following each member shows its value for the **"C"** locale, followed by the category that can affect its value.

A description of each member follows, with an example in parentheses that would be suitable for a USA locale.

currency_symbol — the local currency symbol (**"$"**)

decimal_point — the decimal point for non-monetary values (**"."**)

grouping — the sizes of digit groups for non-monetary values. Successive elements of the string describe groups going away from the decimal point:

- An element value of zero (the terminating null character) calls for the previous element value to be repeated indefinitely.
- An element value of **CHAR_MAX** ends any further grouping (and hence ends the string).

Thus, the array **{3, 2, CHAR_MAX}** calls for a group of three digits, then two, then whatever remains, as in **9876,54,321**, while **"\3"** calls for repeated groups of three digits, as in **987,654,321**. (**"\3"**)

int_curr_symbol — the international currency symbol specified by ISO 4217 (**"USD "**)

mon_decimal_point — the decimal point for monetary values (**"."**)

mon_grouping — the sizes of digit groups for monetary values. Successive elements of the string describe groups going away from the decimal point. The encoding is the same as for **grouping** above:

- An element value of zero (the terminating null character) calls for the previous element value to be repeated indefinitely.
- An element value of **CHAR_MAX** ends any further grouping (and hence ends the string). (**"\3"**)

mon_thousands_sep — the separator for digit groups to the left of the decimal point for monetary values (**","**)

negative_sign — the negative sign for monetary values (**"-"**)

positive_sign — the positive sign for monetary values (**"+"**)

thousands_sep — the separator for digit groups to the left of the decimal point for non-monetary values (**","**)

frac_digits — the number of digits to display to the right of the decimal point for monetary values (**2**)

int_frac_digits — the number of digits to display to the right of the decimal point for international monetary values (**2**)

n_cs_precedes — whether the currency symbol precedes or follows the value for negative monetary values:

- A value of 0 indicates that the symbol follows the value.
- A value of 1 indicates that the symbol precedes the value. (**1**)

n_sep_by_space — whether the currency symbol is separated by a space or by no space from the value for negative monetary values:

- A value of 0 indicates that no space separates symbol and value.
- A value of 1 indicates that a space separates symbol and value. (**0**)

n_sign_posn — the format for negative monetary values:

- A value of 0 indicates that parentheses surround the value and the currency symbol.
- A value of 1 indicates that the negative sign precedes the value and the currency symbol.
- A value of 2 indicates that the negative sign follows the value and the currency symbol.
- A value of 3 indicates that the negative sign immediately precedes the currency symbol.
- A value of 4 indicates that the negative sign immediately follows the currency symbol. (**4**)

p_cs_precedes — whether the currency symbol precedes or follows the value for positive monetary values:

- A value of 0 indicates that the symbol follows the value.
- A value of 1 indicates that the symbol precedes the value. (**1**)

p_sep_by_space — whether the currency symbol is separated by a space or by no space from the value for positive monetary values:

- A value of 0 indicates that no space separates symbol and value.
- A value of 1 indicates that a space separates symbol and value. (**0**)

p_sign_posn — the format for positive monetary values:

- A value of 0 indicates that parentheses surround the value and the currency symbol.
- A value of 1 indicates that the negative sign precedes the value and the currency symbol.
- A value of 2 indicates that the negative sign follows the value and the currency symbol.
- A value of 3 indicates that the negative sign immediately precedes the currency symbol.
- A value of 4 indicates that the negative sign immediately follows the currency symbol. (**4**)

localeconv

```
struct lconv *localeconv(void);
```

The function returns a pointer to a static-duration structure containing numeric formatting information for the current locale. You cannot alter values stored in the static-duration structure. The stored values can change on later calls to **localeconv** or on calls to **setlocale** that alter any of the categories **LC_ALL**, **LC_MONETARY**, or **LC_NUMERIC**.

setlocale

```
char *setlocale(int category, const char *locale);
```

The function either returns a pointer to a static-duration string describing a new locale or returns a null pointer (if the new locale cannot be selected). The value of **category** must match the value of one of the macros defined in this standard header with names that begin with **LC_**.

If **locale** is a null pointer, the locale remains unchanged. If **locale** points to the string **"C"**, the new locale is the **"C"** locale for the category specified. If **locale** points to the string **""**, the new locale is the native locale for the category specified. **locale** can also point to a string returned on an earlier call to **setlocale** or to other strings that the implementation can define.

At program startup, the target environment calls **setlocale(LC_ALL, "C")** before it calls **main**.

Chapter 16: <math.h>

Include the standard header **<math.h>** to declare several functions that perform common mathematical operations on values of type *double.*

A *domain error* exception occurs when the function is not defined for its input argument value or values. A function reports a domain error by storing the value of **EDOM** in **errno** and returning a peculiar value defined for each implementation.

A *range error* exception occurs when the value of the function is defined but cannot be represented by a value of type *double.* A function reports a range error by storing the value of **ERANGE** in **errno** and returning one of three values:

- **HUGE_VAL** — if the value of the function is positive and too large to represent
- zero — if the value of the function is too small to represent with a finite value
- **-HUGE_VAL** — if the value of the function is negative and too large to represent

HUGE_VAL **#define HUGE_VAL** <*double* rvalue>

The macro yields the value returned by some functions on a range error. The value can be a representation of infinity.

acos **double acos(double x);**

The function returns the angle whose cosine is **x**, in the range [0, π] radians.

asin **double asin(double x);**

The function returns the angle whose sine is **x**, in the range [–π/2, +π/2] radians.

atan **double atan(double x);**

The function returns the angle whose tangent is **x**, in the range [–π/2, +π/2] radians.

atan2 `double atan2(double y, double x);`

The function returns the angle whose tangent is **y/x**, in the full angular range $[-\pi, +\pi]$ radians.

ceil `double ceil(double x);`

The function returns the smallest integer value not less than **x**.

cos `double cos(double x);`

The function returns the cosine of **x** for **x** in radians. If **x** is large the value returned may not be meaningful, but the function reports no error.

cosh `double cosh(double x);`

The function returns the hyperbolic cosine of **x**.

exp `double exp(double x);`

The function returns the exponential of **x**, e^{x}.

fabs `double fabs(double x);`

The function returns the absolute value of **x**, |**x**|.

floor `double floor(double x);`

The function returns the largest integer value not greater than **x**.

fmod `double fmod(double x, double y);`

The function returns the remainder of **x/y**, which is defined as follows:

- If **y** is zero, the function either reports a domain error or simply returns zero.
- Otherwise, if $0 \le$ **x**, the value is **x-*i**y** for some integer ***i*** such that $0 \le$ **i***|**y**| $\le$ **x** < (**i**+1)*|**y**|.
- Otherwise, **x** < 0 and the value is **x-*i**y** for some integer *i* such that i*|**y**| $\le$ **x** < (**i**+1)*|**y**| ≤ 0.

frexp `double frexp(double x, int *pexp);`

The function determines a fraction *f* and base-2 integer ***i*** that represent the value of **x**. It returns the value *f* and stores the integer ***i*** in ***pexp**, such that |*f*| is in the interval [1/2, 1) or has the value 0, and **x** equals $f*2^{i}$. If **x** is zero, ***pexp** is also zero.

ldexp `double ldexp(double x, int exp);`

The function returns **x***$2^{\mathbf{exp}}$.

log `double log(double x);`

The function returns the natural logarithm of **x**.

log10 `double log10(double x);`

The function returns the base-10 logarithm of **x**.

modf `double modf(double x, double *pint);`

The function determines an integer i plus a fraction f that represent the value of **x**. It returns the value f and stores the integer i in ***pint**, such that $f + i$ equals **x**, $|f|$ is in the interval [0, 1), and both f and i have the same sign as **x**.

pow `double pow(double x, double y);`

The function returns **x** raised to the power **y**, x^y.

sin `double sin(double x);`

The function returns the sine of **x** for **x** in radians.If **x** is large the value returned might not be meaningful, but the function reports no error.

sinh `double sinh(double x);`

The function returns the hyperbolic sine of **x**.

sqrt `double sqrt(double x);`

The function returns the square root of **x**, $x^{1/2}$.

tan `double tan(double x);`

The function returns the tangent of **x** for **x** in radians.If **x** is large the value returned may not be meaningful, but the function reports no error.

tanh `double tanh(double x);`

The function returns the hyperbolic tangent of **x**.

Chapter 17: <setjmp.h>

Include the standard header **<setjmp.h>** to perform control transfers that bypass the normal function call and return protocol.

jmp_buf `typedef a-type jmp_buf;`

The type is the array type ***a-type*** of an object that you declare to hold the context information stored by **setjmp** and accessed by **longjmp**.

longjmp `void longjmp(jmp_buf env, int val);`

The function causes a second return from the execution of **setjmp** that stored the current context value in **env**. If **val** is nonzero, **setjmp** returns **val**; otherwise, **setjmp** returns the value 1.

The function that was active when **setjmp** stored the current context value must not have returned control to its caller. An object with dynamic duration that does not have a *volatile* type and whose stored value has changed since **setjmp** stored the current context value will have a stored value that is indeterminate.

setjmp `#define setjmp(jmp_buf env) <int rvalue>`

The macro stores the current context value in the array of type **jmp_buf** designated by **env** and returns zero. A later call to **longjmp** that accesses the same context value causes **setjmp** to again return, with a nonzero value. You can use the macro **setjmp** only in an expression that:

- has no operators
- has only the unary operator **!**
- has one of the relational or equality operators (**==**, **!=**, **<**, **<=**, **>**, or **>=**) with the other operand an integer constant expression

You can write such an expression only as the *expression* part of a *do, expression, for, if, if-else, switch,* or *while* statement. (See **STATEMENTS** in ***Chapter 6: Functions***.)

Chapter 18: `<signal.h>`

Include the standard header `<signal.h>` to specify how the program handles *signals* while it executes. A signal can report some exceptional behavior within the program, such as division by zero. Or a signal can report some asynchronous event outside the program, such as someone striking an interactive attention key on a keyboard.

You can report any signal by calling **raise**. Each implementation defines what signals it generates (if any) and under what circumstances it generates them. An implementation can define signals other than the ones listed here. The standard header `<signal.h>` can define additional macros with names beginning with **SIG** to specify the (positive) values of additional signals.

You can specify a *signal handler* for each signal. A signal handler is a function that the target environment calls when the corresponding signal occurs. The target environment suspends execution of the program until the signal handler returns or calls **longjmp**. For maximum portability, an asynchronous signal handler should only:

- make calls (that succeed) to the function **signal**
- assign values to objects of type *volatile* **sig_atomic_t**
- return control to its caller

If the signal reports an error within the program (and the signal is not asynchronous), the signal handler can terminate by calling **abort**, **exit**, or **longjmp**.

SIGABRT **#define SIGABRT** **<integer constant expression>**

The macro yields the **sig** argument value for the abort signal.

SIGFPE **#define SIGFPE** **<integer constant expression>**

The macro yields the **sig** argument value for the arithmetic error signal, such as for division by zero or result out of range.

SIGILL **#define SIGILL** **<integer constant expression>**

The macro yields the **sig** argument value for the invalid execution signal, such as for a corrupted function image.

SIGINT

```
#define SIGINT <integer constant expression>
```

The macro yields the **sig** argument value for the asynchronous interactive attention signal.

SIGSEGV

```
#define SIGSEGV <integer constant expression>
```

The macro yields the **sig** argument value for the invalid storage access signal, such as for an erroneous lvalue.

SIGTERM

```
#define SIGTERM <integer constant expression>
```

The macro yields the **sig** argument value for the asynchronous termination request signal.

SIG_DFL

```
#define SIG_DFL <address constant expression>
```

The macro yields the **func** argument value to **signal** to specify default signal handling.

SIG_ERR

```
#define SIG_ERR <address constant expression>
```

The macro yields the **signal** return value to specify an erroneous call.

SIG_IGN

```
#define SIG_IGN <address constant expression>
```

The macro yields the **func** argument value to **signal** to specify that the target environment is to henceforth ignore the signal.

raise

```
int raise(int sig);
```

The function sends the signal **sig** and returns a value of 0 if the signal is successfully reported.

sig_atomic_t

```
typedef i-type sig_atomic_t;
```

The type is the integer type ***i-type*** for objects whose stored value is altered by an assigning operator as an *atomic operation* (an operation that never has its execution suspended while partially completed). You declare such objects to communicate between signal handlers and the rest of the program.

signal

```
void (*signal(int sig, void (*func)(int)))(int);
```

The function specifies the new handling for signal **sig** and returns the previous handling, if successful; otherwise, it returns **SIG_ERR**.

- If **func** is **SIG_DFL**, the target environment commences default handling (as defined by the implementation).
- If **func** is **SIG_IGN**, the target environment ignores subsequent reporting of the signal.
- Otherwise, **func** must be the address of a function returning *void* that the target environment calls with a single *int* argument. The target environment calls this function to handle the signal when it is next reported, with the value of the signal as its argument.

When the target environment calls a signal handler:

- The target environment can block further occurrences of the corresponding signal until the handler returns, calls **longjmp**, or calls **signal** for that signal.
- The target environment can perform default handling of further occurrences of the corresponding signal.
- For signal **SIGILL**, the target environment can leave handling unchanged for that signal.

Chapter 19: `<stdarg.h>`

Include the standard header **`<stdarg.h>`** to access the unnamed additional arguments in a function that accepts a varying number of arguments. To access the additional arguments:

- The program must first execute the macro **`va_start`** within the body of the function to initialize an object with context information.
- Subsequent execution of the macro **`va_arg`**, designating the same context information, yields the values of the additional arguments in order, beginning with the first unnamed argument. You can execute the macro **`va_arg`** from any function that can access the context information saved by the macro **`va_start`**.
- If you have executed the macro **`va_start`** in a function, you must execute the macro **`va_end`** in the same function, designating the same context information, before the function returns.

You can repeat this sequence (as needed) to access the arguments as often as you want.

You declare an object of type **`va_list`** to store context information. **`va_list`** can be an array type, which affects how the program shares context information with functions that it calls. (The address of the first element of an array is passed, rather than the object itself.)

For example, Figure 19.1 shows a function that concatenates an arbitrary number of strings onto the end of an existing string (assuming that the existing string is stored in an object large enough to hold the resulting string).

Figure 19.1: *Example function with a varying number of arguments.*

```
#include <stdarg.h>
void va_cat(char *s, ...)
     {
     char *t;
     va_list ap;

     va_start(ap, s);
     while (t = va_arg(ap, char *))     NULL terminates list
          {
          s += strlen(s);               skip to end
          strcpy(s, t);                 and copy a string
          }
     va_end(ap);
     }
```

va_arg `#define va_arg(va_list ap, T)` **<*rvalue of type T*>**

The macro yields the value of the next argument in order, specified by the context information designated by **ap**. The additional argument must be of object type ***T*** after applying the rules for promoting arguments in the absence of a function prototype.

va_end `#define va_end(va_list ap)` **<*void* expression>**

The macro performs any cleanup necessary so that the function can return.

va_list `typedef` ***do-type*** `va_list;`

The type is the object type ***do-type*** that you declare to hold the context information initialized by **va_start** and used by **va_arg** to access additional unnamed arguments.

va_start `#define va_start(va_list ap,` ***last-arg***`)` **<*void* expression>**

The macro stores initial context information in the object designated by **ap**. ***last-arg*** is the name of the last argument you declare. For example, ***last-arg*** is **b** for the function declared as **int f(int a, int b, ...)**. The last argument must not have **register** storage class, and it must have a type that is not changed by the translator. It cannot have:

- an array type
- a function type
- type *float*
- any integer type that changes when promoted

Chapter 20: <stddef.h>

Include the standard header **<stddef.h>** to define several types and macros that are of general use throughout the program. The standard header **<stddef.h>** is available even in a freestanding implementation.

NULL `#define NULL <either 0, 0L, or (void *)0>`

The macro yields a null pointer constant that is usable as an address constant expression.

offsetof `#define offsetof(s-type, mbr) <size_t constant expression>`

The macro yields the offset in bytes of member ***mbr*** from the beginning of structure type ***s-type***, where for **x** of type ***s-type***, **&x.*mbr*** is an address constant expression.

ptrdiff_t `typedef si-type ptrdiff_t;`

The type is the signed integer type ***si-type*** of an object that you declare to store the result of subtracting two pointers.

size_t `typedef ui-type size_t;`

The type is the unsigned integer type ***ui-type*** of an object that you declare to hold the result of the *sizeof* operator.

wchar_t `typedef i-type wchar_t;`

The type is the integer type ***i-type*** of the wide-character constant **L'X'**. You declare an object of type **wchar_t** to hold a wide character.

Chapter 21: <stdio.h>

Include the standard header **<stdio.h>** so that you can perform input and output operations on streams and files.

_IOFBF **#define _IOFBF** **<integer constant expression>**

The macro yields the value of the **mode** argument to **setvbuf** to indicate full buffering.

_IOLBF **#define _IOLBF** **<integer constant expression>**

The macro yields the value of the **mode** argument to **setvbuf** to indicate line buffering.

_IONBF **#define _IONBF** **<integer constant expression>**

The macro yields the value of the **mode** argument to **setvbuf** to indicate no buffering.

BUFSIZ **#define BUFSIZ** **<integer constant expression ≥ 256>**

The macro yields the size of the stream buffer used by **setbuf**.

EOF **#define EOF** **<integer constant expression < 0>**

The macro yields the return value used to signal the end of a file or to report an error condition.

FILE **typedef *o-type* FILE;**

The type is an object type ***o-type*** that stores all control information for a stream. The functions **fopen** and **freopen** allocate all **FILE** objects used by the read and write functions.

FILENAME_MAX **#define FILENAME_MAX** **<integer constant expression>**

The macro yields the maximum size array of characters that you must provide to hold a filename string.

FOPEN_MAX **#define FOPEN_MAX** **<integer constant expression ≥ 8>**

The macro yields the maximum number of files that the target environment permits to be simultaneously open (including **stderr**, **stdin**, and **stdout**).

L_tmpnam `#define L_tmpnam` **<integer constant expression>**

The macro yields the number of characters that the target environment requires for representing temporary filenames created by **tmpnam**.

NULL `#define NULL` **<either `0`, `0L`, or `(void *)0`>**

The macro yields a null pointer constant that is usable as an address constant expression.

SEEK_CUR `#define SEEK_CUR` **<integer constant expression>**

The macro yields the value of the **mode** argument to **fseek** to indicate seeking relative to the current file-position indicator.

SEEK_END `#define SEEK_END` **<integer constant expression>**

The macro yields the value of the **mode** argument to **fseek** to indicate seeking relative to the end of the file.

SEEK_SET `#define SEEK_SET` **<integer constant expression>**

The macro yields the value of the **mode** argument to **fseek** to indicate seeking relative to the beginning of the file.

TMP_MAX `#define TMP_MAX` **<integer constant expression ≥ 25>**

The macro yields the minimum number of distinct filenames created by the function **tmpnam**.

clearerr `void clearerr(FILE *stream);`

The function clears the end-of-file and error indicators for the stream **stream**.

fclose `int fclose(FILE *stream);`

The function closes the file associated with the stream **stream**. It returns zero if successful; otherwise, it returns **EOF**. **fclose** writes any buffered output to the file, deallocates the stream buffer if it was automatically allocated, and removes the association between the stream and the file. Do not use the value of **stream** in subsequent expressions.

feof `int feof(FILE *stream);`

The function returns a nonzero value if the end-of-file indicator is set for the stream **stream**.

ferror `int ferror(FILE *stream);`

The function returns a nonzero value if the error indicator is set for the stream **stream**.

fflush `int fflush(FILE *stream);`

The function writes any buffered output to the file associated with the stream **stream** and returns zero if successful; otherwise, it returns **EOF**. If

stream is a null pointer, **fflush** writes any buffered output to all files opened for output.

fgetc `int fgetc(FILE *stream);`

The function reads the next character *c* (if present) from the input stream **stream**, advances the file-position indicator (if defined), and returns **(int)(unsigned char)***c*. If the function sets either the end-of-file indicator or the error indicator, it returns **EOF**.

fgetpos `int fgetpos(FILE *stream, fpos_t *pos);`

The function stores the file-position indicator for the stream **stream** in ***pos** and returns zero if successful; otherwise, the function stores a positive value in **errno** and returns a nonzero value.

fgets `char *fgets(char *s, int n, FILE *stream);`

The function reads characters from the input stream **stream** and stores them in successive elements of the array beginning at **s** and continuing until it stores **n-1** characters, stores an ***NL*** character, or sets the end-of-file or error indicators. If **fgets** stores any characters, it concludes by storing a null character in the next element of the array. It returns **s** if it stores any characters and it has not set the error indicator for the stream; otherwise, it returns a null pointer. If it sets the error indicator, the array contents are indeterminate.

fopen `FILE *fopen(const char *filename, const char *mode);`

The function opens the file with the filename **filename**, associates it with a stream, and returns a pointer to the object controlling the stream. If the open fails, it returns a null pointer. The initial characters of **mode** must be one of the following:

- **"r"** — to open an existing text file for reading
- **"w"** — to create a text file or to open and truncate an existing text file, for writing
- **"a"** — to create a text file or to open an existing text file, for writing. The file-position indicator is positioned at the end of the file before each write
- **"rb"** — to open an existing binary file for reading
- **"wb"** — to create a binary file or to open and truncate an existing binary file, for writing
- **"ab"** — to create a binary file or to open an existing binary file, for writing. The file-position indicator is positioned at the end of the file (possibly after arbitrary null byte padding) before each write
- **"r+"** — to open an existing text file for reading and writing
- **"w+"** — to create a text file or to open and truncate an existing text file, for reading and writing

- **"a+"** — to create a text file or to open an existing text file, for reading and writing. The file-position indicator is positioned at the end of the file before each write
- **"r+b"** or **"rb+"** — to open an existing binary file for reading and writing
- **"w+b"** or **"wb+"** — to create a binary file or to open and truncate an existing binary file, for reading and writing
- **"a+b"** or **"ab+"** — to create a binary file or to open an existing binary file, for reading and writing. The file-position indicator is positioned at the end of the file (possibly after arbitrary null byte padding) before each write

If you open a file for both reading and writing, the target environment can open a binary file instead of a text file. If the file is not interactive, the stream is fully buffered.

fpos_t `typedef o-type fpos_t;`

The type is an object type ***o-type*** of an object that you declare to hold the value of a file-position indicator stored by **fsetpos** and accessed by **fgetpos**.

fprintf `int fprintf(FILE *stream, const char *format, ...);`

The function generates formatted text, under the control of the format **format** and any additional arguments, and writes each generated character to the stream **stream**. It returns the number of characters generated, or it returns a negative value if the function sets the error indicator for the stream. (See **FORMATTED INPUT/OUTPUT** in *Chapter 8: Library*.)

fputc `int fputc(int c, FILE *stream);`

The function writes the character **(unsigned char)c** to the output stream **stream**, advances the file-position indicator (if defined), and returns **(int)(unsigned char)c**. If the function sets the error indicator for the stream, it returns **EOF**.

fputs `int fputs(const char *s, FILE *stream);`

The function accesses characters from the string **s** and writes them to the output stream **stream**. The function does not write the terminating null character. It returns a nonnegative value if it has not set the error indicator; otherwise, it returns **EOF**.

fread

```
size_t fread(void *ptr, size_t size, size_t nelem,
    FILE *stream);
```

The function reads characters from the input stream **stream** and stores them in successive elements of the array whose first element has the address **(char *)ptr** until the function stores **size*nelem** characters or sets the end-of-file or error indicator. It returns *n*/**size**, where *n* is the number of characters it read. If *n* is not a multiple of **size**, the value stored in the last element is indeterminate. If the function sets the error indicator, the file-position indicator is indeterminate.

freopen

```
FILE *freopen(const char *filename, const char *mode,
     FILE *stream);
```

The function closes the file associated with the stream **stream** (as if by calling **fclose**); then it opens the file with the filename **filename** and associates the file with the stream **stream** (as if by calling **fopen(filename, mode)**). It returns **stream** if the open is successful; otherwise, it returns a null pointer.

fscanf

```
int fscanf(FILE *stream, const char *format, ...);
```

The function scans formatted text, under the control of the format **format** and any additional arguments. It obtains each scanned character from the stream **stream**. It returns the number of input items matched and assigned, or it returns **EOF** if the function does not store values before it sets the end-of-file or error indicator for the stream. (See **FORMATTED INPUT/OUTPUT** in *Chapter 8: Library*.)

fseek

```
int fseek(FILE *stream, long offset, int mode);
```

The function sets the file-position indicator for the stream **stream** (as specified by **offset** and **mode**), clears the end-of-file indicator for the stream, and returns zero if successful.

For a binary file, **offset** is a signed offset in bytes:

- If **mode** has the value **SEEK_SET**, **fseek** adds **offset** to the file-position indicator for the beginning of the file.
- If **mode** has the value **SEEK_CUR**, **fseek** adds **offset** to the current file-position indicator.
- If **mode** has the value **SEEK_END**, **fseek** adds **offset** to the file-position indicator for the end of the file (possibly after arbitrary null character padding).

fseek sets the file-position indicator to the result of this addition.

For a text file:

- If **mode** has the value **SEEK_SET**, **fseek** sets the file-position indicator to the file-position indicator encoded in **offset**, which is either a value returned by an earlier successful call to **ftell** or zero to indicate the beginning of the file.
- If **mode** has the value **SEEK_CUR** and **offset** is zero, **fseek** leaves the file-position indicator at its current value.
- If **mode** has the value **SEEK_END** and **offset** is zero, **fseek** sets the file-position indicator to indicate the end of the file.

The function defines no other combination of argument values.

fsetpos `int fsetpos(FILE *stream, const fpos_t *pos);`

The function sets the file-position indicator for the stream **stream** to the value stored in ***pos**, clears the end-of-file indicator for the stream, and returns zero if successful. Otherwise, the function stores a positive value in **errno** and returns a nonzero value.

ftell `long ftell(FILE *stream);`

The function returns an encoded form of the file-position indicator for the stream **stream** or stores a positive value in **errno** and returns the value –1. For a binary file, a successful return value gives the number of bytes from the beginning of the file. For a text file, target environments can vary on the representation and range of encoded file-position indicator values.

fwrite
```
size_t fwrite(const void *ptr, size_t size,
    size_t nelem, FILE *stream);
```

The function writes characters to the output stream **stream**, accessing values from successive elements of the array whose first element has the address **(char *)ptr** until the function writes **size*nelem** characters or sets the error indicator. It returns *n*/**size**, where *n* is the number of characters it wrote. If the function sets the error indicator, the file-position indicator is indeterminate.

getc `int getc(FILE *stream);`

The function has the same effect as **fgetc(stream)** except that a macro version of **getc** can evaluate **stream** more than once.

getchar `int getchar(void);`

The function has the same effect as **fgetc(stdin)**.

gets `char *gets(char *s);`

The function reads characters from the input stream **stdin** and stores them in successive elements of the array whose first element has the address **s** until the function reads an ***NL*** character (which is not stored) or sets the end-of-file or error indicator. If **gets** reads any characters, it concludes by storing a null character in the next element of the array. It returns **s** if it reads any characters and has not set the error indicator for the stream; otherwise, it returns a null pointer. If it sets the error indicator, the array contents are indeterminate. The number of characters that **gets** reads and stores cannot be limited. Use **fgets** instead.

perror `void perror(const char *s);`

The function writes a line of text to **stderr**. If **s** is not a null pointer, the function first writes the string **s** (as if by calling **fputs(s, stderr)**), followed by a colon (**:**) and a ***space***. It then writes the same message string that is returned by **strerror(errno)** followed by an ***NL***.

printf `int printf(const char *format, ...);`

The function generates formatted text, under the control of the format **format** and any additional arguments. It writes each generated character to the stream **stdout**. It returns the number of characters generated, or it returns a negative value if the function sets the error indicator for the stream. (See **FORMATTED INPUT/OUTPUT** in *Chapter 8: Library*.)

putc `int putc(int c, FILE *stream);`

The function has the same effect as **fputc(c, stream)** except that a macro version of **putc** can evaluate **stream** more than once.

putchar `int putchar(int c);`

The function has the same effect as **fputc(c, stdout)**.

puts `int puts(const char *s);`

The function accesses characters from the string **s** and writes them to the output stream **stdout**. The function writes an ***NL*** character to the stream in place of the terminating null character. It returns a nonnegative value if it has not set the error indicator; otherwise, it returns **EOF**.

remove `int remove(const char *filename);`

The function removes the file with the filename **filename** and returns zero if successful. If the file is open when you remove it, the result is implementation-defined. After you remove it, you cannot open it as an existing file.

rename `int rename(const char *old, const char *new);`

The function renames the file with the filename **old** to have the filename **new** and returns zero if successful. If a file with the filename **new** already exists, the result is implementation-defined. After you rename it, you cannot open the file with the filename **old**.

rewind `void rewind(FILE *stream);`

The function calls **fseek(stream, 0L, SEEK_SET)** and then clears the error indicator for the stream **stream**.

scanf `int scanf(const char *format, ...);`

The function scans formatted text, under the control of the format **format** and any additional arguments. It obtains each scanned character from the stream **stdin**. It returns the number of input items matched and assigned, or it returns **EOF** if the function does not store values before it sets the end-of-file or error indicators for the stream. (See **FORMATTED INPUT/OUTPUT** in *Chapter 8: Library*.)

setbuf `void setbuf(FILE *stream, char *buf);`

If **buf** is not a null pointer, the function calls **setvbuf(stream, buf, _IOFBF, BUFSIZ)**; otherwise, the function calls **setvbuf(stream, NULL, _IONBF, BUFSIZ)**.

setvbuf
```
int setvbuf(FILE *stream, char *buf, int mode,
    size_t size);
```

The function sets the buffering mode for the stream **stream** according to **buf**, **mode**, and **size**, and it returns zero if successful. If **buf** is not a null pointer, then **buf** is the address of the first element of an array of *char* of size **size** that can be used as the stream buffer. Otherwise, **setvbuf** can allocate a stream buffer that is freed when the file is closed. For **mode** you must supply one of the following values:

- **_IOFBF** — to indicate full buffering
- **_IOLBF** — to indicate line buffering
- **_IONBF** — to indicate no buffering

You must call **setvbuf** immediately after you call **fopen** to associate a file with that stream and before you call a library function that performs any other operation on the stream.

size_t `typedef` ***ui-type*** `size_t;`

The type is the unsigned integer type ***ui-type*** of an object that you declare to hold the result of the *sizeof* operator.

sprintf `int sprintf(char *s, const char *format, ...);`

The function generates formatted text, under the control of the format **format** and any additional arguments. It stores each generated character in successive locations of the array object whose first element has the address **s**. The function concludes by storing a null character in the next location of the array. It returns the number of characters generated — not including the null character. (See **FORMATTED INPUT/OUTPUT** in ***Chapter 8: Library***.)

sscanf `int sscanf(const char *s, const char *format, ...);`

The function scans formatted text under the control of the format **format** and any additional arguments. It accesses each scanned character from successive locations of the array object whose first element has the address **s**. It returns the number of items matched and assigned, or it returns **EOF** if the function does not store values before it accesses a null character from the array. (See **FORMATTED INPUT/OUTPUT** in ***Chapter 8: Library***.)

stderr `#define stderr` <pointer to **FILE** rvalue>

The macro yields a pointer to the object that controls the standard error output stream.

stdin `#define stdin` **<pointer to `FILE` rvalue>**

The macro yields a pointer to the object that controls the standard input stream.

stdout `#define stdout` **<pointer to `FILE` rvalue>**

The macro yields a pointer to the object that controls the standard output stream.

tmpfile `FILE *tmpfile(void)`

The function creates a temporary binary file with the filename *temp-name* and then has the same effect as calling `fopen(`*temp-name*`, "wb+")`. The file *temp-name* is removed when the program closes it, either by calling `fclose` explicitly or at normal program termination. The filename *temp-name* does not conflict with any filenames that you create. If the open is successful, the function returns a pointer to the object controlling the stream; otherwise, it returns a null pointer.

tmpnam `char *tmpnam(char *s);`

The function creates a unique filename *temp-name* and returns a pointer to the filename. If `s` is not a null pointer, then `s` must be the address of the first element of an array at least of size `L_tmpnam`. The function stores *temp-name* in the array and returns `s`. Otherwise, if `s` is a null pointer, the function stores *temp-name* in a static-duration array and returns the address of its first element. Subsequent calls to `tmpnam` can alter the values stored in this array.

The function returns unique filenames for each of the first `TMP_MAX` times it is called, after which its behavior is implementation-defined. The filename *temp-name* does not conflict with any filenames that you create.

ungetc `int ungetc(int c, FILE *stream);`

If `c` is not equal to `EOF`, the function stores `(unsigned char)c` in the object whose address is `stream` and clears the end-of-file indicator. If `c` equals `EOF` or the store cannot occur, the function returns `EOF`; otherwise, it returns `(unsigned char)c`. A subsequent library function call that reads a character from the stream `stream` obtains this stored value, which is then forgotten.

Thus, you can effectively *push back* a character to a stream after reading a character. (You need not push back the same character that you read.) An implementation can let you push back additional characters before you read the first one. You read the characters in reverse order of pushing them back to the stream. You cannot portably:

- push back more than one character
- push back a character if the file-position indicator is at the beginning of the file
- Call `ftell` for a text file that has a character currently pushed back

A call to the functions **fseek**, **fsetpos**, or **rewind** for the stream causes the stream to forget any pushed-back characters. For a binary stream, the file-position indicator is decremented for each character that is pushed back.

vfprintf

```
int vfprintf(FILE *stream, const char *format,
             va_list ap);
```

The function generates formatted text, under the control of the format **format** and any additional arguments. It writes each generated character to the stream **stream**. It returns the number of characters generated, or it returns a negative value if the function sets the error indicator for the stream. (See **FORMATTED INPUT/OUTPUT** in *Chapter 8: Library*.)

The function accesses additional arguments by using the context information designated by **ap**. The program must execute the macro **va_start** before it calls the function and then execute the macro **va_end** after the function returns. (Both macros are defined in **<stdarg.h>**.)

vprintf

```
int vprintf(const char *format, va_list ap);
```

The function generates formatted text, under control of the format **format** and any additional arguments. It writes each generated character to the stream **stdout**. It returns the number of characters generated, or a negative value if the function sets the error indicator for the stream. (See **FORMATTED INPUT/OUTPUT** in *Chapter 8: Library*.)

The function accesses additional arguments by using the context information designated by **ap**. The program must execute the macro **va_start** before it calls the function, and execute the macro **va_end** after the function returns. (Both macros are defined in **<stdarg.h>**.)

vsprintf

```
int vsprintf(char *s, const char *format, va_list ap);
```

The function generates formatted text, under the control of the format **format** and any additional arguments. It stores each generated character in successive locations of the array object whose first element has the address **s**. The function concludes by storing a null character in the next location of the array. It returns the number of characters generated — not including the null character. (See **FORMATTED INPUT/OUTPUT** in *Chapter 8: Library*.)

The function accesses additional arguments by using the context information designated by **ap**. The program must execute the macro **va_start** before it calls the function and then execute the macro **va_end** after the function returns. (Both macros are defined in **<stdarg.h>**.)

Chapter 22: <stdlib.h>

Include the standard header **<stdlib.h>** to declare an assortment of useful functions and to define the macros and types that help you use them.

EXIT_FAILURE **#define EXIT_FAILURE** <rvalue integer expression>

The macro yields the value of the **status** argument to **exit** that reports unsuccessful termination.

EXIT_SUCCESS **#define EXIT_SUCCESS** <rvalue integer expression>

The macro yields the value of the **status** argument to **exit** that reports successful termination.

MB_CUR_MAX **#define MB_CUR_MAX** <rvalue integer expression ≥ 1>

The macro yields the maximum number of characters that comprise a multibyte character in the current locale. Its value is less than or equal to **MB_LEN_MAX**.

NULL **#define NULL** <either **0**, **0L**, or **(void *)0**>

The macro yields a null pointer constant that is usable as an address constant expression.

RAND_MAX **#define RAND_MAX** <integer constant expression ≥ 32767>

The macro yields the maximum value returned by **rand**.

abort **void abort(void);**

The function calls **raise(SIGABRT)**, which reports the abort signal. Default handling for the abort signal is to cause abnormal program termination and report unsuccessful termination to the target environment. Whether or not the target environment flushes output streams, closes open files, or removes temporary files on abnormal termination is implementation-defined. If you specify handling that causes **raise** to return control to **abort**, the function calls **exit(EXIT_FAILURE)**. **abort** never returns control to its caller.

abs **int abs(int i);**

The function returns the absolute value of **i**, **|i|**.

atexit `int atexit(void (*func)(void));`

The function registers the function whose address is **func** to be called by **exit** and returns zero if successful. **exit** calls functions in reverse order of registry. You can register at least 32 functions.

atof `double atof(const char *s);`

The function converts the initial characters of the string **s** to an equivalent value *x* of type *double* and then returns *x*. The conversion is the same as for **strtod(s, NULL)**, except that an error code is not necessarily stored in **errno** if a conversion error occurs.

atoi `int atoi(const char *s);`

The function converts the initial characters of the string **s** to an equivalent value *x* of type *int* and then returns *x*. The conversion is the same as for **(int)strtol(s, NULL, 10)**, except that an error code is not necessarily stored in **errno** if a conversion error occurs.

atol `long atol(const char *s);`

The function converts the initial characters of the string **s** to an equivalent value *x* of type *long* and then returns *x*. The conversion is the same as for **strtol(s, NULL, 10)**, except that an error code is not necessarily stored in **errno** if a conversion error occurs.

bsearch

```
void *bsearch(const void *key, const void *base,
     size_t nelem, size_t size,
     int (*cmp)(const void *ck, const void *ce));
```

The function searches an array of ordered values and returns the address of an array element that equals the search key **key** (if one exists); otherwise, it returns a null pointer. The array consists of **nelem** elements, each of **size** bytes, beginning with the element whose address is **base**.

bsearch calls the comparison function whose address is **cmp** to compare the search key with elements of the array. The comparison function must return:

- a negative value if the search key **ck** is less than the array element **ce**
- zero if the two are equal
- a positive value if the search key is greater than the array element

bsearch assumes that the array elements are in ascending order according to the same comparison rules that are used by the comparison function.

calloc `void *calloc(size_t nelem, size_t size);`

The function allocates an array object containing **nelem** elements each of size **size**, stores zeros in all bytes of the array, and returns the address of the first element of the array if successful; otherwise, it returns a null pointer. You can safely convert the return value to an object pointer of any type whose size in bytes is not greater than **size**.

div `div_t div(int numer, int denom);`

The function divides **numer** by **denom** and returns both quotient and remainder in the structure **div_t** result *x*, if the quotient can be represented. The structure member *x*.**quot** is the quotient, which is the algebraic quotient truncated toward 0. The structure member *x*.**rem** is the remainder, such that **numer** equals *x*.**quot** * **denom** + *x*.**rem**.

div_t

```
typedef struct {
    int quot, rem;
    } div_t;
```

The type is a structure type that you declare to hold the value returned by the function **div**. The structure contains members that represent the quotient (**quot**) and remainder (**rem**) of a signed integer division with operands of type *int*. The members shown above can occur in either order.

exit `void exit(int status);`

The function calls all functions registered by **atexit**, closes all files, and returns control to the target environment. If **status** is zero or **EXIT_SUCCESS**, the program reports successful termination. If **status** is **EXIT_FAILURE**, the program reports unsuccessful termination. An implementation can define additional values for **status**.

free `void free(void *ptr);`

If **ptr** is not a null pointer, the function deallocates the object whose address is **ptr**; otherwise, it does nothing. You can deallocate only objects that you first allocate by calling **calloc**, **malloc**, or **realloc**.

getenv `char *getenv(const char *name);`

The function searches an *environment list* that each implementation defines for an entry whose name matches the string **name**. If the function finds a match, it returns a pointer to a static-duration object that holds the definition associated with the target environment name. Otherwise, it returns a null pointer. Do not alter the value stored in the object. If you call **getenv** again, the value stored in the object can change. No target environment names are required of all environments.

labs `long labs(long i);`

The function returns the absolute value of **i**, |**i**|

ldiv `ldiv_t ldiv(long numer, long denom);`

The function divides **numer** by **denom** and returns both quotient and remainder in the structure **ldiv_t** result *x*, if the quotient can be represented. The structure member *x*.**quot** is the quotient, which is the algebraic quotient truncated toward zero. The structure member *x*.**rem** is the remainder, such that **numer** equals *x*.**quot** * **denom** + *x*.**rem**.

ldiv_t

```
typedef struct {
    long quot, rem;
    } ldiv_t;
```

The type is a structure type that you declare to hold the value returned by the function **ldiv**. The structure contains members that represent the quotient (**quot**) and remainder (**rem**) of a signed integer division with operands of type *long*. The members shown above can occur in either order.

malloc

```
void *malloc(size_t size);
```

The function allocates an object of size **size**, and returns the address of the object if successful; otherwise, it returns a null pointer. The values stored in the object are indeterminate. You can safely convert the return value to an object pointer of any type whose size is not greater than **size**.

mblen

```
int mblen(const char *s, size_t n);
```

If **s** is not a null pointer, the function returns the number of bytes in the multibyte string **s** that constitute the next multibyte character, or it returns –1 if the next **n** (or the remaining) bytes do not comprise a valid multibyte character. **mblen** does not include the terminating null in the count of bytes. The function can use a shift state stored in an internal static-duration object to determine how to interpret the multibyte character string.

If **s** is a null pointer and if multibyte characters have a state-dependent encoding in the current locale, the function stores the initial shift state in its internal static-duration object and returns nonzero; otherwise, it returns zero.

mbstowcs

```
size_t mbstowcs(wchar_t *wcs, const char *s, size_t n);
```

The function stores a wide character string, in successive elements of the array whose first element has the address **wcs**, by converting, in turn, each of the multibyte characters in the multibyte string **s**. The string begins in the initial shift state. The function converts each character as if by calling **mbtowc** (except that the internal shift state stored for that function is unaffected). It stores at most **n** wide characters, stopping after it stores a null wide character. It returns the number of wide characters it stores, not counting the null wide character, if all conversions are successful; otherwise, it returns –1.

mbtowc

```
int mbtowc(wchar_t *pwc, const char *s, size_t n);
```

If **s** is not a null pointer, the function determines *x*, the number of bytes in the multibyte string **s** that constitute the next multibyte character. (*x* cannot be greater than **MB_CUR_MAX**.) If **pwc** is not a null pointer, the function converts the next multibyte character to its corresponding wide-character value and stores that value in ***pwc**. It then returns *x*, or it returns –1 if the next **n** or the remaining bytes do not constitute a valid multibyte character. **mbtowc** does not include the terminating null in the count of bytes. The function can use a shift state stored in an internal static-duration object to determine how to interpret the multibyte character string.

If `s` is a null pointer and if multibyte characters have a state-dependent encoding in the current locale, the function stores the initial shift state in its internal static-duration object and returns nonzero; otherwise, it returns zero.

qsort

```
void qsort(void *base, size_t nelem, size_t size,
    int (*cmp)(const void *e1, const void *e2));
```

The function sorts, in place, an array consisting of `nelem` elements, each of `size` bytes, beginning with the element whose address is `base`. It calls the comparison function whose address is `cmp` to compare pairs of elements. The comparison function must return a negative value if `e1` is less than `e2`, zero if the two are equal, or a positive value if `e1` is greater than `e2`. Two array elements that are equal can appear in the sorted array in either order.

rand

```
int rand(void);
```

The function computes a pseudo-random number x based on a seed value stored in an internal static-duration object, alters the stored seed value, and returns x. x is in the interval [0, `RAND_MAX`].

realloc

```
void *realloc(void *ptr, size_t size);
```

The function allocates an object of size `size`, possibly obtaining initial stored values from the object whose address is `ptr`. It returns the address of the new object if successful; otherwise, it returns a null pointer. You can safely convert the return value to an object pointer of any type whose size is not greater than `size`.

If `ptr` is not a null pointer, it must be the address of an existing object that you first allocate by calling `calloc`, `malloc`, or `realloc`. If the existing object is not larger than the newly allocated object, `realloc` copies the entire existing object to the initial part of the allocated object. (The values stored in the remainder of the object are indeterminate.) Otherwise, the function copies only the initial part of the existing object that fits in the allocated object. If `realloc` succeeds in allocating a new object, it deallocates the existing object. Otherwise, the existing object is left unchanged.

If `ptr` is a null pointer, the function does not store initial values in the newly created object.

size_t

```
typedef ui-type size_t;
```

The type is the unsigned integer type ***ui-type*** of an object that you declare to hold the result of the *sizeof* operator.

srand

```
void srand(unsigned int seed);
```

The function stores the seed value `seed` in a static-duration object that `rand` uses to compute a pseudo-random number. From a given seed value, `rand` generates the same sequence of return values. The program behaves as if the target environment calls `srand(1)` at program startup.

strtod `double strtod(const char *s, char **endptr);`

The function converts the initial characters of the string **s** to an equivalent value *x* of type *double*. If **endptr** is not a null pointer, the function stores a pointer to the unconverted remainder of the string in ***endptr**. The function then returns *x*.

The initial characters of the string **s** must consist of zero or more characters for which **isspace** returns nonzero, followed by the longest sequence of one or more characters that match the pattern shown in Figure 22.1.

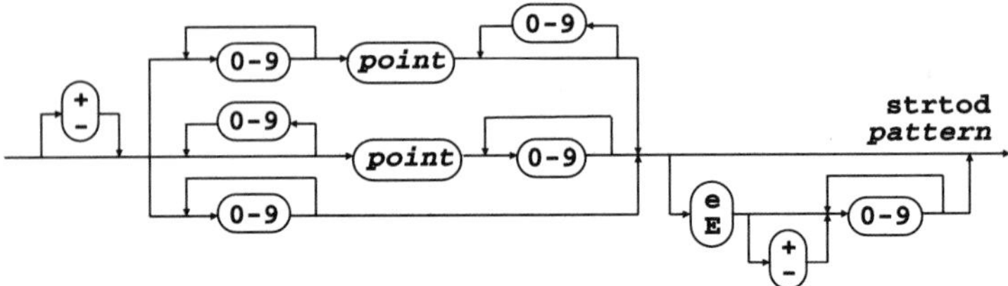

Figure 22.1: *Syntax of strings for* **strtod**.

Here, a ***point*** is the decimal-point character for the current locale. (It is the dot (**.**) in the **"C"** locale.) If the string **s** matches this pattern, its equivalent value is the decimal integer represented by any digits to the left of the ***point***, plus the decimal fraction represented by any digits to the right of the ***point***, times 10 raised to the signed decimal integer power that follows an optional **e** or **E**. A leading minus sign negates the value. In locales other than the **"C"** locale, **strtod** can define additional patterns as well.

If the string **s** does not match a valid pattern, the value stored in ***endptr** is **s**, and *x* is zero. If a range error occurs, **strtod** behaves exactly as the functions declared in **<math.h>**.

strtol `long strtol(const char *s, char **endptr, int base);`

The function converts the initial characters of the string **s** to an equivalent value *x* of type *long*. If **endptr** is not a null pointer, it stores a pointer to the unconverted remainder of the string in ***endptr**. The function then returns *x*.

The initial characters of the string **s** must consist of zero or more characters for which **isspace** returns nonzero, followed by the longest sequence of one or more characters that match the pattern shown in Figure 22.2.

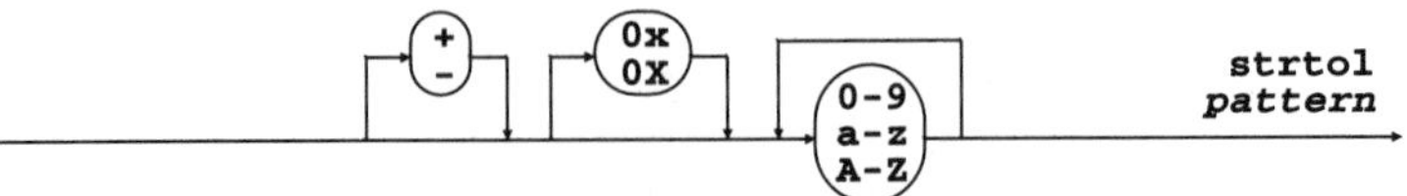

Figure 22.2: *Syntax of strings for* **strtol** *and* **strtoul**.

The function accepts the sequences **0x** or **0X** only when **base** equals zero or 16. The letters **a-z** or **A-Z** represent digits in the range [10, 36). If **base** is in the range [2, 36], the function accepts only digits with values less than

base. If **base** equals zero, then a leading **0x** or **0X** (after any sign) indicates a hexadecimal (base 16) integer, a leading **0** indicates an octal (base 8) integer, and any other valid pattern indicates a decimal (base 10) integer.

If the string **s** matches this pattern, its equivalent value is the signed integer of the appropriate base represented by the digits that match the pattern. (A leading minus sign negates the value.) In locales other than the **"C"** locale, **strtol** can define additional patterns.

If the string **s** does not match a valid pattern, the value stored in ***endptr** is **s**, and *x* is zero. If the equivalent value is too large to represent as type *long*, **strtol** stores the value of **ERANGE** in **errno** and returns either **LONG_MAX** if *x* is positive or **LONG_MIN** if *x* is negative.

strtoul

```
unsigned long strtoul(const char *s, char **endptr,
    int base);
```

The function converts the initial characters of the string **s** to an equivalent value *x* of type *unsigned long*. If **endptr** is not a null pointer, it stores a pointer to the unconverted remainder of the string in ***endptr**. The function then returns *x*.

strtoul converts strings exactly as does **strtol**, but reports a range error only if the equivalent value is too large to represent as type *unsigned long*. In this case, **strtoul** stores the value of **ERANGE** in **errno** and returns **ULONG_MAX**.

system

```
int system(const char *s);
```

If **s** is not a null pointer, the function passes the string **s** to be executed by a *command processor*, supplied by the target environment, and returns the status reported by the command processor. If **s** is a null pointer, the function returns nonzero only if the target environment supplies a command processor. Each implementation defines what strings its command processor accepts.

wchar_t

```
typedef i-type wchar_t;
```

The type is the integer type ***i-type*** of the wide-character constant **L'X'**. You declare an object of type **wchar_t** to hold a wide character.

wcstombs

```
size_t wcstombs(char *s, const wchar_t *wcs, size_t n);
```

The function stores a multibyte string, in successive elements of the array whose first element has the address **s**, by converting in turn each of the wide characters in the string **wcs**. The multibyte string begins in the initial shift state. The function converts each wide character as if by calling **wctomb** (except that the shift state stored for that function is unaffected). It stores no more than **n** bytes, stopping after it stores a null byte. It returns the number of bytes it stores, not counting the null byte, if all conversions are successful; otherwise, it returns –1.

wctomb `int wctomb(char *s, wchar_t wchar);`

If **s** is not a null pointer, the function determines *x*, the number of bytes needed to represent the multibyte character corresponding to the wide character **wchar**. *x* cannot exceed **MB_CUR_MAX**. The function converts **wchar** to its corresponding multibyte character, which it stores in successive elements of the array whose first element has the address **s**. It then returns *x*, or it returns –1 if **wchar** does not correspond to a valid multibyte character. **wctomb** *includes* the terminating null byte in the count of bytes. The function can use a shift state stored in a static-duration object to determine how to interpret the multibyte character string.

If **s** is a null pointer and if multibyte characters have a state-dependent encoding in the current locale, the function stores the initial shift state in its static-duration object and returns nonzero; otherwise, it returns zero.

Chapter 23: <string.h>

Include the standard header **<string.h>** to declare a number of functions that help you manipulate strings and other arrays of characters.

NULL

```
#define NULL <either 0, 0L, or (void *)0>
```

The macro yields a null pointer constant that is usable as an address constant expression.

memchr

```
void *memchr(const void *s, int c, size_t n);
```

The function searches for the first element of an array of *unsigned char*, beginning at the address **s** with size **n**, that equals **(unsigned char)c**. If successful, it returns the address of the matching element; otherwise, it returns a null pointer.

memcmp

```
int memcmp(const void *s1, const void *s2, size_t n);
```

The function compares successive elements from two arrays of *unsigned char*, beginning at the addresses **s1** and **s2** (both of size **n**), until it finds elements that are not equal:

- If all elements are equal, the function returns zero.
- If the differing element from **s1** is greater than the element from **s2**, the function returns a positive number.
- Otherwise, the function returns a negative number.

memcpy

```
void *memcpy(void *s1, const void *s2, size_t n);
```

The function copies the array of *char* beginning at the address **s2** to the array of *char* beginning at the address **s1** (both of size **n**). It returns **s1**. The elements of the arrays can be accessed and stored in any order.

memmove

```
void *memmove(void *s1, const void *s2, size_t n);
```

The function copies the array of *char* beginning at **s2** to the array of *char* beginning at **s1** (both of size **n**). It returns **s1**. If the arrays overlap, the function accesses each of the element values from **s2** before it stores a new value in that element, so the copy is not corrupted.

memset `void *memset(void *s, int c, size_t n);`

The function stores `(unsigned char)c` in each of the elements of the array of *unsigned char* beginning at `s`, with size `n`. It returns `s`.

size_t `typedef` ***ui-type*** `size_t;`

The type is the unsigned integer type ***ui-type*** of an object that you declare to hold the result of the *sizeof* operator.

strcat `char *strcat(char *s1, const char *s2);`

The function copies the string `s2`, including its terminating null character, to successive elements of the array of *char* that stores the string `s1`, beginning with the element that stores the terminating null character of `s1`. It returns `s1`.

strchr `char *strchr(const char *s, int c);`

The function searches for the first element of the string `s` that equals `(char)c`. It considers the terminating null character as part of the string. If successful, the function returns the address of the matching element; otherwise, it returns a null pointer.

strcmp `int strcmp(const char *s1, const char *s2);`

The function compares successive elements from two strings, `s1` and `s2`, until it finds elements that are not equal.

- If all elements are equal, the function returns zero.
- If the differing element from `s1` is greater than the element from `s2` (both taken as *unsigned char*), the function returns a positive number.
- Otherwise, the function returns a negative number.

strcoll `int strcoll(const char *s1, const char *s2);`

The function compares two strings, `s1` and `s2`, using a comparison rule that depends on the current locale. If `s1` is greater than `s2`, the function returns a positive number. If the two strings are equal, it returns zero. Otherwise, it returns a negative number.

strcpy `char *strcpy(char *s1, const char *s2);`

The function copies the string `s2`, including its terminating null character, to successive elements of the array of *char* whose first element has the address `s1`. It returns `s1`.

strcspn `size_t strcspn(const char *s1, const char *s2);`

The function searches for the first element `s1[`*i*`]` in the string `s1` that equals *any one* of the elements of the string `s2` and returns ***i***. Each terminating null character is considered part of its string.

strerror `char *strerror(int errcode);`

The function returns a pointer to an internal static-duration object containing the message string corresponding to the error code **errcode**. The program must not alter any of the values stored in this object. A later call to **strerror** can alter the value stored in this object.

strlen `size_t strlen(const char *s);`

The function returns the number of characters in the string **s**, *not* including its terminating null character.

strncat `char *strncat(char *s1, const char *s2, size_t n);`

The function copies the string **s2**, *not* including its terminating null character, to successive elements of the array of *char* that stores the string **s1**, beginning with the element that stores the terminating null character of **s1**. The function copies no more than **n** characters from **s2**. It then stores a null character, in the next element to be altered in **s1**, and returns **s1**.

strncmp `int strncmp(const char *s1, const char *s2, size_t n);`

The function compares successive elements from two strings, **s1** and **s2**, until it finds elements that are not equal or until it has compared the first **n** elements of the two strings.

- If all elements are equal, the function returns zero.
- If the differing element from **s1** is greater than the element from **s2** (both taken as *unsigned char*), the function returns a positive number.
- Otherwise, it returns a negative number.

strncpy `char *strncpy(char *s1, const char *s2, size_t n);`

The function copies the string **s2**, *not* including its terminating null character, to successive elements of the array of *char* whose first element has the address **s1**. It copies no more than **n** characters from **s2**. The function then stores zero or more null characters in the next elements to be altered in **s1** until it stores a total of **n** characters. It returns **s1**.

strpbrk `char *strpbrk(const char *s1, const char *s2);`

The function searches for the first element **s1[*i*]** in the string **s1** that equals *any one* of the elements of the string **s2**. It considers each terminating null character as part of its string. If **s1[*i*]** is not the terminating null character, the function returns **&s1[*i*]**; otherwise, it returns a null pointer.

strrchr `char *strrchr(const char *s, int c);`

The function searches for the last element of the string **s** that equals **(char)c**. It considers the terminating null character as part of the string. If successful, the function returns the address of the matching element; otherwise, it returns a null pointer.

strspn `size_t strspn(const char *s1, const char *s2);`

The function searches for the first element **s1[*i*]** in the string **s1** that equals *none* of the elements of the string **s2** and returns *i*. It considers the terminating null character as part of the string **s1** only.

strstr `char *strstr(const char *s1, const char *s2);`

The function searches for the first sequence of elements in the string **s1** that matches the sequence of elements in the string **s2**, *not* including its terminating null character. If successful, the function returns the address of the matching first element; otherwise, it returns a null pointer.

strtok `char *strtok(char *s1, const char *s2);`

If **s1** is not a null pointer, the function begins a search of the string **s1**. Otherwise, it begins a search of the string whose address was last stored in an internal static-duration object on an earlier call to the function, as described below. The search proceeds as follows:

1. The function searches the string for *begin*, the address of the first element that equals *none* of the elements of the string **s2** (a set of token separators). It considers the terminating null character as part of the search string only.
2. If the search does not find an element, the function stores the address of the terminating null characterin the internal static-duration object (so that a subsequent search beginning with that address will fail) and returns a null pointer. Otherwise, the function searches from *begin* for *end*, the address of the first element that equals *any one* of the elements of the string **s2**. It again considers the terminating null character as part of the search string only.
3. If the search does not find an element, the function stores the address of the terminating null characterin the internal static-duration object. Otherwise, it stores a null character in the element whose address is *end*. Then it stores the address of the next element after *end* in the internal static-duration object (so that a subsequent search beginning with that address will continue with the remaining elements of the string) and returns *begin*.

strxfrm `size_t strxfrm(char *s1, const char *s2, size_t n);`

The function stores a string in the array of *char* whose first element has the address **s1**. It stores no more than **n** characters, *including* the terminating null character, and returns the number of characters needed to represent the entire string, *not* including the terminating null character. If the value returned is **n** or greater, the values stored in the array are indeterminate. (If **n** is zero, **s1** can be a null pointer.)

strxfrm generates the string it stores from the string **s2** by using a transformation rule that depends on the current locale. For example, if x is a transformation of **s1** and y is a transformation of **s2**, then **strcmp(*x*, *y*)** returns the same value as **strcoll(s1, s2)**.

Chapter 24: `<time.h>`

Include the standard header `<time.h>` to declare several functions that help you manipulate times. Figure 24.1 shows all the functions and the object types that they convert between.

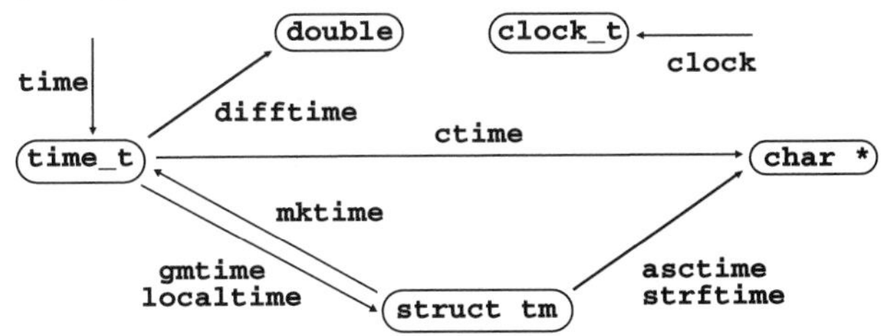

Figure 24.1: *Time conversion functions and object types.*

The functions share two static-duration objects that hold values computed by the functions:

- a *time string* of type array of *char*
- a *time structure* of type **`struct tm`**

A call to one of these functions can alter the value that was stored earlier in a static-duration object by another of these functions.

`CLOCKS_PER_SEC` **`#define CLOCKS_PER_SEC`** **<integer constant expression > 0>**

The macro yields the number of clock ticks, returned by **`clock`**, in one second.

`NULL` **`#define NULL`** **<either `0`, `0L`, or `(void *)0`>**

The macro yields a null pointer constant that is usable as an address constant expression.

`asctime` **`char *asctime(const struct tm *tptr);`**

The function stores in the static-duration time string a 26-character English-language representation of the time encoded in **`*tptr`**. It returns the address of the static-duration time string. The text representation takes the form:

```
Sun Dec  2 06:55:15 1979\n\0
```

clock `clock_t clock(void);`

The function returns the number of clock ticks of elapsed processor time, counting from a time related to program startup, or it returns –1 if the target environment cannot measure elapsed processor time.

clock_t `typedef` ***a-type*** `clock_t;`

The type is the arithmetic type ***a-type*** of an object that you declare to hold the value returned by **`clock`**, representing elapsed processor time.

ctime `char *ctime(const time_t *tod);`

The function converts the calendar time in **`*tod`** to a text representation of the local time in the static-duration time string. It returns the address of the static-duration time string. It is equivalent to **`asctime(localtime(tod))`**.

difftime `double difftime(time_t t1, time_t t0);`

The function returns the difference **`t1 - t0`**, in seconds, between the calendar time **`t0`** and the calendar time **`t1`**.

gmtime `struct tm *gmtime(const time_t *tod);`

The function stores in the static-duration time structure an encoding of the calendar time in **`*tod`**, expressed as Universal Time Coordinated, or UTC. (UTC was formerly Greenwich Mean Time, or GMT). It returns the address of the static-duration time structure.

localtime `struct tm *localtime(const time_t *tod);`

The function stores in the static-duration time structure an encoding of the calendar time in **`*tod`**, expressed as local time. It returns the address of the static-duration time structure.

mktime `time_t mktime(struct tm *tptr);`

The function alters the values stored in **`*tptr`** to represent an equivalent encoded local time, but with the values of all members within their normal ranges. It then determines the values **`tptr->wday`** and **`tptr->yday`** from the values of the other members. It returns the calendar time equivalent to the encoded time, or it returns a value of –1 if the calendar time cannot be represented.

size_t `typedef` ***ui-type*** `size_t;`

The type is the unsigned integer type ***ui-type*** of an object that you declare to hold the result of the *sizeof* operator.

strftime

```
size_t strftime(char *s, size_t n, const char *format,
                const struct tm *tptr);
```

The function generates formatted text, under the control of the format **`format`** and the values stored in the time structure **`*tptr`**. It stores each generated character in successive locations of the array object of size **n** whose first element has the address **s**. The function then stores a null character in the next location of the array. It returns **x**, the number of characters generated, if **x** < **n**; otherwise, it returns zero, and the values stored in the array are indeterminate.

For each multibyte character other than **%** in the format, the function stores that multibyte character in the array object. Each occurrence of **%** followed by another character in the format is a *conversion specifier*. For each conversion specifier, the function stores a replacement character sequence.

Table 24.1 lists all conversion specifiers defined for **strftime**. Example replacement character sequences in parentheses follow each conversion specifier. All examples are for the **"C"** locale, using the date and time Sunday, 2 December 1979 at 06:55:15 AM EST.

The current locale category **LC_TIME** can affect these replacement character sequences.

Table 24.1: *Time conversion specifiers for* **strftime**.

- **%a** — abbreviated weekday name (**Sun**)
- **%A** — full weekday name (**Sunday**)
- **%b** — abbreviated month name (**Dec**)
- **%B** — full month name (**December**)
- **%c** — date and time (**Dec 2 06:55:15 1979**)
- **%d** — day of the month (**02**)
- **%H** — hour of the 24-hour day (**06**)
- **%I** — hour of the 12-hour day (**06**)
- **%j** — day of the year, from 001 (**335**)
- **%m** — month of the year, from 01 (**12**)
- **%M** — minutes after the hour (**55**)
- **%p** — AM/PM indicator (**AM**)
- **%S** — seconds after the minute (**15**)
- **%U** — Sunday week of the year, from 00 (**48**)
- **%w** — day of the week, from 0 for Sunday (**6**)
- **%W** — Monday week of the year, from 00 (**47**)
- **%x** — date (**Dec 2 1979**)
- **%X** — time (**06:55:15**)
- **%y** — year of the century, from 00 (**79**)
- **%Y** — year (**1979**)
- **%Z** — time zone name, if any (**EST**)
- **%%** — percent character **%**

time **time_t time(time_t *tod);**

If **tod** is not a null pointer, the function stores the current calendar time in ***tod**. The function returns the current calendar time, if the target environment can determine it; otherwise, it returns –1.

time_t `typedef a-type time_t;`

The type is the arithmetic type ***a-type*** of an object that you declare to hold the value returned by **time**. The value represents calendar time.

tm
```
struct tm {
    int tm_sec;       seconds after the minute (from 0)
    int tm_min;       minutes after the hour (from 0)
    int tm_hour;      hour of the day (from 0)
    int tm_mday;      day of the month (from 1)
    int tm_mon;       month of the year (from 0)
    int tm_year;      years since 1900 (from 0)
    int tm_wday;      days since Sunday (from 0)
    int tm_yday;      day of the year (from 0)
    int tm_isdst;     daylight saving time flag
    };
```

struct tm contains members that describe various properties of the calendar time. The members shown above can occur in any order, interspersed with additional members. The comment following each member briefly describes its meaning.

The member **tm_isdst** contains:

- a positive value if daylight saving time is in effect
- zero if daylight saving time is not in effect
- a negative value if the status of daylight saving time is not known (so the target environment should attempt to determine its status)

Chapter 25: <wchar.h>

Amendment 1 (entire header) Include the standard header **<wchar.h>** so that you can perform input and output operations on wide streams or manipulate wide strings.

NULL `#define NULL <either 0, 0L, or (void *)0>`

The macro yields a null pointer constant that is usable as an address constant expression.

WCHAR_MAX `#define WCHAR_MAX <#if expression ≥ 127>`

The macro yields the maximum value for type **wchar_t**.

WCHAR_MIN `#define WCHAR_MIN <#if expression>`

The macro yields the minimum value for type **wchar_t**.

WEOF `#define WEOF <wint_t constant expression>`

The macro yields the return value used to signal the end of a wide file or to report an error condition.

btowc `wint_t btowc(int c);`

The function returns **WEOF** if **c** equals **EOF**. Otherwise, it converts **(unsigned char)c** as a one-byte multibyte character beginning in the initial shift state, as if by calling **mbrtowc**. If the conversion succeeds, the function returns the wide-character conversion. Otherwise, it returns **WEOF**.

fgetwc `wint_t fgetwc(FILE *stream);`

The function reads the next wide character *c* (if present) from the input stream **stream**, advances the file-position indicator (if defined), and returns **(wint_t)***c*. If the function sets either the end-of-file indicator or the error indicator, it returns **WEOF**.

fgetws `wchar_t *fgetws(wchar_t *s, int n, FILE *stream);`

The function reads wide characters from the input stream **stream** and stores them in successive elements of the array beginning at **s** and continuing until it stores **n-1** wide characters, stores an ***NL*** wide character, or sets the end-of-file or error indicators. If **fgets** stores any wide characters, it concludes by storing a null wide character in the next element of the array. It returns **s** if it stores any wide characters and it has not set the error indicator for the stream; otherwise, it returns a null pointer. If it sets the error indicator, the array contents are indeterminate.

fputwc `wint_t fputwc(wchar_t c, FILE *stream);`

The function writes the wide character **c** to the output stream **stream**, advances the file-position indicator (if defined), and returns **(wint_t)c**. If the function sets the error indicator for the stream, it returns **WEOF**.

fputws `int fputws(const wchar_t *s, FILE *stream);`

The function accesses wide characters from the string **s** and writes them to the output stream **stream**. The function does not write the terminating null wide character. It returns a nonnegative value if it has not set the error indicator; otherwise, it returns **WEOF**.

fwide `int fwide(FILE *stream, int mode);`

The function determines the orientation of the stream **stream**. If **mode** is greater than zero, it first attempts to make the stream wide oriented. If **mode** is less than zero, it first attempts to make the stream narrow oriented. In any event, the function returns:

- a value greater than zero if the stream is left with wide orientation
- zero if the stream is left unoriented
- a value less than zero if the stream is left with byte orientation

In no event will the function alter the orientation of a stream once it has been oriented. (See **FILES AND STREAMS** in ***Chapter 8: Library***. In particular, see Figure 8.1 under **Controlling Streams** in that section.)

fwprintf `int fwprintf(FILE *stream, const wchar_t *format, ...);`

The function generates formatted text, under the control of the format **format** and any additional arguments, and writes each generated wide character to the stream **stream**. It returns the number of wide characters generated, or it returns a negative value if the function sets the error indicator for the stream. (See **FORMATTED INPUT/OUTPUT** in ***Chapter 8: Library***.)

fwscanf `int fwscanf(FILE *stream, const wchar_t *format, ...);`

The function scans formatted text, under the control of the format **format** and any additional arguments. It obtains each scanned wide character from the stream **stream**. It returns the number of input items matched and assigned, or it returns **WEOF** if the function does not store values before it sets the end-of-file or error indicator for the stream. (See **FORMATTED INPUT/OUTPUT** in ***Chapter 8: Library***.)

getwc `wint_t getwc(FILE *stream);`

The function has the same effect as **fgetwc(stream)** except that a macro version of **getwc** can evaluate **stream** more than once.

getwchar `wint_t getwchar(void);`

The function has the same effect as `fgetwc(stdin)`.

mbrlen `size_t mbrlen(const char *s, size_t n, mbstate_t *ps);`

The function is equivalent to the call:

```
mbrtowc(NULL, s, n, ps != NULL ? ps : &internal)
```

where ***internal*** is an object of type `mbstate_t` internal to the `mbrlen` function. At program startup, ***internal*** is initialized to the initial conversion state. No other library function alters the value stored in ***internal***.

The function returns:

- `(size_t)-2` if, after converting all `n` characters, the resulting conversion state indicates an incomplete multibyte character
- `(size_t)-1` if the function detects an encoding error before completing the next multibyte character, in which case the function stores the value `EILSEQ` in `errno` (both defined in `<errno.h>`) and leaves the resulting conversion state undefined
- zero, if the next completed character is a null character, in which case the resulting conversion state is the initial conversion state
- *x*, the number of bytes needed to complete the next muitibyte character, in which case the resulting conversion state indicates that *x* bytes have been converted

Thus, `mbrlen` effectively returns the number of bytes that would be consumed in successfully converting a multibyte character to a wide character (without storing the converted wide character), or an error code if the conversion cannot succeed.

mbrtowc

```
size_t mbrtowc(wchar_t *pwc, const char *s, size_t n,
     mbstate_t *ps);
```

The function determines the number of bytes in a multibyte string that completes the next multibyte character, if possible.

If `ps` is not a null pointer, the conversion state for the multibyte string is assumed to be `*ps`. Otherwise, it is assumed to be `&`*internal*, where *internal* is an object of type `mbstate_t` internal to the `mbrtowc` function. At program startup, *internal* is initialized to the initial conversion state. No other library function alters the value stored in *internal*.

If `s` is not a null pointer, the function determines *x*, the number of bytes in the multibyte string `s` that complete or contribute to the next multibyte character. (*x* cannot be greater than `n`.) Otherwise, the function effectively returns `mbrtowc(NULL, "", 1, ps)`, ignoring `pwc` and `n`. (The function thus returns zero only if the conversion state indicates that no incomplete multibyte character is pending from a previous call to `mbrlen`, `mbrtowc`, or `mbsrtowcs` for the same string and conversion state.)

If `pwc` is not a null pointer, the function converts a completed multibyte character to its corresponding wide-character value and stores that value in `*pwc`.

The function returns:

- **`(size_t)-2`** if, after converting all **`n`** characters, the resulting conversion state indicates an incomplete multibyte character
- **`(size_t)-1`** if the function detects an encoding error before completing the next multibyte character, in which case the function stores the value **`EILSEQ`** in **`errno`** (both defined in **`<errno.h>`**) and leaves the resulting conversion state undefined
- zero, if the next completed character is a null character, in which case the resulting conversion state is the initial conversion state
- *x*, the number of bytes needed to complete the next muitibyte character, in which case the resulting conversion state indicates that *x* bytes have been converted

`mbsinit`

```
int mbsinit(const mbstate_t *ps);
```

The function returns a nonzero value if **`ps`** is a null pointer or if **`*ps`** designates an initial conversion state. Otherwise, it returns zero.

`mbsrtowcs`

```
size_t mbsrtowcs(wchar_t *dst, const char **src,
     size_t len, mbstate_t *ps);
```

The function converts the multibyte string beginning at **`*src`** to a sequence of wide characters as if by repeated calls of the form:

```
X = mbrtowc(dst, *src, n, ps != NULL ? ps : &internal)
```

where ***n*** is some value greater than zero and ***internal*** is an object of type **`mbstate_t`** internal to the **`mbsrtowcs`** function. At program startup, ***internal*** is initialized to the initial conversion state. No other library function alters the value stored in ***internal***.

If **`dst`** is not a null pointer, the **`mbsrtowcs`** function stores at most **`len`** wide characters by calls to **`mbrtowc`**. The function effectively increments **`dst`** by one and **`*src`** by ***X*** after each call to **`mbrtowc`** that stores a converted wide character. After a call to **`mbrtowc`** that returns zero, **`mbsrtowcs`** stores a null wide character at **`dst`** and stores a null pointer at **`*src`**.

If **`dst`** is a null pointer, **`len`** is effectively assigned a large value.

The function returns:

- **`(size_t)-1`**, if a call to **`mbrtowc`** returns **`(size_t)-1`**, indicating that it has detected an encoding error before completing the next multibyte character
- the number of multibyte characters successfully converted, not including the terminating null character

`mbstate_t`

```
typedef o-type mbstate_t;
```

The type is an object type ***o-type*** that can represent a *conversion state* for any of the functions **`mblen`**, **`mbrtowc`**, **`mbsrtowcs`**, **`wcrtomb`**, or **`wcsrtomb`**. The conversion state has two components:

- a *parse state,* that remembers any partially converted (for **mbrtowc**) or partially generated (for **wcrtomb**) multibyte character
- a *shift state,* for multibyte encodings that are state dependent

A definition of the form:

```
mbstate_t mbst = {0};
```

ensures that **mbst** represents the *initial conversion state:*

- between multibyte characters
- in the initial shift state, for a state-dependent encoding

Note, however, that other values stored in an object of type **mbstate_t** can also represent the initial conversion state. (See the function **mbsinit**, earlier in this chapter.)

putwc

```
wint_t putwc(wchar_t c, FILE *stream);
```

The function has the same effect as **fputwc(c, stream)** except that a macro version of **putwc** can evaluate **stream** more than once.

putwchar

```
wint_t putwchar(wchar_t c);
```

The function has the same effect as **fputwc(c, stdout)**.

size_t

```
typedef ui-type size_t;
```

The type is the unsigned integer type ***ui-type*** of an object that you declare to hold the result of the *sizeof* operator.

swprintf

```
int swprintf(wchar_t *s, size_t n, const wchar_t *format,
        ...);
```

The function generates formatted text, under the control of the format **format** and any additional arguments. It stores each generated wide character in successive locations of the array object whose first element has the address **s**. The function concludes by storing a null wide character in the next location of the array. It returns the number of wide characters generated — not including the null wide character. (See **FORMATTED INPUT/OUTPUT** in ***Chapter 8: Library***.)

swscanf

```
int swscanf(const wchar_t *s, const wchar_t *format, ...);
```

The function scans formatted text under the control of the format **format** and any additional arguments. It accesses each scanned character from successive locations of the array object whose first element has the address **s**. It returns the number of items matched and assigned, or it returns **EOF** if the function does not store values before it accesses a null wide character from the array. (See **FORMATTED INPUT/OUTPUT** in ***Chapter 8: Library***.)

tm

```
struct tm;
```

struct tm contains members that describe various properties of the calendar time. The declaration in this header leaves **struct tm** an incomplete type. Include the header **<time.h>** to complete the type.

ungetwc `wint_t ungetwc(wint_t c, FILE *stream);`

If **c** is not equal to **WEOF**, the function stores **(wchar_t)c** in the object whose address is **stream** and clears the end-of-file indicator. If **c** equals **WEOF** or the store cannot occur, the function returns **WEOF**; otherwise, it returns **(wchar_t)c**. A subsequent library function call that reads a wide character from the stream **stream** obtains this stored value, which is then forgotten.

Thus, you can effectively *push back* a wide character to a stream after reading a wide character. (You need not push back the same wide character that you read.) An implementation can let you push back additional wide characters before you read the first one. You read the wide characters in reverse order of pushing them back to the stream.

You cannot portably:

- Push back more than one wide character.
- Push back a wide character if the file-position indicator is at the beginning of the file.
- Call **ftell** for a text file that has a wide character currently pushed back.

A call to the functions **fseek**, **fsetpos**, or **rewind** for the stream causes the stream to forget any pushed-back wide characters.

vwfprintf

```
int vfwprintf(FILE *stream, const wchar_t *format,
     va_list arg);
```

The function generates formatted text, under the control of the format **format** and any additional arguments. It writes each generated wide character to the stream **stream**. It returns the number of wide characters generated, or it returns a negative value if the function sets the error indicator for the stream. (See **FORMATTED INPUT/OUTPUT** in ***Chapter 8: Library***.)

The function accesses additional arguments by using the context information designated by **ap**. The program must execute the macro **va_start** before it calls the function and then execute the macro **va_end** after the function returns. (Both macros are defined in **<stdarg.h>**.)

vswprintf

```
int vswprintf(wchar_t *s, size_t n,
     const wchar_t *format, va_list arg);
```

The function generates formatted text, under the control of the format **format** and any additional arguments. It stores each generated wide character in successive locations of the array object whose first element has the address **s**. The function concludes by storing a null wide character in the next location of the array. It returns the number of characters generated — not including the null wide character. (See **FORMATTED INPUT/OUTPUT** in ***Chapter 8: Library***.)

The function accesses additional arguments by using the context information designated by **ap**. The program must execute the macro **va_start** before it calls the function and then execute the macro **va_end** after the function returns. (Both macros are defined in **<stdarg.h>**.)

vwprintf `int vwprintf(const wchar_t *format, va_list arg);`

The function generates formatted text, under control of the format **format** and any additional arguments. It writes each generated wide character to the stream **stdout**. It returns the number of characters generated, or a negative value if the function sets the error indicator for the stream. (See **FORMATTED INPUT/OUTPUT** in *Chapter 8: Library*.)

The function accesses additional arguments by using the context information designated by **ap**. The program must execute the macro **va_start** before it calls the function, and execute the macro **va_end** after the function returns. (Both macros are defined in **<stdarg.h>**.)

wchar_t `typedef` *i-type* `wchar_t;`

The type is the integer type ***i-type*** of the wide-character constant **L'X'**. You declare an object of type **wchar_t** to hold a wide character.

wcrtomb `size_t wcrtomb(char *s, wchar_t wc, mbstate_t *ps);`

The function determines the number of bytes needed to represent the wide character **wc** as a multibyte character, if possible. (Not all values representable as type **wchar_t** are valid wide-character codes.)

If **ps** is not a null pointer, the conversion state for the multibyte string is assumed to be ***ps**. Otherwise, it is assumed to be **&***internal*, where *internal* is an object of type **mbstate_t** internal to the **wcrtomb** function. At program startup, *internal* is initialized to the initial conversion state. No other library function alters the value stored in *internal*.

If **s** is not a null pointer and **wc** is a valid wide-character code, the function determines *x*, the number of bytes needed to represent **wc** as a multibyte character, and stores the converted bytes in the array of *char* beginning at **s**. (*x* cannot be greater than **MB_CUR_MAX**.) If **wc** is a null wide character, the function stores any shift sequence needed to restore the initial shift state, followed by a null byte. The resulting conversion state is the initial conversion state.

If **s** is a null pointer, the function effectively returns **wcrtomb(***buf***, L'0', ps)**, where *buf* is buffer internal to the function. (The function thus returns the number of bytes needed to restore the initial shift state and to terminate the multibyte string pending from a previous call to **wcrtomb** or **wcsrtombs** for the same string and conversion state.)

The function returns:

- **(size_t)-1** if **wc** is an invalid wide-character code, in which case the function stores the value **EILSEQ** in **errno** (both defined in **<errno.h>**) and leaves the resulting conversion state undefined
- *x*, the number of bytes needed to complete the next muitibyte character, in which case the resulting conversion state indicates that *x* bytes have been generated

wcscat `wchar_t *wcscat(wchar_t *s1, const wchar_t *s2);`

The function copies the wide string **s2**, including its terminating null wide character, to successive elements of the array of **wchar_t** that stores the wide string **s1**, beginning with the element that stores the terminating null wide character of **s1**. It returns **s1**.

wcschr `wchar_t *wcschr(const wchar_t *s, wchar_t c);`

The function searches for the first element of the wide string **s** that equals **c**. It considers the terminating null wide character as part of the wide string. If successful, the function returns the address of the matching element; otherwise, it returns a null pointer.

wcscmp `int wcscmp(const wchar_t *s1, const wchar_t *s2);`

The function compares successive elements from two wide strings, **s1** and **s2**, until it finds elements that are not equal.

- If all elements are equal, the function returns zero.
- If the differing element from **s1** is greater than the element from **s2** (both taken as **wchar_t**), the function returns a positive number.
- Otherwise, the function returns a negative number.

wcscoll `int wcscoll(const wchar_t *s1, const wchar_t *s2);`

The function compares two wide strings, **s1** and **s2**, using a comparison rule that depends on the current locale. If **s1** is greater than **s2**, the function returns a positive number. If the two wide strings are equal, it returns zero. Otherwise, it returns a negative number.

wcscpy `wchar_t *wcscpy(wchar_t *s1, const wchar_t *s2);`

The function copies the wide string **s2**, including its terminating null wide character, to successive elements of the array of **wchar_t** whose first element has the address **s1**. It returns **s1**.

wcscspn `size_t wcscspn(const wchar_t *s1, const wchar_t *s2);`

The function searches for the first element **s1[**i**]** in the wide string **s1** that equals *any one* of the elements of the wide string **s2** and returns i. Each terminating null wide character is considered part of its wide string.

wcsftime
```
size_t wcsftime(wchar_t *s, size_t maxsize,
    const wchar_t *format, const struct tm *timeptr);
```

The function generates formatted text, under the control of the format **format** and the values stored in the time structure ***tptr**. It stores each generated wide character in successive locations of the array object of size **n** whose first element has the address **s**. The function then stores a null wide character in the next location of the array. It returns x, the number of wide characters generated, if x **< n**; otherwise, it returns zero, and the values stored in the array are indeterminate.

For each wide character other than `%` in the format, the function stores that wide character in the array object. Each occurrence of `%` followed by another character in the format is a *conversion specifier*. For each conversion specifier, the function stores a replacement wide character sequence. Conversion specifiers are the same as for the function **strftime** (defined in **<time.h>**). The current locale category **LC_TIME** can affect these replacement character sequences.

wcslen

```
size_t wcslen(const wchar_t *s);
```

The function returns the number of wide characters in the wide string **s**, *not* including its terminating null wide character.

wcsncat

```
wchar_t *wcsncat(wchar_t *s1, const wchar_t *s2,
    size_t n);
```

The function copies the wide string **s2**, *not* including its terminating null wide character, to successive elements of the array of **wchar_t** that stores the wide string **s1**, beginning with the element that stores the terminating null wide character of **s1**. The function copies no more than **n** wide characters from **s2**. It then stores a null wide character, in the next element to be altered in **s1**, and returns **s1**.

wcsncmp

```
int wcsncmp(const wchar_t *s1, const wchar_t *s2,
    size_t n);
```

The function compares successive elements from two wide strings, **s1** and **s2**, until it finds elements that are not equal or until it has compared the first **n** elements of the two wide strings.

- If all elements are equal, the function returns zero.
- If the differing element from **s1** is greater than the element from **s2** (both taken as **wchar_t**), the function returns a positive number.
- Otherwise, it returns a negative number.

wcsncpy

```
wchar_t *wcsncpy(wchar_t *s1, const wchar_t *s2,
    size_t n);
```

The function copies the wide string **s2**, *not* including its terminating null wide character, to successive elements of the array of **wchar_t** whose first element has the address **s1**. It copies no more than **n** wide characters from **s2**. The function then stores zero or more null wide characters in the next elements to be altered in **s1** until it stores a total of **n** wide characters. It returns **s1**.

wcspbrk

```
wchar_t *wcspbrk(const wchar_t *s1, const wchar_t *s2);
```

The function searches for the first element **s1[*i*]** in the wide string **s1** that equals *any one* of the elements of the wide string **s2**. It considers each terminating null wide character as part of its wide string. If **s1[*i*]** is not the terminating null wide character, the function returns **&s1[*i*]**; otherwise, it returns a null pointer.

wcsrchr `wchar_t *wcsrchr(const wchar_t *s, wchar_t c);`

The function searches for the last element of the wide string `s` that equals `c`. It considers the terminating null wide character as part of the wide string. If successful, the function returns the address of the matching element; otherwise, it returns a null pointer.

wcsrtombs

```
size_t wcsrtombs(char *dst, const wchar_t **src,
     size_t len, mbstate_t *ps);
```

The function converts the wide-character string beginning at `*src` to a sequence of multibyte characters as if by repeated calls of the form:

```
X = wcrtomb(dst ? dst : buf, *src,
     ps != NULL ? ps : &internal)
```

where ***buf*** is an array of type *char* and ***internal*** is an object of type `mbstate_t`, both internal to the `wcsrtombs` function. At program startup, ***internal*** is initialized to the initial conversion state. No other library function alters the value stored in ***internal***.

If `dst` is not a null pointer, the `wcsrtombs` function stores at most `len` bytes by calls to `wcrtomb`. The function effectively increments `dst` by ***X*** and `*src` by one after each call to `wcrtomb` that stores a *complete* converted multibyte character in the remaining space available. After a call to `wcrtomb` that stores a complete null multibyte character at `dst` (including any shift sequence needed to restore the initial shift state), the function stores a null pointer at `*src`.

If `dst` is a null pointer, `len` is effectively assigned a large value.

The function returns:

- `(size_t)-1`, if a call to `wcrtomb` returns `(size_t)-1`, indicating that it has detected an invalid wide-character code
- the number of bytes successfully converted, not including the terminating null byte

wcsspn `size_t wcsspn(const wchar_t *s1, const wchar_t *s2);`

The function searches for the first element `s1[i]` in the wide string `s1` that equals *none* of the elements of the wide string `s2` and returns *i*. It considers the terminating null wide character as part of the wide string `s1` only.

wcsstr `wchar_t *wcsstr(const wchar_t *s1, const wchar_t *s2);`

The function searches for the first sequence of elements in the wide string `s1` that matches the sequence of elements in the wide string `s2`, *not* including its terminating null wide character. If successful, the function returns the address of the matching first element; otherwise, it returns a null pointer.

wcstod `double wcstod(const wchar_t *nptr, wchar_t **endptr);`

The function converts the initial wide characters of the wide string `s` to an equivalent value *x* of type *double*. If `endptr` is not a null pointer, the function stores a pointer to the unconverted remainder of the wide string in ***endptr**. The function then returns *x*.

The initial wide characters of the wide string **s** must consist of zero or more wide characters **c** for which **isspace(wctob(c))** returns nonzero, followed by the longest sequence of one or more wide characters that match the same pattern as recognized by the function **strtod** (defined in **<stdlib.h>**). The pattern is shown as a railroad-track diagram in Figure 22.1 in *Chapter 22:* **<stdlib.h>**.

Here, a ***point*** is the wide-character equivalent of the decimal-point character **c** for the current locale, or **btowc(c)**. (It is the dot (**.**) in the **"C"** locale.) If the wide string **s** matches this pattern, its equivalent value is the decimal integer represented by any digits to the left of the ***point***, plus the decimal fraction represented by any digits to the right of the ***point***, times 10 raised to the signed decimal integer power that follows an optional **e** or **E**. A leading minus sign negates the value. In locales other than the **"C"** locale, **wcstod** can define additional patterns as well.

If the wide string **s** does not match a valid pattern, the value stored in ***endptr** is **s**, and *x* is zero. If a range error occurs, **wcstod** behaves exactly as the functions declared in **<math.h>**.

wcstok

```
wchar_t *wcstok(wchar_t *s1, const wchar_t *s2,
    wchar_t **ptr);
```

If **s1** is not a null pointer, the function begins a search of the wide string **s1**. Otherwise, it begins a search of the wide string whose address was last stored in ***ptr** on an earlier call to the function, as described below. The search proceeds as follows:

1. The function searches the wide string for *begin,* the address of the first element that equals *none* of the elements of the wide string **s2** (a set of token separators). It considers the terminating null character as part of the search wide string only.
2. If the search does not find an element, the function stores the address of the terminating null wide character in ***ptr** (so that a subsequent search beginning with that address will fail) and returns a null pointer. Otherwise, the function searches from *begin* for *end,* the address of the first element that equals *any one* of the elements of the wide string **s2**. It again considers the terminating null wide character as part of the search string only.
3. If the search does not find an element, the function stores the address of the terminating null wide character in ***ptr**. Otherwise, it stores a null wide character in the element whose address is *end.* Then it stores the address of the next element after *end* in ***ptr** (so that a subsequent search beginning with that address will continue with the remaining elements of the string) and returns *begin.*

wcstol

```
long int wcstol(const wchar_t *nptr, wchar_t **endptr,
    int base);
```

The function converts the initial wide characters of the wide string **s** to an equivalent value *x* of type *long*. If **endptr** is not a null pointer, it stores a pointer to the unconverted remainder of the wide string in ***endptr**. The function then returns *x*.

The initial wide characters of the wide string **s** must consist of zero or more wide characters **c** for which **isspace(wctob(c))** returns nonzero, followed by the longest sequence of one or more wide characters that match the same pattern as recognized by the function **strtol** (defined in **<stdlib.h>**). The pattern is shown as a railroad-track diagram in Figure 22.2 in *Chapter 22:* **<stdlib.h>**.

The function accepts the sequences **0x** or **0X** only when **base** equals zero or 16. The letters **a-z** or **A-Z** represent digits in the range [10, 36). If **base** is in the range [2, 36], the function accepts only digits with values less than **base**. If **base** equals zero, then a leading **0x** or **0X** (after any sign) indicates a hexadecimal (base 16) integer, a leading **0** indicates an octal (base 8) integer, and any other valid pattern indicates a decimal (base 10) integer.

If the wide string **s** matches this pattern, its equivalent value is the signed integer of the appropriate base represented by the digits that match the pattern. (A leading minus sign negates the value.) In locales other than the **"C"** locale, **wcstol** can define additional patterns.

If the wide string **s** does not match a valid pattern, the value stored in ***endptr** is **s**, and *x* is zero. If the equivalent value is too large to represent as type *long*, **wcstol** stores the value of **ERANGE** in **errno** and returns either **LONG_MAX** if *x* is positive or **LONG_MIN** if *x* is negative.

wcstoul

```
unsigned long int wcstoul(const wchar_t *nptr,
    wchar_t **endptr, int base);
```

The function converts the initial wide characters of the wide string **s** to an equivalent value *x* of type *unsigned long*. If **endptr** is not a null pointer, it stores a pointer to the unconverted remainder of the wide string in ***endptr**. The function then returns *x*.

wcstoul converts strings exactly as does **wcstol**, but reports a range error only if the equivalent value is too large to represent as type *unsigned long*. In this case, **wcstoul** stores the value of **ERANGE** in **errno** and returns **ULONG_MAX**.

wcsxfrm

```
size_t wcsxfrm(wchar_t *s1, const wchar_t *s2, size_t n);
```

The function stores a wide string in the array of **wchar_t** whose first element has the address **s1**. It stores no more than **n** wide characters, *including* the terminating null wide character, and returns the number of wide characters needed to represent the entire wide string, *not* including the terminating null wide character. If the value returned is **n** or greater, the values stored in the array are indeterminate. (If **n** is zero, **s1** can be a null pointer.)

wcsxfrm generates the wide string it stores from the wide string **s2** by using a transformation rule that depends on the current locale. For example, if *x* is a transformation of **s1** and *y* is a transformation of **s2**, then **wcscmp(***x***,** *y***)** returns the same value as **wcscoll(s1, s2)**.

wctob `int wctob(wint_t c);`

The function determines whether **c** can be represented as a one-byte multibyte character *x*, beginning in the initial shift state. (It effectively calls **wcrtomb** to make the conversion.) If so, the function returns *x*. Otherwise, it returns **WEOF**.

wint_t `typedef` ***i_type*** `wint_t;`

The type is the integer type ***i_type*** that can represent all values of type **wchar_t** as well as the value of the macro **WEOF**, and that doesn't change when promoted.

wmemchr `wchar_t *wmemchr(const wchar_t *s, wchar_t c, size_t n);`

The function searches for the first element of an array of **wchar_t**, beginning at the address **s** with size **n**, that equals **c**. If successful, it returns the address of the matching element; otherwise, it returns a null pointer.

wmemcmp
```
int wmemcmp(const wchar_t *s1, const wchar_t *s2,
    size_t n);
```

The function compares successive elements from two arrays of **wchar_t**, beginning at the addresses **s1** and **s2** (both of size **n**), until it finds elements that are not equal:

- If all elements are equal, the function returns zero.
- If the differing element from **s1** is greater than the element from **s2**, the function returns a positive number.
- Otherwise, the function returns a negative number.

wmemcpy
```
wchar_t *wmemcpy(wchar_t *s1, const wchar_t *s2,
    size_t n);
```

The function copies the array of **wchar_t** beginning at the address **s2** to the array of **wchar_t** beginning at the address **s1** (both of size **n**). It returns **s1**. The elements of the arrays can be accessed and stored in any order.

wmemmove
```
wchar_t *wmemmove(wchar_t *s1, const wchar_t *s2,
    size_t n);
```

The function copies the array of **wchar_t** beginning at **s2** to the array of **wchar_t** beginning at **s1** (both of size **n**). It returns **s1**. If the arrays overlap, the function accesses each of the element values from **s2** before it stores a new value in that element, so the copy is not corrupted.

wmemset `wchar_t *wmemset(wchar_t *s, wchar_t c, size_t n);`

The function stores **c** in each of the elements of the array of **whar_t** beginning at **s**, with size **n**. It returns **s**.

wprintf `int wprintf(const wchar_t *format, ...);`

The function generates formatted text, under the control of the format **format** and any additional arguments. It writes each generated wide character to the stream **stdout**. It returns the number of wide characters generated, or it returns a negative value if the function sets the error indicator for the stream. (See **FORMATTED INPUT/OUTPUT** in ***Chapter 8: Library***.)

wscanf `int wscanf(const wchar_t *format, ...);`

The function scans formatted text, under the control of the format **format** and any additional arguments. It obtains each scanned wide character from the stream **stdin**. It returns the number of input items matched and assigned, or it returns **WEOF** if the function does not store values before it sets the end-of-file or error indicators for the stream. (See **FORMATTED INPUT/OUTPUT** in ***Chapter 8: Library***.)

Chapter 26: `<wctype.h>`

Amendment 1 (entire header)

Include the standard header `<wctype.h>` to declare several functions that are useful for classifying and mapping codes from the target wide-character set. This header is supplied only with Amendment 1.

Every function that has a parameter of type `wint_t` can accept the value of the macro `WEOF` or any valid wide-character code (of type `wchar_t`). Thus, the argument can be the value returned by any of the functions:

```
btowc    fgetwc  fputwc      getwc
getwchar putwc   putwchar    ungetwc
```

(declared in `<wchar.h>`), or by:

```
towctrans
towlower towupper
```

(declared in `<wctype.h>`). You must not call these functions with other wide-character argument values.

The wide-character classification functions are strongly related to the byte classification functions declared in `<ctype.h>`. (See *Chapter 10:* `<ctype.h>`.) Each byte function **`isXXX`** has a corresponding wide-character function **`iswXXX`**. Moreover, the wide-character classification functions are interrelated much the same way as their corresponding byte functions shown in Figure 10.1.

There are two added provisos, however:

- The function `iswprint`, unlike `isprint`, can return a nonzero value for additional space characters besides the wide-character equivalent of ***space***. (The additional characters return a nonzero value for `iswspace` and return zero for `iswgraph` or `iswpunct`.)
- The characters in each wide-character class are a superset of the characters in the corresponding byte class. (If the call **`isXXX(c)`** returns a nonzero value, then the corresponding call **`iswXXX(btowc(c))`** also returns a nonzero value.)

An implementation can define additional characters that return nonzero for some of these functions. Any character set can contain additional characters that return nonzero for:

- `iswpunct` (provided the characters cause `iswalnum` to return zero)
- `iswcntrl` (provided the characters cause `iswprint` to return zero)

Moreover, locales other than the **"C"** locale can define additional characters for:

- **iswalpha**, **iswupper**, and **iswlower** (provided the characters cause **iswcntrl**, **iswdigit**, **iswpunct**, and **iswspace** to return zero)
- **iswspace** (provided the characters cause **iswpunct** to return zero)

Note that the last rule differs slightly from the corresponding rule for the function **isspace**, as indicated above.

Note also that an implementation can define locales other than the **"C"** locale in which a character can cause **iswalpha** (and hence **iswalnum**) to return nonzero, yet still cause **iswupper** and **iswlower** to return zero.

WEOF **#define WEOF <wint_t constant expression>**

The macro yields the return value used to signal the end of a wide file or to report an error condition.

iswalnum **int iswalnum(wint_t c);**

The function returns nonzero if **c** is any of:

```
a b c d e f g h i j k l m n o p q r s t u v w x y z
A B C D E F G H I J K L M N O P Q R S T U V W X Y Z
0 1 2 3 4 5 6 7 8 9
```

or any other locale-specific alphabetic character.

iswalpha **int iswalpha(wint_t c);**

The function returns nonzero if **c** is any of:

```
a b c d e f g h i j k l m n o p q r s t u v w x y z
A B C D E F G H I J K L M N O P Q R S T U V W X Y Z
```

or any other locale-specific alphabetic character.

iswcntrl **int iswcntrl(wint_t c);**

The function returns nonzero if **c** is any of:

BEL BS CR FF HT NL VT

or any other implementation-defined control character.

iswctype **int iswctype(wint_t c, wctype_t category);**

The function returns nonzero if **c** is any character in the category **category**. The value of **category** must have been returned by an earlier successful call to **wctype**.

iswdigit **int iswdigit(wint_t c);**

The function returns nonzero if **c** is any of:

```
0 1 2 3 4 5 6 7 8 9
```

iswgraph **int iswgraph(wint_t c);**

The function returns nonzero if **c** is any character for which either **iswalnum** or **iswpunct** returns nonzero.

iswlower `int iswlower(wint_t c);`

The function returns nonzero if **c** is any of:

a b c d e f g h i j k l m n o p q r s t u v w x y z

or any other locale-specific lowercase character.

iswprint `int iswprint(wint_t c);`

The function returns nonzero if **c** is ***space***, a character for which **isgraph** returns nonzero, or an implementation-defined subset of the characters for which **iswspace** returns nonzero.

iswpunct `int iswpunct(wint_t c);`

The function returns nonzero if **c** is any of:

! " # % & ' ( ) ; < = > ? [\ ] * + , - . / : ^ _ { | } ~

or any other implementation-defined punctuation character.

iswspace `int iswspace(wint_t c);`

The function returns nonzero if **c** is any of:

CR FF HT NL VT space

or any other locale-specific space character.

iswupper `int iswupper(wint_t c);`

The function returns nonzero if **c** is any of:

A B C D E F G H I J K L M N O P Q R S T U V W X Y Z

or any other locale-specific uppercase character.

iswxdigit `int iswxdigit(wint_t c);`

The function returns nonzero if **c** is any of

a b c d e f
A B C D E F
0 1 2 3 4 5 6 7 8 9

towctrans `wint_t towctrans(wint_t c, wctrans_t category);`

The function returns the transformation of the character **c**, using the transform in the category **category**. The value of **category** must have been returned by an earlier successful call to **wctrans**.

towlower `wint_t towlower(wint_t c);`

The function returns the corresponding lowercase letter if one exists and if **iswupper(c)**; otherwise, it returns **c**.

towupper `wint_t towupper(wint_t c);`

The function returns the corresponding uppercase letter if one exists and if **iswlower(c)**; otherwise, it returns **c**.

wctrans `wctrans_t wctrans(const char *property);`

The function determines a mapping from one set of wide-character codes to another. If the **LC_CTYPE** category of the current locale does not define a mapping whose name matches the property string **property**, the function returns zero. Otherwise, it returns a nonzero value suitable for use as the second argument to a subsequent call to **towctrans**.

The following pairs of calls have the same behavior in all locales (but an implementation can define additional mappings even in the **"C"** locale):

```
towlower(c)   same as   towctrans(c, wctrans("tolower"))
towupper(c)   same as   towctrans(c, wctrans("toupper"))
```

wctrans_t `typedef` *s_type* `wctrans_t;`

The type is the scalar type ***s-type*** that can represent locale-specific character mappings.

wctype `wctype_t wctype(const char *property);`
`wctrans_t wctrans(const char *property);`

The function determines a classification rule for wide-character codes. If the **LC_CTYPE** category of the current locale does not define a classification rule whose name matches the property string **property**, the function returns zero. Otherwise, it returns a nonzero value suitable for use as the second argument to a subsequent call to **towctype**.

The following pairs of calls have the same behavior in all locales (but an implementation can define additional mappings even in the **"C"** locale):

```
iswalnum(c)    same as   iswctype(c, wctype("alnum"))
iswalpha(c)    same as   iswctype(c, wctype("alpha"))
iswcntrl(c)    same as   iswctype(c, wctype("cntrl"))
iswdigit(c)    same as   iswctype(c, wctype("digit"))
iswgraph(c)    same as   iswctype(c, wctype("graph"))
iswlower(c)    same as   iswctype(c, wctype("lower"))
iswprint(c)    same as   iswctype(c, wctype("print"))
iswpunct(c)    same as   iswctype(c, wctype("punct"))
iswspace(c)    same as   iswctype(c, wctype("space"))
iswupper(c)    same as   iswctype(c, wctype("upper"))
iswxdigit(c)   same as   iswctype(c, wctype("xdigit"))
```

wctype_t `typedef` *i_type* `wctype_t;`

The type is the scalar type ***s-type*** that can represent locale-specific character classifications.

wint_t `typedef` *i_type* `wint_t;`

The type is the integer type ***i_type*** that can represent all values of type **wchar_t** as well as the value of the macro **WEOF**, and that doesn't change when promoted.

Appendixes

Appendix A: Portability

A *portable* program is one that you can move with little or no extra investment of effort to a computer that differs from the one on which you originally developed the program. Writing a program in Standard C does not guarantee that it will be portable. You must be aware of the aspects of the program that can vary among implementations. You can then write the program so that it does not depend critically on implementation-specific aspects.

This appendix describes what you must be aware of when writing a portable program. It also tells you what to look for when you alter programs written in older dialects of C so that they behave properly under a Standard C implementation. It briefly summarizes the features added with Amendment 1 to the C Standard. And it suggests ways to write C code that is also valid as C++ code.

WRITING PORTABLE PROGRAMS

Although the language definition specifies most aspects of Standard C, it intentionally leaves some aspects unspecified. The language definition also permits other aspects to vary among implementations. If the program depends on behavior that is not fully specified or that can vary among implementations, then there is a good chance that you will need to alter the program when you move it to another computer.

This section identifies issues that affect portability, such as how the translator interprets the program and how the target environment represents files. The list of issues is not complete, but it does include the common issues that you confront when you write a portable program.

An implementation of Standard C must include a document that describes any behavior that is *implementation-defined*. You should read this document to be aware of those aspects that can vary, to be alert to behavior that can be peculiar to a particular implementation, and to take advantage of special features in programs that need not be portable.

Translation-Time Issues

A program can depend on peculiar properties of the translator.

The filenames acceptable to an *include* directive can vary considerably among implementations. If you use filenames that consist of other than six letters (of a single case), followed by a dot (`.`), followed by a single letter, then an implementation can find the name unacceptable. Each implementation defines the filenames that you can create.

How preprocessing uses a filename to locate a file can also vary. Each implementation defines where you must place files that you want to include with an *include* directive.

If you write two or more of the operators **##** within a macro definition, the order in which preprocessing concatenates tokens can vary. If any order produces an invalid preprocessing token as an intermediate result, the program can misbehave when you move it.

A translator can limit the size and complexity of a program that it can translate. Such limits can also depend on the environment in which the translator executes. Thus, no translation unit you write can assuredly survive all Standard C translators. Obey the following individual limits, however, to ensure the highest probability of success:

- Nest statements — such as *if* and *while* statements — no more than fifteen levels deep. The braces surrounding a block add a level of nesting.
- Nest conditional directive — such as *if* and *ifdef* directives — no more than eight levels deep.
- Add no more than twelve decorations — to derive pointer, array, and function types — to a declarator.
- Write no more than 31 nested pairs of parentheses in a declarator.
- Write no more than 32 nested pairs of parentheses within an expression.
- Ensure that all distinct names differ in their first 31 characters. Also ensure that all characters match for names that the translator should treat as the same.
- Ensure that all distinct names with external linkage differ in the first six characters, even if the translator converts all letters to a single case. Also ensure that all characters match for such names that the translator should treat as the same.
- Write no more than 511 distinct names with external linkage within a translation unit.
- Write no more than 127 distinct names in block-level declarations that share a single name space.
- Define no more than 1,024 distinct names as macros at any point within a translation unit.
- Write no more than 31 parameters in a function decoration.
- Write no more than 31 arguments in a function call.
- Write no more than 31 parameters in a macro definition.
- Write no more than 31 arguments in a macro invocation.

- Write no logical source line that exceeds 509 characters.
- Construct no string literal that contains more than 509 characters or wide characters.
- Declare no object whose size exceeds 32,767 bytes.
- Ensure that *include* directives nest no more than eight files deep.
- Write no more than 257 *case* labels for any one *switch* statement. (*Case* labels within nested *switch* statements do not affect this limit.)
- Write no more than 127 members in any one structure or union.
- Write no more than 127 enumeration constants in any one enumeration.
- Nest structure or union definitions no more than fifteen deep in any one list of member declarations.

Character-Set Issues

The program can depend on peculiar properties of the character set.

If you write in the source files any characters not in the basic C character set, a corresponding character might not be in another character set, or the corresponding character might not be what you want. The set of characters is defined for each implementation. (See **CHARACTER SETS** in ***Chapter 1: Characters***.

Similarly, if the program makes special use of characters not in the basic C character set when it executes, you might get different behavior when you move the program.

If you write a character constant that specifies more than one character, such as `'ab'`, the result might change when you move the program. Each implementation defines what values it assigns such character constants.

If the program depends on a particular value for one or more character codes, it can behave differently on an implementation with a different character set. The codes associated with each character are implementation-defined.

Representation Issues

The program can depend on how an implementation represents objects. All representations are implementation-defined.

If the program depends on the representation of an object type (such as its size in bits or whether type *char* or the plain *bitfield* types can represent negative values), the program can change behavior when you move it.

If you treat an arithmetic object that has more than one byte as an array of characters, you must be aware that the order of significant bytes can vary among implementations. You cannot write an integer or floating-point type object to a binary file on one implementation, then later read those bytes into an object of the same type on a different implementation, and portably obtain the same stored value.

The method of encoding integer and floating-point values can vary widely. For signed integer types, negative values have several popular encodings. Floating-point types have numerous popular encodings. This means that, except for the minimum guaranteed range of values for each type, the range of values can vary widely.

Both signed integer and floating-point types can have invalid values on some implementations. Performing an arithmetic operation or a comparison on an invalid value can report a signal or otherwise terminate execution. Initialize all such objects before accessing them, and avoid overflow or underflow, to avoid invalid values.

The alignment requirements of various object types can vary widely. The placement and size of holes in structures is implementation-defined. You can portably determine the offset of a given member from the beginning of a structure, but only by using the **`offsetof`** macro (defined in **`<stddef.h>`**).

Each implementation defines how bitfields pack into integer objects and whether bitfields can straddle two or more underlying objects. You can declare bitfields of 16 bits or less in all implementations.

How an implementation represents enumeration types can vary. You can be certain that all enumeration constants can be represented as type *int*.

Expression-Evaluation Issues

The program can depend on how an implementation evaluates expressions.

The order in which the program evaluates subexpressions can vary widely, subject to the limits imposed by the sequence points within and between expressions. Therefore, the timing and order of side effects can vary between any two sequence points. A common error is to depend on a particular order for the evaluation of argument expressions on a function call. Any order is permissible.

Whether you can usefully type cast a pointer value to an integer value or type cast a nonzero integer value to a pointer value depends on the implementation. Each implementation defines how it converts between scalar types.

If the quotient of an integer division is negative, the sign of a nonzero remainder can be either positive or negative. The result is implementation-defined. Use the **`div`** and **`ldiv`** functions (defined in **`<stdlib.h>`**) for consistent behavior across implementations.

When the program right shifts a negative integer value, different implementations can define different results. To get consistent results across implementations, you can right shift only positive (or unsigned) integer values.

When the program converts a *long double* value to another floating-point type, or a *double* to a *float*, it can round the result to either a nearby higher or a nearby lower representation of the original value. Each implementation defines how such conversions behave.

When the program accesses or stores a value in a *volatile* object, each implementation defines the number and nature of the accesses and stores. Three possibilities exist:

- multiple accesses to different bytes
- multiple accesses to the same byte
- no accesses at all

You cannot write a program that assuredly produces the same pattern of accesses across multiple implementations.

The expansion of the null pointer constant macro `NULL` can be any of `0`, `0L`, or `(void *)0`. The program should not depend on a particular choice. You should not assign `NULL` to a pointer to a function, and you should not use `NULL` as an argument to a function call that has no type information for the corresponding parameter.

The actual integer types corresponding to the type definitions `ptrdiff_t`, `size_t`, and `wchar_t` (defined in `<stddef.h>`) can vary. Use the type definitions.

Library Issues

The behavior of the standard library can vary.

What happens to the file-position indicator for a text stream immediately after a successful call to `ungetc` (declared in `<stdio.h>`) is not defined. Avoid mixing file-positioning operations with calls to this function.

When the function `bsearch` can match either of two equal elements of an array, different implementations can return different matches.

When the function `qsort` sorts an array containing two elements that compare equal, different implementations can leave the elements in different order.

Whether or not floating-point underflow causes the value `ERANGE` to be stored in `errno` can vary. Each implementation defines how it handles floating-point underflow.

What library functions store values in `errno` varies considerably. To determine whether the function of interest reported an error, you must store the value zero in `errno` before you call a library function and then test the stored value before you call another library function.

You can do very little with signals in a portable program. A target environment can elect not to report signals. If it does report signals, any handler you write for an asynchronous signal can only:

- make a successful call to `signal` for that particular signal
- alter the value stored in an object of type `volatile sig_atomic_t`
- return control to its caller

Asynchronous signals can disrupt proper operation of the library. Avoid using signals, or tailor how you use them to each target environment.

Scan functions can give special meaning to a minus (**.**) that is not the first or the last character of a scan set. The behavior is implementation-defined. Write this character only first or last in a scan set.

If you allocate an object of zero size by calling one of the functions **calloc**, **malloc**, or **realloc** (defined in **<stdlib.h>**), the behavior is implementation-defined. Avoid such calls.

If you call the function **exit** with a status argument value other than zero (for successful termination), **EXIT_FAILURE**, or **EXIT_SUCCESS**, the behavior is implementation-defined. Use only these values to report status.

CONVERTING TO STANDARD C

If you have a program written in an earlier dialect of C that you want to convert to Standard C, be aware of all the portability issues described earlier in this appendix. You must also be aware of issues peculiar to earlier dialects of C. Standard C tries to codify existing practice wherever possible, but existing practice varied in certain areas. This section discusses the major areas to address when moving an older C program to a Standard C environment.

Function-Call Issues

In earlier dialects of C, you cannot write a function prototype. Function types do not have argument information, and function calls occur in the absence of any argument information. Many implementations let you call any function with a varying number of arguments.

You can directly address many of the potential difficulties in converting a program to Standard C by writing function prototypes for all functions. Declare functions with external linkage that you use in more than one file in a separate file, and then include that file in all source files that call or define the functions.

The translator will check that function calls and function definitions are consistent with the function prototypes that you write. It will emit a diagnostic if you call a function with an incorrect number of arguments. It will emit a diagnostic if you call a function with an argument expression that is not assignment compatible with the corresponding function parameter. It will convert an argument expression that is assignment-compatible but that does not have the same type as the corresponding function parameter.

Older C programs often rely on argument values of different types having the same representation on a given implementation. By providing function prototypes, you can ensure that the translator will diagnose, or quietly correct, any function calls for which the representation of an argument value is not always acceptable.

For functions intended to accept a varying number of arguments, different implementations provide different methods of accessing the unnamed arguments. When you identify such a function, declare it with the ellipsis notation, such as `int f(int x, ...)`. Within the function, use the macros defined in `<stdarg.h>` to replace the existing method for accessing unnamed arguments.

Preprocessing Issues

Perhaps the greatest variation in dialects among earlier implementations of C occurs in preprocessing. If the program defines macros that perform only simple substitutions of preprocessing tokens, then you can expect few problems. Otherwise, be wary of variations in several areas.

Some earlier dialects expand macro arguments after substitution, rather than before. This can lead to differences in how a macro expands when you write other macro invocations within its arguments.

Some earlier dialects do not rescan the replacement token sequence after substitution. Macros that expand to macro invocations work differently, depending on whether the rescan occurs.

Dialects that rescan the replacement token sequence work differently, depending on whether a macro that expands to a macro invocation can involve preprocessing tokens in the text following the macro invocation.

The handling of a macro name during an expansion of its invocation varies considerably.

Some dialects permit empty argument sequences in a macro invocation. Standard C does not always permit empty arguments.

The concatenation of tokens with the operator **##** is new with Standard C. It replaces several earlier methods.

The creation of string literals with the operator **#** is new with Standard C. It replaces the practice in some earlier dialects of substituting macro parameter names that you write within string literals in macro definitions.

Library Issues

The Standard C library is largely a superset of existing libraries. Some conversion problems, however, can occur.

Many earlier implementations offer an additional set of input/output functions with names such as `close`, `creat`, `lseek`, `open`, `read`, and `write`. You must replace calls to these functions with calls to other functions defined in `<stdio.h>`.

Standard C has several minor changes in the behavior of library functions, compared with popular earlier dialects. These changes generally occur in areas where practice also varied.

Quiet Changes

Most differences between Standard C and earlier dialects of C cause a Standard C translator to emit a diagnostic when it encounters a program written in the earlier dialect of C. Some changes, unfortunately, require no diagnostic. What was a valid program in the earlier dialect is also a valid program in Standard C, but with different meaning.

While these *quiet changes* are few in number and generally subtle, you need to be aware of them. They occasionally give rise to unexpected behavior in a program that you convert to Standard C. The principal quiet changes are discussed below.

Trigraphs do not occur in earlier dialects of C. An older program that happens to contain a sequence of two question marks (`??`) can change meaning in a variety of ways.

Some earlier dialects effectively promote any declaration you write that has external linkage to file level. Standard C keeps such declarations at block level.

Earlier dialects of C let you use the digits `8` and `9` in an octal escape sequence, such as in the string literal `"\08"`. Standard C treats this as a string literal with two characters (plus the terminating null character).

Hexadecimal escape sequences, such as `\xff`, and the escape sequence `\a` are new with Standard C. In certain earlier implementations, they could have been given different meaning.

Some earlier dialects guarantee that identical string literals share common storage, and others guarantee that they do not. Some dialects let you alter the values stored in string literals. You cannot be certain that identical string literals overlap in Standard C. Do not alter the values stored in string literals in Standard C.

Some earlier dialects have different rules for promoting the types *unsigned char, unsigned short,* and *unsigned bitfields.* On most implementations, the difference is detectable only on a few expressions where a negative value becomes a large positive value of unsigned type. Add type casts to specify the types you require.

Earlier dialects convert lvalue expressions of type *float* to *double,* in a value context, so all floating-point arithmetic occurs only in type *double.* A program that depends on this implicit increase in precision can behave differently in a Standard C environment. Add type casts if you need the extra precision.

On some earlier dialects of C, shifting an *int* or *unsigned int* value left or right by a *long* or *unsigned long* value first converts the value to be shifted to the type of the shift count. In Standard C, the type of the shift count has no such effect. Use a type cast if you need this behavior.

Some earlier dialects guarantee that the *if* directive performs arithmetic to the same precision as the target environment. (You can write an *if* directive that reveals properties of the target environment.) Standard C makes no such guarantee. Use the macros defined in **<float.h>** and **<limits.h>** to test properties of the target environment.

Earlier dialects vary considerably in the grouping of values within an object initializer, when you omit some (but not all) of the braces within the initializer. Supply all braces for maximum clarity.

Earlier dialects convert the expression in any *switch* statement to type *int*. Standard C also performs comparisons within a *switch* statement in other integer types. A *case* label expression that relies on being truncated when converted to *int*, in an earlier dialect, can behave differently in a Standard C environment.

Some earlier preprocessing expands parameter names within string literals or character constants that you write within a macro definition. Standard C does not. Use the string literal creation operator **#**, along with string literal concatenation, to replace this method.

Some earlier preprocessing concatenates preprocessor tokens separated only by a comment within a macro definition. Standard C does not. Use the token concatenation operator **##** to replace this method.

NEWER DIALECTS

Making standards for programming languages is an on-going activity. As of this writing, the C Standard has been formally amended. A standard for C++, which is closely related to C, is in the late stages of development. One aspect of portability is writing code that is compatible with these newer dialects, whether or not the code makes use of the newer features.

Amendment 1 Most of the features added with Amendment 1 are declared or defined in three new headers — **<iso646.h>**, **<wchar.h>**, and **<wctype.h>**. A few take the form of capabilities added to the functions declared in **<stdio.h>**. While not strictly necessary, it is best to avoid using any of the names declared or defined in these new headers. (See *Appendix B: Names*.)

C++ Maintaining compatibility with C++ takes considerably more work. It can be useful, however, to write in a common dialect called "typesafe C" (**P&S91**). Here is a brief summary of the added constraints:

- Avoid using any C++ keywords. As of this writing, the list includes:

```
and          and_eq      asm          bitand       bitor
bool         catch       class        compl        delete
explicit     false       friend       inline       mutable
namespace    new         not          not_eq       operator
or           or_eq       private      protected    public
template     this        throw        true         try
typeid       typename    using        virtual      wchar_t
xor          xor_eq      const_cast   dynamic_cast
reinterpret_cast         static_cast
```

- Write function prototypes for all functions you call.
- Define each tag name also as a type, as in:

```
typedef struct x x;
```

- Assume each enumerated type is a distinct type that promotes to an integer type. Type cast an integer expression that you assign to an object of enumerated type.
- Write an explicit storage class for each constant object declaration at file level.
- Do not write tentative definitions.
- Do not apply the operator **`sizeof`** to an rvalue operand.

Appendix B: Names

PREDEFINED NAMES

Standard C predefines many names. The list below shows all predefined names that can collide with names that you create. The list does not include preprocessing directive names, such as **`include`**, because the translator can tell from context when it expects a preprocessing directive name. Nor does it include member names from structures declared in standard headers, for the same reason.

You can reuse any of these names for a different purpose, with suitable precautions:

- You can reuse a library name in a name space other than the one in which a standard header declares or defines it. (See **VISIBILITY AND NAME SPACES** in *Chapter 5: Declarations*.)
- You can reuse a library name with no linkage in a translation unit that does not include a standard header that declares or defines it.

Amendment 1

- You can reuse a library name with external linkage declared in either **`<wchar.h>`** or **`<wctype.h>`** provided *no* translation unit in the program includes either of these headers.

Otherwise, you can reuse no library name with external linkage even if you do not include a standard header that declares or defines it. For maximum readability, however, avoid giving new meaning to any library names.

If a standard header is not listed next to the name, then the name is in scope even if you include no standard headers. Otherwise, you include that standard header in the program to make use of the name. Five names are defined in multiple standard headers — **`NULL`**, **`size_t`**, **`wchar_t`**, **`wint_t`**, and **`WEOF`**. You can include any one, or any combination, of their defining standard headers to define the name.

Two names are *not* predefined, but are referenced by the Standard C environment — **`NDEBUG`** and **`main`**. You *must* provide a definition for **`main`**. You *can* provide a definition for **`NDEBUG`** to disable testing in the **`assert`** macro.

If a name is shown in ***`boldface italics`***, then it has external linkage. Any declaration you write for that name that has external linkage must agree in type and meaning with the definition provided by the translator. Do not write a definition for that name.

For example, the line:

`stdlib.h` *`bsearch`* function or macro

tells you that **bsearch** is declared in **<stdlib.h>** as a function with external linkage. **stdlib.h** can also provide a macro definition for **bsearch** that masks the declaration.

And the line:

`time.h` `time_t` arithmetic type definition

tells you that **time_t** is declared in **<time.h>** as a type definition. **time_t** can have integer or floating-point type. It is not reserved in the space of names with external linkage.

An *old function or macro* has been retained in the Standard C library for compatibility with earlier C dialects. Use the replacement indicated in the description of the function in programs that you write.

Header	Identifier	Usage
	__DATE__	string literal macro
	__FILE__	string literal macro
	__LINE__	decimal constant macro
	__STDC__	decimal constant macro
	__STDC_VERSION__	decimal constant macro
	__TIME__	string literal macro
stdio.h	**_IOFBF**	integer constant macro
stdio.h	**_IOLBF**	integer constant macro
stdio.h	**_IONBF**	integer constant macro
stdio.h	**BUFSIZ**	integer constant macro
limits.h	**CHAR_BIT**	*#if* macro
limits.h	**CHAR_MAX**	*#if* macro
limits.h	**CHAR_MIN**	*#if* macro
time.h	**CLOCKS_PER_SEC**	arithmetic rvalue macro
float.h	**DBL_DIG**	integer rvalue macro
float.h	**DBL_EPSILON**	*double* rvalue macro
float.h	**DBL_MANT_DIG**	integer rvalue macro
float.h	**DBL_MAX**	*double* rvalue macro
float.h	**DBL_MAX_10_EXP**	integer rvalue macro
float.h	**DBL_MAX_EXP**	integer rvalue macro
float.h	**DBL_MIN**	*double* rvalue macro
float.h	**DBL_MIN_10_EXP**	integer rvalue macro
float.h	**DBL_MIN_EXP**	integer rvalue macro
errno.h	**EDOM**	integer constant macro
errno.h	**EFPOS**	integer constant macro
stdio.h	**EOF**	integer constant macro
errno.h	**ERANGE**	integer constant macro
stdlib.h	**EXIT_FAILURE**	integer rvalue macro
stdlib.h	**EXIT_SUCCESS**	integer rvalue macro
stdio.h	**FILE**	object type definition
stdio.h	**FILENAME_MAX**	integer constant macro

Header	Identifier	Usage
float.h	FLT_DIG	integer rvalue macro
float.h	FLT_EPSILON	*float* rvalue macro
float.h	FLT_MANT_DIG	integer rvalue macro
float.h	FLT_MAX	*float* rvalue macro
float.h	FLT_MAX_10_EXP	integer rvalue macro
float.h	FLT_MAX_EXP	integer rvalue macro
float.h	FLT_MIN	*float* rvalue macro
float.h	FLT_MIN_10_EXP	integer rvalue macro
float.h	FLT_MIN_EXP	integer rvalue macro
float.h	FLT_RADIX	*#if* macro
float.h	FLT_ROUNDS	integer rvalue macro
stdio.h	FOPEN_MAX	integer constant macro
math.h	HUGE_VAL	*double* rvalue macro
limits.h	INT_MAX	*#if* macro
limits.h	INT_MIN	*#if* macro
stdio.h	L_tmpnam	integer constant macro
locale.h	LC_ALL	integer constant macro
locale.h	LC_COLLATE	integer constant macro
locale.h	LC_CTYPE	integer constant macro
locale.h	LC_MONETARY	integer constant macro
locale.h	LC_NUMERIC	integer constant macro
locale.h	LC_TIME	integer constant macro
float.h	LDBL_DIG	integer rvalue macro
float.h	LDBL_EPSILON	*long double* rvalue macro
float.h	LDBL_MANT_DIG	integer rvalue macro
float.h	LDBL_MAX	*long double* rvalue macro
float.h	LDBL_MAX_10_EXP	integer rvalue macro
float.h	LDBL_MAX_EXP	integer rvalue macro
float.h	LDBL_MIN	*long double* rvalue macro
float.h	LDBL_MIN_10_EXP	integer rvalue macro
float.h	LDBL_MIN_EXP	integer rvalue macro
limits.h	LONG_MAX	*#if* macro
limits.h	LONG_MIN	*#if* macro
stdlib.h	MB_CUR_MAX	integer rvalue macro
limits.h	MB_LEN_MAX	*#if* macro
assert.h	NDEBUG	macro ***reference***
locale.h	NULL	pointer constant macro
stddef.h	" "	" "
stdio.h	" "	" "
stdlib.h	" "	" "
string.h	" "	" "
time.h	" "	" "
wchar.h	" "	" "
stdlib.h	RAND_MAX	integer constant macro
limits.h	SCHAR_MAX	*#if* macro

Header	Identifier	Usage
limits.h	SCHAR_MIN	*#if* macro
stdio.h	SEEK_CUR	integer constant macro
stdio.h	SEEK_END	integer constant macro
stdio.h	SEEK_SET	integer constant macro
limits.h	SHRT_MAX	*#if* macro
limits.h	SHRT_MIN	*#if* macro
signal.h	SIGABRT	integer constant macro
signal.h	SIGFPE	integer constant macro
signal.h	SIGILL	integer constant macro
signal.h	SIGINT	integer constant macro
signal.h	SIGSEGV	integer constant macro
signal.h	SIGTERM	integer constant macro
signal.h	SIG_DFL	pointer constant macro
signal.h	SIG_ERR	pointer constant macro
signal.h	SIG_IGN	pointer constant macro
stdio.h	TMP_MAX	integer constant macro
limits.h	UCHAR_MAX	*#if* macro
limits.h	UINT_MAX	*#if* macro
limits.h	ULONG_MAX	*#if* macro
limits.h	USHRT_MAX	*#if* macro
wchar.h	WCHAR_MAX	integer constant macro
wchar.h	WCHAR_MIN	integer constant macro
wchar.h	WEOF	integer constant macro
wctype.h	" "	" "
stdlib.h	*abort*	function or macro
stdlib.h	*abs*	function or macro
math.h	*acos*	function or macro
iso646.h	and	operator macro
iso646.h	and_eq	operator macro
time.h	*asctime*	function or macro
math.h	*asin*	function or macro
assert.h	assert	*void* macro
math.h	*atan*	function or macro
math.h	*atan2*	function or macro
stdlib.h	*atexit*	function or macro
stdlib.h	*atof*	old function or macro
stdlib.h	*atoi*	old function or macro
stdlib.h	*atol*	old function or macro
	auto	keyword
iso646.h	bitand	operator macro
iso646.h	bitor	operator macro
	break	keyword
stdlib.h	*bsearch*	function or macro
wchar.h	*btowc*	function or macro
stdlib.h	*calloc*	function or macro

Header	Identifier	Usage
	`case`	keyword
`math.h`	*`ceil`*	function or macro
	`char`	keyword
`stdio.h`	*`clearerr`*	function or macro
`time.h`	*`clock`*	function or macro
`time.h`	`clock_t`	arithmetic type definition
`iso646.h`	`compl`	operator macro
	`const`	keyword
	`continue`	keyword
`math.h`	*`cos`*	function or macro
`math.h`	*`cosh`*	function or macro
`time.h`	*`ctime`*	function or macro
	`default`	keyword
	`defined`	*#if* macro operator
`time.h`	*`difftime`*	function or macro
`stdlib.h`	*`div`*	function or macro
`stdlib.h`	`div_t`	structure type definition
	`do`	keyword
	`double`	keyword
	`else`	keyword
	`enum`	keyword
`errno.h`	*`errno`*	*int* modifiable lvalue macro
`stdlib.h`	*`exit`*	function or macro
`math.h`	*`exp`*	function or macro
	`extern`	keyword
`math.h`	*`fabs`*	function or macro
`stdio.h`	*`fclose`*	function or macro
`stdio.h`	*`feof`*	function or macro
`stdio.h`	*`ferror`*	function or macro
`stdio.h`	*`fflush`*	function or macro
`stdio.h`	*`fgetc`*	function or macro
`stdio.h`	*`fgetpos`*	function or macro
`stdio.h`	*`fgets`*	function or macro
`wchar.h`	*`fgetwc`*	function or macro
`wchar.h`	*`fgetws`*	function or macro
	`float`	keyword
`math.h`	*`floor`*	function or macro
`math.h`	*`fmod`*	function or macro
`stdio.h`	*`fopen`*	function or macro
	`for`	keyword
`stdio.h`	`fpos_t`	assignable type definition
`stdio.h`	*`fprintf`*	function or macro
`stdio.h`	*`fputc`*	function or macro
`stdio.h`	*`fputs`*	function or macro
`wchar.h`	*`fputwc`*	function or macro

Header	Identifier	Usage
`wchar.h`	*`fputws`*	function or macro
`stdio.h`	*`fread`*	function or macro
`stdlib.h`	*`free`*	function or macro
`stdio.h`	*`freopen`*	function or macro
`math.h`	*`frexp`*	function or macro
`stdio.h`	*`fscanf`*	function or macro
`stdio.h`	*`fseek`*	function or macro
`stdio.h`	*`fsetpos`*	function or macro
`stdio.h`	*`ftell`*	function or macro
`wchar.h`	*`fwide`*	function or macro
`wchar.h`	*`fwprintf`*	function or macro
`stdio.h`	*`fwrite`*	function or macro
`wchar.h`	*`fwscanf`*	function or macro
`stdio.h`	*`getc`*	function or unsafe macro
`stdio.h`	*`getchar`*	function or macro
`stdlib.h`	*`getenv`*	function or macro
`stdio.h`	*`gets`*	old function or macro
`wchar.h`	*`getwc`*	function or macro
`wchar.h`	*`getwchar`*	function or macro
`time.h`	*`gmtime`*	function or macro
	`goto`	keyword
	`if`	keyword
	`int`	keyword
`ctype.h`	*`isalnum`*	function or macro
`ctype.h`	*`isalpha`*	function or macro
`ctype.h`	*`iscntrl`*	function or macro
`ctype.h`	*`isdigit`*	function or macro
`ctype.h`	*`isgraph`*	function or macro
`ctype.h`	*`islower`*	function or macro
`ctype.h`	*`isprint`*	function or macro
`ctype.h`	*`ispunct`*	function or macro
`ctype.h`	*`isspace`*	function or macro
`ctype.h`	*`isupper`*	function or macro
`wctype.h`	*`iswalnum`*	function or macro
`wctype.h`	*`iswalpha`*	function or macro
`wctype.h`	*`iswcntrl`*	function or macro
`wctype.h`	*`iswctype`*	function or macro
`wctype.h`	*`iswdigit`*	function or macro
`wctype.h`	*`iswgraph`*	function or macro
`wctype.h`	*`iswlower`*	function or macro
`wctype.h`	*`iswprint`*	function or macro
`wctype.h`	*`iswpunct`*	function or macro
`wctype.h`	*`iswspace`*	function or macro
`wctype.h`	*`iswupper`*	function or macro
`wctype.h`	*`iswxdigit`*	function or macro

Header	Identifier	Usage
ctype.h	*isxdigit*	function or macro
setjmp.h	jmp_buf	array type definition
stdlib.h	*labs*	function or macro
locale.h	lconv	structure tag
math.h	*ldexp*	function or macro
stdlib.h	*ldiv*	function or macro
stdlib.h	ldiv_t	structure type definition
locale.h	*localeconv*	function or macro
time.h	*localtime*	function or macro
math.h	*log*	function or macro
math.h	*log10*	function or macro
	long	keyword
setjmp.h	*longjmp*	function or macro
	main	function ***reference***
stdlib.h	*malloc*	function or macro
stdlib.h	*mblen*	function or macro
wchar.h	*mbrlen*	function or macro
wchar.h	*mbrtowc*	function or macro
wchar.h	*mbsinit*	function or macro
wchar.h	*mbsrtowcs*	function or macro
stdlib.h	*mbstowcs*	function or macro
stdlib.h	*mbtowc*	function or macro
string.h	*memchr*	function or macro
string.h	*memcmp*	function or macro
string.h	*memcpy*	function or macro
string.h	*memmove*	function or macro
string.h	*memset*	function or macro
time.h	*mktime*	function or macro
math.h	*modf*	function or macro
iso646.h	not	operator macro
iso646.h	not_eq	operator macro
stddef.h	offsetof	size_t constant macro
iso646.h	or	operator macro
iso646.h	or_eq	operator macro
stdio.h	*perror*	function or macro
math.h	*pow*	function or macro
stdio.h	*printf*	function or macro
stddef.h	ptrdiff_t	integer type definition
stdio.h	*putc*	function or unsafe macro
stdio.h	*putchar*	function or macro
stdio.h	*puts*	function or macro
wchar.h	*putwc*	function or macro
wchar.h	*putwchar*	function or macro
stdlib.h	*qsort*	function or macro
signal.h	*raise*	function or macro

Header	Identifier	Usage
stdlib.h	*rand*	function or macro
stdlib.h	*realloc*	function or macro
	register	keyword
stdio.h	*remove*	function or macro
stdio.h	*rename*	function or macro
	return	keyword
stdio.h	*rewind*	function or macro
stdio.h	*scanf*	function or macro
stdio.h	*setbuf*	old function or macro
setjmp.h	*setjmp*	integer rvalue macro
locale.h	*setlocale*	function or macro
stdio.h	*setvbuf*	function or macro
	short	keyword
signal.h	sig_atomic_t	integer type definition
signal.h	*signal*	function or macro
	signed	keyword
math.h	*sin*	function or macro
math.h	*sinh*	function or macro
stddef.h	size_t	unsigned type definition
stdio.h	" "	" "
stdlib.h	" "	" "
string.h	" "	" "
time.h	" "	" "
wchar.h	" "	" "
	sizeof	keyword
stdio.h	*sprintf*	function or macro
math.h	*sqrt*	function or macro
stdlib.h	*srand*	function or macro
stdio.h	*sscanf*	function or macro
	static	keyword
stdio.h	*stderr*	*pointer to* **FILE** rvalue macro
stdio.h	*stdin*	*pointer to* **FILE** rvalue macro
stdio.h	*stdout*	*pointer to* **FILE** rvalue macro
string.h	*strcat*	function or macro
string.h	*strchr*	function or macro
string.h	*strcmp*	function or macro
string.h	*strcoll*	function or macro
string.h	*strcpy*	function or macro
string.h	*strcspn*	function or macro
string.h	*strerror*	function or macro
time.h	*strftime*	function or macro
string.h	*strlen*	function or macro
string.h	*strncat*	function or macro
string.h	*strncmp*	function or macro
string.h	*strncpy*	function or macro

Header	Identifier	Usage
string.h	*strpbrk*	function or macro
string.h	*strrchr*	function or macro
string.h	*strspn*	function or macro
string.h	*strstr*	function or macro
stdlib.h	*strtod*	function or macro
string.h	*strtok*	function or macro
stdlib.h	*strtol*	function or macro
stdlib.h	*strtoul*	function or macro
	struct	keyword
string.h	*strxfrm*	function or macro
	switch	keyword
wchar.h	*swprintf*	function or macro
wchar.h	*swscanf*	function or macro
stdlib.h	*system*	function or macro
math.h	*tan*	function or macro
math.h	*tanh*	function or macro
time.h	*time*	function or macro
time.h	time_t	arithmetic type definition
time.h	tm	structure tag
wchar.h	tm	incomplete structure tag
stdio.h	*tmpfile*	function or macro
stdio.h	*tmpnam*	function or macro
ctype.h	*tolower*	function or macro
ctype.h	*toupper*	function or macro
wctype.h	*towctrans*	function or macro
wctype.h	*towlower*	function or macro
wctype.h	*towupper*	function or macro
	typedef	keyword
stdio.h	*ungetc*	function or macro
wchar.h	*ungetwc*	
	union	keyword
	unsigned	keyword
stdarg.h	va_arg	assignable rvalue macro
stdarg.h	va_end	*void* macro
stdarg.h	va_list	object type definition
stdarg.h	va_start	*void* macro
stdio.h	*vfprintf*	function or macro
wchar.h	*vfwprintf*	function or macro
	void	keyword
	volatile	keyword
stdio.h	*vprintf*	function or macro
stdio.h	*vsprintf*	function or macro
wchar.h	*vswprintf*	function or macro
wchar.h	*vwprintf*	function or macro
stddef.h	wchar_t	integer type definition

Header	Identifier	Usage
stdlib.h	wchar_t	integer type definition
wchar.h	" "	" "
wchar.h	*wcrtomb*	function or macro
wchar.h	*wcscat*	function or macro
wchar.h	*wcschr*	function or macro
wchar.h	*wcscmp*	function or macro
wchar.h	*wcscoll*	function or macro
wchar.h	*wcscpy*	function or macro
wchar.h	*wcscspn*	function or macro
wchar.h	*wcsftime*	function or macro
wchar.h	*wcslen*	function or macro
wchar.h	*wcsncat*	function or macro
wchar.h	*wcsncmp*	function or macro
wchar.h	*wcsncpy*	function or macro
wchar.h	*wcspbrk*	function or macro
wchar.h	*wcsrchr*	function or macro
wchar.h	*wcsrtombs*	function or macro
wchar.h	*wcsspn*	function or macro
wchar.h	*wcsstr*	function or macro
wchar.h	*wcstod*	function or macro
wchar.h	*wcstok*	function or macro
wchar.h	*wcstol*	function or macro
stdlib.h	*wcstombs*	function or macro
wchar.h	*wcstoul*	function or macro
wchar.h	*wcsxfrm*	function or macro
wchar.h	*wctob*	function or macro
stdlib.h	*wctomb*	function or macro
wctype.h	wctrans_t	scalar type definition
wctype.h	wctype_t	scalar type definition
wchar.h	wint_t	integer type definition
wctype.h	" "	" "
wchar.h	*wmemchr*	function or macro
wchar.h	*wmemcmp*	function or macro
wchar.h	*wmemcpy*	function or macro
wchar.h	*wmemmove*	function or macro
wchar.h	*wmemset*	function or macro
wchar.h	*wprintf*	function or macro
wchar.h	*wscanf*	function or macro
	while	keyword
iso646.h	xor	operator macro
iso646.h	xor_eq	operator macro

RESERVED NAMES

As with the predefined names, you should not use other sets of names when you write programs. To specify a set of names:

- `[0-9]` stands for any digit
- `[a-z]` stands for any lowercase letter
- `[A-Z]` stands for any uppercase letter
- `...` stands for zero or more letters, digits, and underscores

These sets are reserved for various uses by implementations:

- To provide *additional* functions and macros
- For *future* C standards to add functions and macros
- For implementations to create *hidden* names

The list of reserved names shown in the table below uses the same notation as for predefined names. (See **PREDEFINED NAMES** earlier in this appendix.) For example, the lines:

`__...`	hidden macros
`_[A-Z]...`	hidden macros

tell you that all names that begin either with two underscores or with a single underscore followed by an uppercase letter are reserved for naming macros intended not to be directly visible to you. The line:

`_...`	hidden external names

tells you that all names that have external linkage and that begin with a single underscore are reserved for naming functions and objects intended not to be directly visible to you.

An implementation can define only names that are predefined or reserved. Any other names that you create cannot conflict with names defined by the implementation.

Header	Identifier	Usage
	`__...`	hidden macros
	`_[A-Z]...`	hidden macros
	`_...`	hidden external names
errno.h	`E[0-9]...`	added macros
errno.h	`E[A-Z]...`	added macros
locale.h	`LC_[A-Z]...`	added macros
signal.h	`SIG_...`	added macros
signal.h	`SIG[A-Z]...`	added macros
math.h	*acosf*	future function or macro
math.h	*acosl*	future function or macro
math.h	*asinf*	future function or macro
math.h	*asinl*	future function or macro
math.h	*atanf*	future function or macro
math.h	*atanl*	future function or macro

Header	Identifier	Usage
math.h	*atan2f*	future function or macro
math.h	*atan2l*	future function or macro
math.h	*ceilf*	future function or macro
math.h	*ceill*	future function or macro
math.h	*cosf*	future function or macro
math.h	*cosl*	future function or macro
math.h	*coshf*	future function or macro
math.h	*coshl*	future function or macro
math.h	*expf*	future function or macro
math.h	*expl*	future function or macro
math.h	*fabsf*	future function or macro
math.h	*fabsl*	future function or macro
math.h	*floorf*	future function or macro
math.h	*floorl*	future function or macro
math.h	*fmodf*	future function or macro
math.h	*fmodl*	future function or macro
math.h	*frexpf*	future function or macro
math.h	*frexpl*	future function or macro
ctype.h	*is[a-z]...*	future functions or macros
math.h	*ldexpf*	future function or macro
math.h	*ldexpl*	future function or macro
math.h	*logf*	future function or macro
math.h	*logl*	future function or macro
math.h	*log10f*	future function or macro
math.h	*log10l*	future function or macro
string.h	*mem[a-z]...*	future functions or macros
math.h	*modff*	future function or macro
math.h	*modfl*	future function or macro
math.h	*powf*	future function or macro
math.h	*powl*	future function or macro
math.h	*sinf*	future function or macro
math.h	*sinl*	future function or macro
math.h	*sinhf*	future function or macro
math.h	*sinhl*	future function or macro
math.h	*sqrtf*	future function or macro
math.h	*sqrtl*	future function or macro
stdlib.h	*str[a-z]...*	future functions or macros
string.h	" "	" "
math.h	*tanf*	future function or macro
math.h	*tanl*	future function or macro
math.h	*tanhf*	future function or macro
math.h	*tanhl*	future function or macro
ctype.h	*to[a-z]...*	future functions or macros
string.h	*wcs[a-z]...*	future functions or macros

Appendix C: References

ANS89 *ANSI Standard X3.159-1989* (New York NY: American National Standards Institute, 1989). The original C Standard, developed by the ANSI-authorized committee X3J11. The Rationale that accompanies the C Standard explains many of the decisions that went into it, if you can get your hands on a copy.

ISO90 *ISO/IEC Standard 9899:1990* (Geneva: International Standards Organization, 1990). The official C Standard around the world. Aside from formatting details and section numbering, the ISO C Standard is identical to the ANSI C Standard.

ISO94 *ISO/IEC Amendment 1 to Standard 9899:1990* (Geneva: International Standards Organization, 1994). The first (and only) amendment to the C Standard. It provides substantial support for manipulating large character sets.

K&R78 Brian Kernighan and Dennis Ritchie, *The C Programming Language* (Englewood Cliffs NJ: Prentice Hall, 1978). Served for years as the de facto standard for the C language. It also provides a very good tutorial overview of C.

K&R89 Brian Kernighan and Dennis Ritchie, *The C Programming Language, Second Edition* (Englewood Cliffs NJ: Prentice Hall, 1989). An update to **K&R78**, above, upgraded to reflect the ANSI C Standard.

Pla92 P.J. Plauger, *The Standard C Library* (Englewood Cliffs NJ: Prentice Hall, 1992). Contains a complete implementation of the Standard C library, as well as text from the library portion of the C Standard and guidance in using the Standard C library. It is the predecessor and companion volume to this book.

Pla95 P.J. Plauger, *The Draft Standard C++ Library* (Englewood Cliffs NJ: Prentice Hall, 1995). Contains a complete implementation of the draft Standard C++ library as of early 1994, as well as text from the library portion of the draft C++ Standard and guidance in using the Standard C++ library. It is another useful companion volume to this book.

P&B89 P.J. Plauger and Jim Brodie, *Standard C: A Programmer's Reference* (Redmond WA: Microsoft Press, 1989). The first complete but succinct reference to the entire C Standard. It covers both the language and the library.

P&B92 P.J. Plauger and Jim Brodie, *ANSI and ISO Standard C: Programmer's Reference* (Redmond WA: Microsoft Press, 1992). An update to **P&B89**, above.

Plu89 Thomas Plum, *C Programming Guidelines* (Cardiff NJ: Plum Hall, Inc., 1989). An excellent style guide for writing C programs. It also contains a good discussion of first-order correctness testing, on pp. 194-199.

P&S91 Thomas Plum and Dan Saks, *C++ Programming Guidelines* (Cardiff NJ: Plum Hall, Inc., 1991). An excellent style guide for writing C++ programs and a useful companion to **Plu89**. It describes in detail how to write "type-safe C," a dialect common to C and C++.

Sch93 Herbert Schildt, *The Annotated ANSI C Standard* (Berkeley CA: Osborne McGraw Hill, 1993). A reprint of **ISO90** with accompanying commentary. This is the least expensive and most available version of the C Standard.

Index

D

F

M

N

Q

R

S

T

U

V

W

X